THE
TELEVI
SERIES

indicates date for
...st...ner v

Alan Bennett

MANCHESTER
1824

Manchester University Press

THE TELEVISION SERIES

series editors

SARAH CARDWELL
JONATHAN BIGNELL

KARA McKECHNIE

Alan Bennett

Manchester University Press

MANCHESTER AND NEW YORK

distributed exclusively in the USA by Palgrave

Published by Manchester University Press
Oxford Road, Manchester M13 9NR, UK
and Room 400, 175 Fifth Avenue, New York, NY 10010, USA
www.manchesteruniversitypress.co.uk

Distributed exclusively in the USA by
Palgrave, 175 Fifth Avenue, New York, NY 10010, USA

Distributed exclusively in Canada by
UBC Press, University of British Columbia, 2029 West Mall,
Vancouver, BC, Canada V6T 1Z2

British Library Cataloguing-in-Publication Data
A catalogue record for this book is available from the British Library

Library of Congress Cataloging-in-Publication Data applied for

ISBN 978 0 7190 6805 8 *hardback*
ISBN 978 0 7190 6806 5 *paperback*

First published 2007

16 15 14 13 12 11 10 09 08 07   10 9 8 7 6 5 4 3 2 1

Typeset in Scala with Meta display
by Koinonia, Manchester
Printed in Great Britain
by The Cromwell Press, Trowbridge

For Peter Davidson

Contents

General editors' preface

Television is part of our everyday experience, and is one of the most significant features of our cultural lives today. Yet its practitioners and its artistic and cultural achievements remain relatively unacknowledged. The books in this series aim to remedy this by addressing the work of major television writers and creators. Each volume provides an authoritative and accessible guide to a particular practitioner's body of work, and assesses his or her contribution to television over the years. Many of the volumes draw on original sources, such as specially conducted interviews and archive material, and all of them list relevant bibliographic sources and provide full details of the programmes discussed. The author of each book makes a case for the importance of the work considered therein, and the series includes books on neglected or overlooked practitioners alongside well-known ones.

In comparison with some related disciplines, Television Studies scholarship is still relatively young, and the series aims to contribute to establishing the subject as a vigorous and evolving field. This series provides resources for critical thinking about television. Whilst maintaining a clear focus on the writers, on the creators and on the programmes themselves, the books in this series also take account of key critical concepts and theories in Television Studies. Each book is written from a particular critical or theoretical perspective, with reference to pertinent issues, and the approaches included in the series are varied and sometimes dissenting. Each author explicitly outlines the reasons for his or her particular focus, methodology or perspective. Readers are invited to think critically about the subject matter and approach covered in each book.

Although the series is addressed primarily to students and scholars of television, the books will also appeal to the many people who are interested in how television programmes have been commissioned, made and enjoyed. Since television has been so much a part of personal and public life in the twentieth and twenty-first centuries, we hope that the series will engage with, and sometimes challenge, a broad and diverse readership.

Sarah Cardwell
Jonathan Bignell

List of illustrations

Acknowledgements

I would like to express my appreciation and gratitude to everyone who has contributed to this study, which began at the University of Heidelberg in 1994, and appropriately reaches its conclusion in West Yorkshire in 2006.

First of all, the man himself, Alan Bennett, provided encouragement and graciously answered questions. He ended a letter with 'And good luck with the book … I won't promise to read it but I hope lots of people will!' Thank you.

At various stages of my work, I received help from Eva Hornstein, former resident of Gloucester Crescent and London correspondent, Renate Schmidt and Chris Green. My thanks also go to Kirsten Hertel, Manfred Bernhard, Horst Meller, Daniela Saccà Reuter, Wolf Reuter, Gudula Kienemund and Julie Anderson. The late Jim Green's considerable support is remembered fondly and gratefully.

My thanks for valuable pieces of information go to Audrey Booth, Michael Raab, Andreas Höfele, and my Yorkshire neighbours Simon Child and Roy Radcliffe. I am grateful to Ian Brown, Alex Chisholm and Sarah Punshon of the West Yorkshire Playhouse, for providing me with insight to productions of Alan Bennett's plays performed at the theatre.

I would like to thank my students on the BA (Hons) Theatre Dramaturgy degree at Leeds University, particularly Graham Whitehead, who patiently transcribed inaudible interview material. I owe thanks to my colleagues at the School of Performance and Cultural Industries, and particularly the following: Mick Wallis for his generous support of the illustrations, Susan Daniels, Arthur Pritchard, Tony Green, George Rodosthenous Linda Smith, the School Office, and the School Research Committee for support and teaching buyout. The most heartfelt thanks to the late Wendy Johnson, who enabled me to go on partial study leave in 2002 by acting Programme Manager, as well as providing encouragement, fun and friendship. I miss her an awful lot.

My interviewees, Sir Peter Hall, Paul Kerryson and Jonathan Stedall are owed special thanks for giving me their time and expertise. Stephen Frears has contributed a lot to my work, through a long interview and ongoing correspondence. I am extremely appreciative of the interest he has taken in this study.

Thanks are due to Faber & Faber, Profile Books and Williams UK Ltd for allowing the reproduction of quotations and excerpts from poems and songs.

At De Montfort University, Steve Chibnall contributed interdisciplinary thought, as well as research and valuable film material. Tim O'Sullivan and John R. Cook and the late Nicholas Zurbrugg showed trust in my abilities, allowing me to develop a module on Alan Bennett's television drama while still a PhD student. My PhD supervisors, Peter Davison, Judy Simons and Andy Mousley, are owed thanks for their considerable help at the thesis stage of this project. I would especially like to express my gratitude to Peter Davison for continuing to supervise and motivate me, even after his retirement in 2001. He continues to be a mentor and role model, and it is to him that this book is dedicated.

Paul Cowen, formerly my Head of School, has supported my work beyond his retirement, and his excellent contributions at the late stages are very much appreciated, as is his and Chris' friendship. My parents, Antje and Gordon McKechnie, have patiently followed and encouraged my work. Thank you.

Thanks to my series editors, Sarah Cardwell and Jonathan Bignell, for their feedback on the draft manuscript, and to my copy-editor, Solveig Gardner Servian. At MUP, Matthew Frost was the driving force at every stage of the project, way beyond the call of duty. This book would not have been conceived or completed without his considerable help.

Finally, thank you to Malcolm Johnson for everything he has contributed to the book, and for everything else.

List of abbreviations

CTH	The Complete Talking Heads
Dinner	Dinner at Noon
Englishman	An Englishman Abroad
George III	The Madness of George III
Insurance Man	in Two Kafka Plays
Kafka's Dick	in Two Kafka Plays
King George	The Madness of King George
LRB	London Review of Books
Me	Me, I'm Afraid of Virginia Woolf (2003 collection of television plays)
Objects	Objects of Affection
Poetry	Poetry in Motion 1
Portrait	Portrait or Bust
Private Function	A Private Function (2004 collection of television and film scripts)
Question	A Question of Attribution
TH 1	Talking Heads 1
TH 2	Talking Heads 2
TT	Telling Tales
US	Untold Stories
Van	The Lady in the Van
WH	Writing Home
Writer	The Writer in Disguise

Introduction: 'Treat me as a dead author'

> I always say to people who are studying my stuff that it's best to treat me
> as a dead author and so not available for comment. Make it up – no-one
> will know.[1]

This is a quotation from a letter in which Alan Bennett politely declined
to give any information on his work. I share the experience with most
authors working on Bennett. He explains his reasons for not wanting
others to write about his life in the introduction to *Telling Tales* (*TT*):

> If there are any tales to be told, then I want to tell them, and I want to tell
> them unmediated. (*TT*: 9)

This book is an academic study, and therefore discusses and interprets
Bennett's works for television in their context. It is not a biographical
investigation, although it discusses Bennett's biographical and autobiographical modes within his television work.

Positioning

Alan Bennett is one of the most popular contemporary British dramatists. Successful across a range of media and forms, he has gained
public (and some critical) acclaim through his television work. Bennett
started writing for television in the mid-1960s and was a prolific writer
of television plays from the 1970s to the late 1990s.

> The idea that he [Bennett] might be the most important and innova-
> tive British television playwright since Dennis Potter initially seems
> laughable. But it's hard to think of a stronger contender. His prolific
> output has stretched to nineteen individual television plays, four tele-
> vision series and three cinema films, together with numerous stage
> works, short stories, assorted journalism and his inimitable diaries. *An
> Englishman Abroad* and the two *Talking Heads* series are ranked amongst
> British television's greatest achievements, and he is widely recognised as
> the master of the television monologue. (Brooke 2002)[2]

Born in Leeds in 1934 as the son of a violin-playing butcher, Alan Bennett claims to have spent a typically provincial, uneventful childhood. Awarded a civic scholarship from the city of Leeds after A-level success, he received Russian language training during his National Service. This possibly accounts for an enduring interest in the concepts of espionage and treachery. Bennett then read medieval history at Oxford, and seemed destined for a career as a don. However, a growing interest in writing and performing led, in 1960, to his involvement in *Beyond the Fringe*, considered a defining moment for satire. The revue, created for the Edinburgh Festival, launched Bennett as a public persona alongside his collaborators, Peter Cook, Jonathan Miller and Dudley Moore. While Bennett still continued research into Richard II at Oxford in the 1960s, he gradually realised that he was probably not suited to academe, and more attracted to performing and writing. Since the mid-1960s, Bennett has acted, written, directed, presented and edited in almost every conceivable medium, including stage, television, radio, film and print media.

Bennett's first work for television was the comedy series *On the Margin* in 1966. In the 1970s, the single play, set in the north of England, emerged as one of the main forms of production. The realist dramas about unassuming northern lives continued until the mid-1980s, Bennett, with increasing popularity, delivering his plays in 'seasons'. Bennett's single plays of mid-1980s constituted a departure from northern backdrops, as they are mainly biographical studies, often of writers and their works. The form of the documentary entered Bennett's work in the late 1980s, making significant statements about Englishness through specific studies, all linked by their concern with the recent and remote past. The first series of *Talking Heads*, a series of six one-person plays, was broadcast in 1988, followed by a second series of six plays in 1998. The television monologue has turned into Bennett's signature form, and the *Talking Heads* series constitute his biggest success for television. In 2000, Bennett wrote, produced and presented a series of ten autobiographical reflections on his childhood and youth: *Telling Tales*. These pieces draw on conventions of both drama and documentary, employing monologic conventions. Bennett has not written any works for television since 2000. He has since produced dramatic and prose works that have been considerable critical and commercial successes. Bennett's stage adaptation of *The Lady in the Van* (*Van*) took record advance sales in the West End in 1999, and *The History Boys* (2004) was the best-selling show the National Theatre ever produced. In 2006, it opened to critical superlatives on Broadway, winning six Tony Awards,[3] and its film adaptation went on UK release in October 2006. Bennett's short stories[4] have steadily sold well. His autobiographical volume *Untold Stories* (*US*), following the success of *Writing Home* (*WH*) in 1994, was one of the big selling, heavily marketed titles in the run up to Christmas 2005, and was still selling a large number of copies six months later.[5] The paperback version, released in August 2006, saw another surge in sales and media coverage.

Should Bennett, after a long pause, start writing television plays again, his work would be met with huge expectations and earn big viewing figures, as well as widespread critical attention. However, Bennett is sceptical about any future writing for television. In a question and answer session in 2004,[6] he said it was unlikely he was going to write in the 'social realist style' of his earlier television drama again, conceding he did not know how people spoke these days, and felt left behind by the developments of modern language. When asked whether there were any plans to re-release his earlier television work, say on DVD, Bennett said that this was also unlikely as he was 'not considered a big earner.' In the light of the figures above and Bennett's enduring commercial success, whether prose, stage plays, film or audio books, his comments sound self-deprecating. But to anyone familiar with the dissemination and availability of earlier television drama, his comment will not come as a surprise. Of course, Bennett responds to the question with characteristic (almost trade mark) reticence, but there seems to be reluctance among broadcasters to revisit older material. When *Telling Tales* was shown in November 2000, the BBC put on an 'Alan Bennett Night', grouping his most successful works, such as *A Woman of No Importance*, first of the *Talking Heads* style monologues, and *An Englishman Abroad*. Material from the 1970s and most of Bennett's plays from the 1980s, however, have not been repeated or made available for a very long time. There is hope that this material will be revived with the arrival and popular success of the digital channel BBC4, which specialises in archive material and topical 'theme nights'. However, there will be no such revival for Bennett's BBC comedy series *On the Margin* (1966), as it has been deleted and thus belongs to the notorious and unfortunate category of 'missing, believed wiped'.[7]

Bennett himself, in a traditional attitude that harks back to the very early days of television drama, sees television as being of lower status than theatre. In the 1980s, he named this lower status, and its opportunity to escape critical scorn, as the very reason for his being more comfortable writing for television than for the stage:

> [W]hen I'm writing for TV it doesn't feel as though I'm going to be marked on it in the same way as I am with theatre. (Bennett in Anty 1984: 13)

At the beginning of the twenty-first century, however, television drama does not provide a sanctuary to avoid critical scrutiny any more. The expansion of television, screenwriting and media degrees and the increasing flexibility of what constitutes high and popular culture have meant that the academic profile of television studies has been enhanced. Although television is still occasionally put into less 'serious' categories than other art forms, television plays are perceived to be at the high end of television's cultural hierarchy (see also Caughie 2000: 12–13). Bignell and Lacey (2005: 2) agree that the form of television play, and within this the single play, has been placed by academics 'at the centre of its curriculum and at the head of its hierarchy of canonical programme texts'.

> Television drama has both reproduced distinctions between 'serious' drama and 'popular' forms and also challenged them. (Bignell and Lacey 2005: 4)

As a result, the erstwhile 'poor relation' of theatre has been receiving considerable critical attention.[8] Given this development, Alan Bennett's television work has been somewhat overlooked. This study is partly motivated by this critical neglect and Bennett's problematic, atypical position within the canon. Although establishing himself as a writer of television, Bennett generally does not appear in generic works on television drama. Albert Hunt discusses *Bed Among the Lentils* (*Talking Heads I*) in detail in Brandt 1993, but neither Caughie (2000), Nelson (1997), Day-Lewis (1998) nor Creeber (2001) mention his considerable body of work. Bignell and Lacey, in their edited collection *Popular Television Drama* (2005), do not mention Bennett's work either, but nevertheless offer an explanation why he might have been left out of critical considerations: television programmes can become 'marginalised because of their lack of fit with dominant paradigms. ... The continual generation of new objects of analysis in the ongoing production of television drama produces both new points of discussion but also new marginalisations' (Bignell and Lacey 2005: 1).

Bennett's fame is centred around his public persona, which is seen as shy, self-deprecating and gently ironic. The sheer diversity of the work he is associated with (starting with *Beyond the Fringe*, but including recordings of bestselling audio books such as *Winnie-the-Pooh*, work in comedy, prose, stage plays and journalism) means he can fall between all stools, as well as occupy all of them. More pragmatically, Bennett is outside mainstream developments and trends in television drama, and it would upset tidy timelines to include him. Instead, consistently high viewing figures and sales for audiovisual material and scripts of his television works have to make the point that Bennett is a successful television author:

> [C]anonicity and quality have a relationship ... There is no necessary separation, then, between the 'canonical' and the 'popular', and each term shifts in its meaning according to its referent, its user's critical agenda and the discursive context. (Bignell and Lacey 2005: 5)

In Bennett's case, the 'critical agenda' does seem to exclude him from the 'canonical', associating him solely with the 'popular'. His work is greeted with huge public acclaim, meriting frequently repeated attributes such as 'everyone's favourite Yorkshireman' or 'National Treasure'.[9] It seems to be this very popular appeal that results in his critical perception as 'cosy' or 'lightweight'. The following excerpt from a review is an example of the language used in connection with Bennett:

> They [*Green Forms* and *A Visit from Miss Prothero*] evince a bittersweet nostalgia ... the production lets this conviction permeate through to us at its own pace, not so much wagging a finger as tentatively gesturing with a Rich Tea biscuit.[10]

Bennett has become a cultural icon, lovingly mocked as a reactionary northern remnant of times past, or as having 'a nice cup of tea' with Thora Hird.[11] On the occasions when he is subjected to the critical gaze, he is often presented as a reactionary playwright who glorifies the past,[12] and is seen within a framework of northern homeliness. Apart from his classification as apolitical and provincial, another reason for Bennett's problematic relationship with the critics may be his awareness of the audience, and the high expectations this places on him to repeat winning formulas. Bennett respects but also fears his public's reaction to his work. He gives the example of 'sabre-toothed pensioners' warning him outside a theatre that his work 'had better be good ... We're big fans of yours.'[13]

This study argues that Bennett, as the author of single plays, seasons and mini-series, has an influential position within the canon and the field of television drama. It suggests possibilities of reading and contexts for Bennett's television plays. Autobiography has been at the centre of his work in a number of media since the 1990s. The main critical approaches within this study are therefore related to areas of autobiography and the presentation of self, particularly taking into account Bennett's authorial self-fashioning, which sometimes clashes with and at other times responds to public perception. Bennett's public self, known through voice-overs, documentaries and public appearances, is referred to as the 'Bennett persona' in this study.[14] In his works, Bennett's autobiographical voice is at first disguised, his persona transferred to his protagonists, and then gradually moves towards a direct and confessional approach. His biographical works explore questions and ideas that can often be related to Bennett and his self-perception as a writer. Latterly, Bennett has provided increasingly frank autobiographical offerings and useful approaches to the evolution of his work.

This study takes an organic approach, as chapters follow on from each other, and mostly also follow the chronology of Bennett's career. There are exceptions: it seems appropriate, for example, to discuss the plays on spies and writers in the same chapter, dates ranging from 1983 to 1991. However, as chapters are also grouped thematically, they also can be read discretely.

In the overall structure, Chapter 1 furnishes the reader with concepts and influences instrumental to the understanding of Bennett's television work. On its own, it provides an overview of Bennett's career, as well as giving information on his non-televisual work. The chapter maps Bennett's early development as a performer and writer previous to his writing for television. In a wider context, the issues of provincialism and parochialism are introduced, as well as touching on social, domestic and so-called northern realism. For the first ten years, 1972 to 1982, all of Bennett's television plays are set in the north of England. This section therefore offers an examination of these northern contexts and influences, such as Richard Hoggart's seminal study *The Uses of Literacy*. It can be argued that Bennett's take on 'the provincial' creates regionally and culturally specific discourses which insist on the relevance of 'ordinary lives'. An excursus provides information on Bennett's non-televisual work for stage, film, prose and journalism.

Chapter 2 introduces and interprets all Bennett's television plays between 1972 and 1982, also providing the necessary context of British television drama and its developments. Following the study's chronology, it shows Bennett's beginnings in the field of television drama, examining his contribution to the category of the single play in his earlier works, including *A Day Out* and *Sunset Across the Bay*. These plays are populated by people with seemingly ordinary lives, the middle-aged couples, the aunties, the ladies in sensible shoes. Bennett's two seasons of plays, *Six Plays* (1978/79), later published as *The Writer in Disguise* (*Writer*, 1985), and *Objects of Affection* (*Objects*, 1982) show similarly ordinary types of characters. Protagonists find themselves on the margins, with 'life' happening elsewhere, observing, rather than participating. These plays can also be – and have been – read applying autobiographical subtexts. *The Old Crowd*, a collaboration with Lindsay Anderson, provides a departure from typical 'Bennettland', and shows critical and public dissatisfaction with Bennett, assumed to be the cosy northern playwright with a knack for writing 'typical' dialogue.

Chapter 3 is an exploration of the recurring figures of spies and writers in Bennett's work. Within the structure of the study, it documents Bennett's move from disguised autobiography to producing works on the lives of others. Centred around ideas Bennett was in two minds about, the single plays between 1983 and 1991 are all biographical studies, and all include autobiographical subtext and exploration. After the northern, deliberately provincial plays, Bennett takes the themes of his television plays into 'southern', upper class contexts. Bennett has written three plays about treachery, exile and (in two cases) spying: the stage play *The Old Crowd* (1977), and the two biographical studies of Cambridge Spies Guy Burgess in *An Englishman Abroad* (John Schlesinger, 1983) and Anthony Blunt in *A Question of Attribution* (1988; television adaptation John Schlesinger, 1991). The two television plays on spies can be read as studies in Englishness associated with a specific class, and as examinations of treachery and nostalgia.

The Insurance Man (Richard Eyre, 1986) and *102 Boulevard Haussmann* (Udayan Prasad, 1991) document Bennett's recurring engagement with the work and the lives of other writers, with Kafka and Proust respectively as their protagonists. Harold Bloom's arguments on *The Anxiety of Influence* are in Bennett's case extended from the work other writers produce to the lives they lead – uncomfortable comparisons and a complex biographical argument. The cinematography of *The Insurance Man*, a collaboration with Richard Eyre, offers a stunning visual realisation of Kafkaesque interiors and scenarios. *102 Boulevard Haussman* translates Marcel Proust's insularity and his sensitively selfish life into text and images with the underlying and continuing concept of 'art as pain'. The theme of the observer on the outside looking in is extended to the writer. The other dominant theme, one that has resonated in many of Bennett's works over the years, is the question of the ethics of using other people's lives. This impacts on the portrayal of Franz Kafka in *The Insurance Man*, and also in the comedy for the stage, *Kafka's Dick*, from the same period.

Chapter 4 shows Bennett's move towards 'undisguised' autobiography, but through forms that are not associated with life writing, such as the documentary, and the introductions or the prefaces to his works. It also discusses Bennett's persona in the documentaries he has authored, and its presentation on screen. Standing on its own, the chapter is a study of Bennett's and director Jonathan Stedall's distinctive approach to the documentary. *Dinner at Noon* (1988), *Portrait or Bust* (1994) and *The Abbey* (1995) all explore issues of Englishness. *Dinner* started as a behaviourist investigation into the way people perform in public spaces, in this case a hotel. It turned into a rather more personal narrative.

Portrait was created alongside an exhibition curated by Bennett for Leeds City Art Gallery in 1993. The documentary is a personal approach to visual art and its reception, and is here aligned with the increasingly popular public face of Bennett, the Bennett persona.

The Abbey, a documentary in three parts, shows Bennett in the role of a commenting historian and often subversive art historian, with less biographical additions than in the other documentaries (including the series *Poetry in Motion*).

Bennett's strategies and trajectories of biography and autobiography are also analysed, with the contradicting notions of autobiographical exposure and the urge to withdraw from public scrutiny as a focal point.

Two series of television monologues constitute Alan Bennett's most successful work for television: *Talking Heads 1* and *2* (1988 and 1998). They are, together with the autobiographical monologues *Telling Tales* (2000), discussed in Chapter 5. In Bennett's career, generic and formal boundaries become increasingly insignificant. Forms are created to carry content and context of a work, and are 'customised' to suit Bennett's needs, resulting in forms unique to Bennett. The *Talking Heads* monologues illustrate this point in showing how Bennett has reinvented the monologue for television and stage by creating a generic composite. The result is a format that seems familiar, but is innovative and tailor-made to suit its author's and its performers' strengths. *Telling Tales*, features Bennett himself narrating his early life, marking a culmination of his increasingly autobiographical writing for the screen. Both the form and the content show his dispensation with the protection of the writer in disguise and present carefully measured and stage-managed revelations. Again, *Telling Tales* is a generic hybrid, but continues the trajectory towards autobiographical dominance, with Bennett as the executive producer, writer, presenter and subject of the ten monologues.

Within the structure, the chapter demonstrates Bennett's continuing reduction of form and character, arriving at the monologue. Standing on its own, the chapter presents a study of Bennett's reinvention of the monologue, with particular reference to the characters' addressee, as well as a perspective on the influences of music hall, stage monologue, soliloquy, photography and others.

Telling Tales, Bennett's last work for television at the time of writing, was broadcast in November 2000 to largely positive critical reactions. Bennett himself felt, however, that the monologues and accompanying book passed 'almost unnoticed' (*US*: xii), claiming them 'a bit of an indulgence' (*US*: 618). As Bennett was gravely ill with cancer at the time, he remarked:

> Had I said more about being ill and the impending curtailment that caused the memoirs to be written there would, I'm sure, have been more attention paid and sympathy extended. But cancer is not a career move and I kept quiet, which since I'm still here, turned out to be the right thing to have done. Had I done otherwise I might have died of embarrassment. (*US*: xii)

In *Untold Stories* (2005), his second autobiographical volume, Bennett provides forensic and detailed accounts of his life, including cancer and chemotherapy, sexual development, family skeletons in the closet and an account of a homophobic attack on himself and his partner. Bennett's writing now almost exclusively centres around his life, and for the first time includes life beyond his youth. Having insisted on being treated as a dead author in the mid-1990s, Bennett's writing has since acquired an open and confessional quality. It seems that Bennett has stopped worrying about what readers might think about him, having instead embraced the part of surviving author, no longer dying of embarrassment.

Notes

1 Alan Bennett, letter to K. McKechnie, October 1995.
2 www.screenonline.org.uk/people/id/504794/index.html.
3 Best Play, Best Director (Nicholas Hytner), Best Actor (Richard Griffiths), Best Supporting Actress (Frances de la Tour), Best Set (Bob Crowley), Best Lighting Design (Mark Henderson).
4 'The Clothes They Stood Up In' and 'Father! Father! Burning Bright!' in 1998 and 'The Laying on of Hands' in 2001, published together as *Three Short Stories* in 2003 by Profile Books.
5 '*Untold Stories* has shifted 333,268 copies in hardback in the eight months since it was published [i.e. between 25 October 2005 and 24 March 2006], considered an extraordinary performance for a work with literary qualities. It sold more than £150,000-worth of copies at Christmas alone'. http//books.guardian.co.uk/samueljohnson2006/story/0,,1781745,00.html.
6 'An Audience with Alan Bennett', Queen Elizabeth Hall, South Bank, London, June 2004.
7 See also Fiddy, Dick (2002) *Missing, Believed Wiped*, London: BFI.
8 Examples for the expansion of research on television drama are the AHRB-funded, Reading University based research project 'The BBC Wednesday Play and Postwar British Drama', and The Television Series (MUP), the series in which this study is published. Other monographs are on authors such as Terry Nation, Perry and Croft, Andrew Davies and Trevor Griffiths.
9 This term is often used in connection with Bennett, although he has allegedly threatened the unknown inventor of this soubriquet with a violent death. See,

for example, the *Sunday Telegraph* headline (David Sexton, 23 December 2001) 'National treasure'.

10 Originally written for the *Financial Times*, accessed 21 January 2004, www.cix. co.uk/~shutters/reviews/96076.htm.

11 The satirical series *Spitting Image* (1984–96) used to portray Bennett and Thora Hird in this way.

12 See, for example, Bull, J. (1994) *Stage Right: Crisis and Recovery in British Contemporary Mainstream Theatre*, London: St Martin's Press, pp. 10–11.

13 'Alan Bennett gives a personal view of 25 years of the National on the South Bank', www.nationaltheatre.org.uk/platforms/Alan_Bennett_NT25_article.html.

14 The term 'Bennett persona' is used throughout this study to make the distinction between the (unknown) 'real' person Bennett and the person that is perceived to be Bennett. Bennett's self-presentation and its interpretation by media and public contribute to this 'persona'.

1

'Above all ordinary': contexts and critical approaches

> On my own subjective scale writing for the theatre comes first, feature films second and television (whether film or tape) last. This is partly because at the moment I find television easiest to write, theatre well nigh impossible and feature films (or grown-up films as I tend to think of them) somewhere in between. But the scale has more to do with the permanence of the various forms. A theatre play, once put on, will normally get into print and so can be read and reproduced. A feature film, once shown in the cinema, starts out on its career and has a history, a life. A BBC television film has no history. It is an incident, with luck an occasion, the bait for the writer a nationwide audience and his work a topic of general discussion the next day. (Bennett 1984: 121)

Bennett made this statement in 1984, when television did not have the cultural status or prestige that was awarded to works for theatre and film. Bennett here also draws attention to the ephemerality of television, both due to the way it is consumed and, very specifically, the broadcaster's lack of conservation of programmes. However, the status of television has changed considerably since 1984, due to greatly improved policies of conservation and archiving, home recording facilities, and the post-programme marketing of recordings. Bennett's hierarchy also indicates that he did not grow up with television. In the essay 'Cheeky Chappies' (US: 416), Bennett describes himself as 'brought up during the Second World War', 'a child of the BBC Home Service'. The biggest constant in his childhood and youth was the 'wireless'. Bennett remarks on radio plays leading the way towards later developments in social realism: 'Radio was at the kitchen sink long before Arnold Wesker' (US: 419).

The Bennett family went to 'the pictures' at least twice weekly, and there is a useful account of this other significant influence on the play-wright in the essay 'Seeing Stars' (US: 157). There was also the annual outing to the pantomime at Leeds Town Hall, where Bennett saw come-dians like Norman Evans and Albert Modley perform. Many of these performers started their careers in radio and made the transition to television later on. Even at an early age, Bennett showed a preference for northern 'lugubriousness' and a dislike for relentlessly cheerful 'cheeky chappies' like Tommy Handley and Max Miller (*US*: 418). He preferred types closer to home like Mona Lott and Al Read, whose humour was 'rooted in everyday life':

> And though Cinderella was hardly social realism it came much closer to my life than ever *ITMA* [*It's that Man Again* – Tommy Handley's weekly wartime radio show] did, particularly as every pantomime would include a slapstick routine based on some household chore ... wallpapering, say, or making pastry or doing the washing, procedures with which I was familiar and so found very funny. It was a lesson, though I didn't realise it at the time, that comedy and real life were in some relation. (*US*: 419)

In the late 1940s and 1950s, television was something Bennett and his family associated with 'Down South and certainly not ... Leeds' (*US*: 417). It has a certain irony that television, having come into Bennett's life relatively late, turned out to be the medium for which he produced some of his most personal work, most connected with his northern origins. First of all, he wrote in acquired voices, considered to be appropriate for the stage, the main medium of his early career:

> If Literature and Down South symbolised to Bennett places where life was to be found, it is hardly surprising that, as a young writer in *Beyond the Fringe* and *Forty Years On*, he used the language of literature and the south, and often exaggerated it and used it as parody. (Turner 1997: 149)

Bennett chose television as a medium for the low-key, everyday stories that are characteristic of his northern plays. It is suggested here that this was precisely because it was lower on his personal scale of cultural value, and thus less intimidating and less fraught with expectation.

Beyond the Fringe

The satirical revue *Beyond the Fringe* in 1960 is considered a significant watershed for British satire[1] and comedy, its political edge and its stylistic simplicity. Its importance is still debated among critics, and those involved continue to be interviewed about their place in history:

> It can justly be argued against the show that it is too parochial, too much obsessed with BBC voices and BBC attitudes, too exclusively concerned with taunting the accents and values of John Betjeman's suburbia. *Beyond the Fringe* is anti-reactionary without being progressive. It goes less far

than one could have hoped, but immeasurably farther than one had any right to expect. (Kenneth Tynan, quoted in Wilmut 1980: 17)

When discussing his involvement with the revue and his relationship with its other writers and performers, Jonathan Miller, Dudley Moore and Peter Cook, Bennett characteristically and habitually presents himself as an outsider. This is both in terms of his significance in contributing to the revue, and socially, feeling helplessly inadequate faced with the confidence and free-flowing wit of the other three. Jonathan Miller, on the other hand, acknowledges Bennett's characteristic attention to detail, both in his writing and in his performance:

> He [Bennett] had a sort of pin-sharp accuracy – an absolutely unflinching accuracy of portraiture. Everything else I have ever seen other people do since has always seemed to be extremely blurred. He was a miniaturist. Perfect when he came on. (Miller in Wilmut 1980: 20)

Looking at the revue's significance for Bennett's later career in general and his television plays in particular, there are several strong connections. The most famous of Bennett's contributions to *Beyond the Fringe* is 'Take a Pew', a parodic Anglican sermon, which exemplifies his ability to reproduce familiar speech. The economy with which he carefully mines material from a relatively limited source can also be seen:

> It took about half an hour to write, and was, I suppose, the most profitable half hour of work I had ever done. Once I had hit on the form I used to be able to run up sermons for all sorts of occasions, choosing texts almost at random from any book that came to hand. (Bennett in Wilmut 1980: 10)

Bennett's other solo contribution to *Beyond the Fringe*, the monologue 'The Northern Way of Death', had connections with the acts of northern music hall and radio comics, 'whose comedy comes from talking about life to an audience with whom they share a set of social assumptions and a set of references' (Turner 1997: 152). The piece seemed to be an attempt to include his northern, original voice in the material of *Beyond the Fringe*, for Bennett to 'be himself'. However significant the comic monologue 'The Northern Way of Death' may have been for future television developments, its reception by American audiences delayed the emergence of Bennett's northern voice. This seems understandable, as the Broadway audience would have lacked the specific socio-linguistic knowledge to appreciate the piece. Bennett, however, deemed the monologue a failure that confirmed his suspicions about the pitfalls of 'being yourself':

> This [the monologue] was also death as met with in Morecambe and Blackpool, neither of them settings which an American audience could

be expected to know about or want to. I performed the sketch nightly for six months to the embarrassment of my colleagues and stunned silence of the audience, and when the revue ended it was nearly ten years before I ventured to write about the North of England again. So much for 'being myself'. The first round had gone to T.S. Eliot. (*WH* 1997: xii)

In 1994, decades after the encounter took place, Bennett describes what he calls a 'useful parable' (*WH* 1997: xi) to 'make sense' of his two different modes of writing. Bennett's father was a butcher, and Mrs Fletcher one of his clients to whom Bennett delivered meat. Her daughter, Valerie, worked for the publisher Faber & Faber in London, and later became T.S. Eliot's second wife. Bennett's mother once met Mrs Fletcher with an elegant gentleman she did not know, and Bennett realised later that his mother had been introduced to T.S. Eliot. Already torn between the bright lights of literary London and his 'authentic' northern roots, Bennett saw his mother and T.S. Eliot as the exponents of the two worlds he has been torn between throughout his career: the provincial North, at first uninspiring, uneventful and breeding escapist fantasies, and the metropolitan South, promising fulfilment of intel- lectual and literary ambitions. This encounter,[2] Bennett imagining his mother in awkward conversation with T.S Eliot, has provided an impor- tant interpretative subtext to Bennett's career, and a comic epiphany for a career shaped by being in two minds:

> [I]f we take T.S. Eliot to represent Art and Literature and Culture and everything in the upper case, my mother indefatigably in the lower case to represent life, then it seems to me that what I've written teeters rather indecisively between the two. Because what I've written for the stage, I suppose, aspires more towards culture. What I've written for television is really much more to do with life with a capital 'L'.[3]

The conflict is made more universal by the fact that the voices also repre- sent a literary north–south conflict, or, more specifically in Bennett's case, the conflict between a biographical environment and one that had been acquired through education and assimilation. From the 1970s onwards, Bennett has retained a foot in both camps, writing in both the northern, 'the inner voice he hears most clearly', and in the southern voice, 'speaking properly', he has acquired through education and ambition.[4]

On the Margin

One would never have suspected that a Yorkshire accent could be so camp. (Wilmut 1980: 94)

Positioned roughly halfway between the satirical revue *Beyond the Frv.* (1960) and the revue-style play *Forty Years On* (1968), *On the Margin* was conceived as a television comedy series including sketches, clips of music hall comedians and excerpts from and parodies of poems. Written as six half-hour programmes for BBC 2, it was first broadcast on 9 November 1966, and in a weekly slot for six weeks after that. The practice of 'observation without passing judgement' (Wilmut 1980: 94), for which Bennett's television plays were to be praised in later decades, was already in place.

Bennett's performance is in line with many northern comedians who use camp conventions as part of their inventory, such as *The League of Gentlemen* or Les Dawson (himself influenced by Norman Evans and the persona he adopted in *Over the Garden Wall*). In the following sketch with John Sergeant, Bennett played an antique shop owner:

> Sergeant: Have you any camp teapot stands?
> Bennett: Do you know, if only you'd come here a week ago, I was knee deep in camp teapot stands. I've had teapot stands in this show as camp as a row of pink tents.
> I tell a lie – as camp as a row of pink *frilly* tents.
> (On the Margin, quoted in Wilmut 1980: 96)

Wilmut (1980: 98) remarks that in *On the Margin* we can see 'the transition between Bennett the comedian, and Bennett the playwright – or rather we could see the transition had not the BBC, in an act of criminal vandalism, allowed the recordings to be destroyed.'

In summary, many of the elements that have made Bennett's work distinctive were assembled in content, if not in form, from the early 1960s onwards.

Northern matters

In his first ten years as a television playwright, Alan Bennett often writes in the voices of familiar, ordinary character types from the 'provinces', and is credited as having 'a gift for naturalistic dialogue' (Badder 1978: 73). Most of Bennett's television work from the 1970s and early 1980s can be seen in a naturalistic or realist mode,[5] although he does not comment on the influence of conventions such as kitchen sink or domestic realism. Bennett's forms of production are too diverse to confine him to northern domestic realism. O'Mealy (2001: xiv) also comments that 'to see Bennett as merely an old-fashioned realist is also to underestimate the protean nature of his gifts and his appeal'. Real-life figures from his past are often the models for Bennett's characters, and he equips them with the language in which he remembers them speaking.

...gins, these characters are often northern working-
...middle-class – all these characteristics are associated
...omestic realism. With the specification of realism as
...alism around the early 1960s,[6] writers and directors,
...king-class backgrounds themselves, and with strong
... were aiming to produce drama that paid attention
to (and was supposed to attract) audiences from a similar class background. This was not always easy, and often assumptions similar to the
one Hoggart describes below patronised the working classes:

> The working-classes are at bottom in excellent health – so the pastoral
> descriptions run – in better health than other classes; rough and unpol-
> ished perhaps, but diamonds nevertheless; rugged, but 'of sterling
> worth': not refined, not intellectual, but with both feet on the ground;
> capable of a good belly-laugh, charitable and forthright. They are, more-
> over, possessed of a racy and salty speech, touched with wit, but always
> with its hard grain of common sense. (Hoggart 1957: 14–15)

This statement is an example of one of the central problems for writers
from a northern, working-class background. They have moved onwards
and upwards through education and aspiration, and now turn their
attention back to their 'unrefined, common sense' origins, wanting a
position of insideness, but no longer able to be part of the environment
from which they came.

Alan Bennett originates from the kind of 1930s and 1940s northern
working-class background that Richard Hoggart describes in his influential work *The Uses of Literacy* (1957). The book was a strong influence
on Bennett, as he and Hoggart had similar Leeds backgrounds and were
both 'scholarship boys'. Bennett could not be described as a writer *of*
the working classes, but rather as an author who writes *about* aspiring
working-class and lower middle-class characters, from an – admittedly
reluctant – position of upward mobility.

> In some of Betjeman's poems he defines the snobberies and the disap-
> pointments of family holidays on the beach with equal precision but
> greater charity. These Lancashire folks [in the television play *All Day
> on the Sands*] were sourly regarded by Alan Bennett, like specimen fish
> upon a slab. (Clayton 1979)

The debate about Bennett's class perspective (is he patronising the
working classes? is he parodying the middle classes? is he unmasking
the upper classes?) can be linked to his relationship with his past.
Someone who has always felt out of place, unable to join in with whatever grouping he found himself, Bennett seems to have acquired a sense
of detachment from his surroundings at an earlier stage than most. As

he has argued, someone who observes cannot be amidst the action, but has to stay separate from it. This principle might be applied to his own situation of disjuncture, as one who originated from a specific class, environment and region, but left it while he was still young. Bennett has never described himself as one who was part of or wrote about the working classes, once claiming that it was not 'class' he was interested in or liked, but 'classes, types' (*Dinner at Noon* in *WH*: 42). The 'types' that Bennett portrays in his works are mostly outsiders, characters on the sidelines; separated from others by class, social embarrassment, lack of confidence or lack of eloquence. When it comes to writing about his parents' generation, Bennett frequently focuses on what he terms 'an almost ecological loss of habitat' (*Me, I'm Afraid of Virginia Woolf*: ix). Texts like the television play *Sunset Across the Bay* (1975) contain important social commentary on the exclusion of people of Bennett's parents' generation in the course of the 'modernisation' of cities in the 1960s and 1970s. Here, he shares a concern with John Betjeman, whose famous anti-modernist poem 'Come friendly bombs and fall on Slough' sums up the brutalist destruction of cityscapes. While *Sunset Across the Bay* shows the flattening of a complete neighbourhood in Leeds, the stage play *Enjoy* exposes the hypocrisy of authorities insensitive to the needs of the population, but wanting to cash in on the 'heritage' industry. Daphne Turner (1997: 16) argues that Bennett's presentation of the North as 'fake' in *Enjoy* is a symptom of his own disillusionment with it, and a realisation of the staying power of destructive northern clichés. Hence, Turner comments, the northern plays stopped in 1982 with the television play *Intensive Care*. I would argue, however, that, while the northern landscape is less prominent in works of the late 1980s and thereafter, the northern idiom has remained one of the main forms of expression for Bennett's characters (in the *Talking Heads* monologues, for example). With usual characteristic ambivalence, Bennett embraces his northerness, but refuses to be too 'typical' by continuing to parody romanticised perceptions of the North. He demonstrates this in a sketch about Ivy Compton-Burnett living in Pontefract and toiling up the slag heaps, in order to write her mining novel 'The Pit and its Pithfalls':[7]

> We were all miners in our family. My father was a miner. My mother is a miner. These are miner's hands. But we were all artists, I suppose, really. But I was the first one who had this urge to express myself on paper rather than at the coalface. But, under the skin, I suppose I'm still a writer. I suppose, in a very real sense, I'm a miner writer. Miners are very strong, very tough, but, in a way, very gentle creatures. But because they're very strong and very tough, they can afford to be very gentle. Just as, being very gentle, they can also be very tough. (*WH* 1997: 590)

This short piece parodies the hypocrisy of having risen above one's origins, and fake nostalgia about 'roots'. It also reflects the public's stereotypical view of the North as a literary landscape.

Bennett is just one example of the scholarship boys turned social critics (and thus turned into social successes): Richard Hoggart, Raymond Williams, and, across the channel, Pierre Bourdieu.[8] Where Hoggart blames the infiltration of new and mass media for the decline in working-class identity, Bennett is more ambivalent, stating that the risk when writing 'about a childhood in the North, is that you may end up writing an extended Hovis commercial' (*TT*: 10). Bennett has written pastoral pieces about the North as it once was (for example, *A Day Out* in 1972), but has also produced scathing satires on false notions of northern heritage, where people are encouraged to 'be typical' (for example, *Enjoy* in 1980). He acknowledges that the North he describes is that of his childhood and youth, but that many of his northern plays are still set in the present, making for a certain 'hybridic' quality.[9]

Bennett's ambivalent relationship with his northern origins has its foundations in the books he read as a child.[10] His early reading featured children who lived either in extremely idyllic or extremely deprived surroundings, and he could detect neither in his own childhood. Leeds, with its nineteenth-century civic architecture, did not have the 'right' kind of old buildings for a youth 'famished for antiquity'; the surrounding landscape was not sufficiently pastoral. Bennett even took it as a sign of Leeds' insignificance that the city suffered little damage from German bombers during World War II (*TT*: 26). Thinking that books represented life as it should be, Bennett at first asked himself what was wrong with his life, and then resigned himself to the fact that it was never going to live up to the expectations set by literature.[11] This notion can be detected in Bennett's works across all genres and forms. It impacts, for example, on his work on other writers, his documentaries, and on the typical Bennett protagonist's belief that 'Life is generally something that happens elsewhere'.

Bennett calls his childhood 'above all ordinary', in accordance with the description his parents would have given of themselves: 'not working-class, certainly not middle-class, but ordinary ... being ordinary was a state to which they almost aspired' (*TT*: 10–11). The importance of 'knowing one's place' for this generation, not pretending to be something one was not, clashed with the wish for their children to have more educational opportunities than they had enjoyed. Bennett, who has described himself as a 'frightful little creep' (*Poetry in Motion 2*: 9), was a bright child and was among the top of the class throughout his time at school. While this was welcomed by his parents, they called his homework and revising 'your swotting', an expression they later transferred to his work as a writer. On the one hand, they wanted him to 'speak properly', to demonstrate the effect of educational opportunities; on the other hand, they did not want their son to rise above their station by 'putting it on'. Bennett's father particularly was 'hot on anything smacking of social pretension' (*WH*: x): 'As a child I was clever and knew it and when I showed off, as I often did, Dad would not trouble to hide his distaste' (*US*: 15). Bennett admits in hindsight that he was always subconsciously including his father's judgement in his considerations about his writing right up to Walter Bennett's death in the early 1970s. It was only after his father died that Bennett started to keep a diary. Like many artists from a similar background, Bennett feels the guilt that can be associated with upward mobility, the fear of being labelled 'pretentious'. Hoggart's *The Uses of Literacy*, published in 1957, appeared around the same time that 'ordinary' lives were exposed as the subject of plays and films: *Look Back in Anger*, for instance, premiered in 1956 at the Royal Court Theatre. The working class was thus moving into the dramatic mainstream, and Bennett self-ironically states in retrospect 'had I known it was going to become fashionable I might have enjoyed it more' (*TT*: 14). Bennett's loyalty to and belief in the importance of his origins clashed with his desire for self-improvement and his appreciation of 'high' art. While always expressing gratitude for his educational opportunities, Bennett has openly admitted that he sometimes deliberately downgrades his background on the social scale, conveniently forgetting some of the privileges and successes he enjoyed during his early years. This paradoxical aspiration to deprivation suggests that Bennett does not want to be seen as showing off. In a traditional Yorkshire environment one must not get above oneself, one must not forget where one came from, and one must always deny that success is deserved. Bennett's work is accordingly characterised by the tension between a natural tendency to perform and the self-deprecation engraved in him through his upbringing.

Bennett belonged to a civic community which invested in academic potential: Leeds. A good performance at secondary level and acceptance by a university automatically provided a scholarship by the city, and state scholarships were topped up by the Corporation Education Department: 'the city educates its own' (*TT*: 91). Bennett is thus a classic case of the scholarship boy from the provinces, excelling at grammar school, chosen to learn Russian for Intelligence purposes at Cambridge during his National Service, and winning a place at Oxford. Education often created separation between parents and child, a dilemma that often befell scholarship boys returning home from university. Bennett was no exception, hearing that he had achieved a first while working at Tetley's.

He received the following communication from his father: 'We haven't let on to your aunties yet that that you're getting your cap and gown. You won't be wanting a lot of splother' (*US*: 26).

Although they share a similar educational trajectory, Bennett and Hoggart's views collide when it comes to surveying the impact of change on their working class origins. Initially, Bennett referred to his origins as something to be ashamed of, and to react against. His mother's fear of 'folks knowing all her business' drove her to delusion and depression. Bennett was made sharply aware of what he presumed were social inadequacies when he went to Oxford with a new set of Antler suitcases:

> That I still had not acquired a past hit me the minute I entered the lodge of my college. It was piled high with trunks: trunks pasted with ancient labels, trunks that had holidayed in Grand Hotels, travelled first-class on liners, trunks painted with four, nay, even *five*, initials. ... These trunks spoke memory. I had two shameful Antler suitcases that I had gone with my mother to buy at Schofields in Leeds.... (*WH*: 501)

At first, Bennett longed for escape, change and excitement; later he realised that he was linked to his 'roots', and was anxious to preserve what was left of his past. He admits that, by the time his parents started to embrace change, 'branching out' after his father had retired, their son did not want them to change anymore. Bennett celebrates the value of inertia in his comments on *The Dalesman*:

> [T]his Yorkshire magazine doesn't change – or does so in a way that you scarcely notice. Its form and contents, the cover, the recipes, the illustrations and the jokes – they're all as they were 30-odd years ago. And none the worse for that. 'When it's not necessary to change,' said the 17th century Lord Falkland, 'it's necessary not to change.' (Bennett in Mitchell 1988: 1)

Bennett's childhood has become the most prolific source and the most important influence in his works. The child's perspective is evident from the 1970s onwards, in works such as *All Day on the Sands* (1979) or *Intensive Care* (1982), whereas the 'undisguised' child Bennett enters his work at a later stage. It is not until *Telling Tales* (2000), *Hymn* (2001) and the largely autobiographical volume *Untold Stories* (2005) that Bennett directly confronts his own childhood, and the relationship with his parents, especially his father. It took him a long time to realise that, despite their ambition not to be different from other people, Bennett's parents were far from commonplace. He writes about the past from the perspective of the present, and works his way backwards, as indeed he claims he does when reading biographies (*Poetry* 2: 9). Just as childhood was the last thing he wanted to learn about when reading about other people's lives, childhood is last to be revealed in the chronology of his own life. In a preface to the short story 'Father! Father! Burning Bright' (*LRB* 1998) he calls this 'tidying up my Nachlass':

> To younger readers they [the plays] may seem old-fashioned and even antique, but they always were even at the time of writing. Writing and recollection are inextricable and I never felt that I was chronicling my own times, simply because so much of the dialogue came out of remembrance of childhood. (Introduction, *Me*: vii)

Bennett is positioned as a writer who observes the social sphere he originates from rather than declaring himself a part of it.

Provincialism

As Bennett's origins and formative influences are contextualised, a case for linking Bennett with the poetics and the politics of provincialism emerges. A northern childhood is inextricably associated with provincialism.[12] Definitions such as 'narrowness of view or interest' or 'wanting the polish of the capital' suggests that 'provincial' is an unsatisfactory condition. Provincialism, or even regionalism, a term less burdened with negative connotations, have hardly received any critical attention within the field of drama, there being a tacit understanding that modernity and regionalism are mutually exclusive (Mecklenburg 1986: 7).[13] If 'great' art aspires to the universal, the provincial carries the notion of the monocultural with a corresponding implication of a rejection of the cosmopolitan. Alan Bennett's northern characters certainly have the manners or speech of 'the provinces', although it would be an insult to the individuals they resemble and the author to assume automatically that they wanted 'the culture or polish of the capital'. On the one hand, the theme of escape is prominent in Bennett's work:

> [L]ife is elsewhere and one of the incentives to get away to university is just to be somewhere else and lead the life and see the places I read about in books. Leeds and a childhood in Leeds do not figure in any of the books I read, the provinces still – well – provincial. (*TT*: 14)[14]

On the other hand, Bennett's work contains the realisation that he underestimated the formative influence and relevance of his upbringing. Thus, gradually, his northern voice increases in importance. Bennett, of course, *has* a non-provincial or metropolitan voice at his disposal, and the two have always co-existed:

> Frears: One didn't think of the provinces in that way. It's much worse now. We were all from the provinces; it was just part of our lives.

McKechnie: Maybe that's what made the plays work. What I like about
your collaborations is that they were just about people, not about class
in that rather anthropological way.

Frears: The films were just a set of assumptions we made. ... The realism
was so central to it all. Morecambe, that was lovely, wonderful town.
We were just given these amazing shots.

(Interview with Stephen Frears)

Bennett's works at first carry strong notions of escapism, traditionally
associated with northern writing. In his later works, with the centring
on his life and persona, he demonstrates a deliberation to be regionally specific, to overcome clichés of northern provincial nostalgia, and
insists on a deliberate parochial approach to his subjects and landscapes. The case for literary parochialism has been formulated by the
critic Andy Medhurst.[15] Its propagation here is not considered to devalue
the political poignancy of Bennett's writing, but simply to personalise
and specify the politics in question. The expression 'parochial' generally has connotations just as negative as 'provincial', but its definition
includes the regionally specific, as identifiable to one particular parish.
What is generally described as narrow-minded, concerned only with
local concerns without any regard for more general or wider issues
should, according to Medhurst, rather be considered as 'speaking from
a position of insideness'.

> When we change scale we think and behave differently: nations are
> abstractions, regions are generally defined from the outside in, they are
> about form and function, they are academic, institutional or political
> creations. Locality needs to be defined from the inside, with a cultural and
> natural base, less abstraction, more detail. (Clifford and King 2002)

Although the concept of equating 'northern' and 'provincial' has
been destabilised, I would still argue that Bennett's television work of
the 1970s and early 1980s adheres to what is *deemed* provincial. His
northern work does not show characters who engage with the recent
northern renaissance, neither is it driven by sentimental working-class
nostalgia, 'we were poor but we were happy' narratives. His characters
do not live in loft apartments, 'nouveau northern' style, nor do they play
in brass bands, 'rugged-but-beautiful northern' style. Instead, Bennett's
writing simply states how unspectacular, dull and humdrum lives could
be in his native Leeds in the 1940s and 1950s. His style is never sentimental, despite his undeniable nostalgia for the past, but precise and
often of sociological quality. Bennett has been accused of being stuck in
the past, in his representation of the language and tone of the 1950s. As
a 'much-loved' writer, critics hold he simply *cannot* be cutting edge, and
as a 'family favourite', writing about northern characters who are not

demonstrating against the closure of a pit and who are not escaping to realise their full potential down south, he *has* to be provincial. However, the pleasure of engaging with a specific, deliberately parochial setting on stage or screen cannot be dismissed merely as a refusal to move with the times. Rather, it has to be seen as the need to have one's identity confirmed, and to be treated as significant. The desire for a knowable community where '...it was all clean and you could walk down the street and folks smiled and passed the time of day' (*CTH*: 116) is an unfashionable, anti-modernist appeal to restore things to their former order. More importantly, however, it has notions of a deep unease about an environment that is becoming less and less identifiable as belonging to a regional or social setting, and where people unable to keep up with changes become redundant. In Bennettland, globalisation creates isolation:

> The more we look at working-class life, the more we try to reach the core of working-class attitudes, the more surely does it appear that the core is the sense of the personal, the concrete, the local: it is embodied in the idea of, first, the family and, second, the neighbourhood. This remains, though much works against it, and partly because so much works against it. (Hoggart 1957: 33)

Hoggart and Bennett are on common ground with the notion of the concrete and the local, although they evaluate it in different ways. Bennett's work shows notions of the deliberately, sometimes defiantly parochial. Characters are anchored in their environment and do not often move out far away from it: a bicycle trip from Halifax to Fountain's Abbey, a move from Leeds to Morecambe, a life between a drab office and a suburban semi, a trip to the cemetery. Some of these scenarios are exchangeable, anonymous, only identifiable as part of the North through the air of hopelessness. This reaches back to the view out of the windows from drab attic rooms in kitchen sink films, *A Taste of Honey* or *Room at the Top*. Bennett's northern locations have the same kind of quality, showing the characters' interaction with their environment.

Social, domestic or provincial realism?

Samantha Lay (2002: 5) suggests that the term 'realism' should not be used without a prefix, but it is difficult to determine which one should be applied to Bennett: working-class realism, social realism? The confusing variety of 'realisms' is narrowed down by using definitions drawn up by Raymond Williams who has described domestic realism as 'the injection of new content into an orthodox dramatic form' (Williams

1977: 498; see also Lay 2002: 9). It is generally described as secular, contemporary and relevant in its linking of characters and the impact on them through politics, and intent on extending the boundaries of representation, both socially and geographically. Williams also defines it as distinguishable from naturalism by the clarity of expression of authorial intent.

In the following, Bennett's work is examined under criteria that are typically associated with social realism. They are combined with more general criteria for categorising television drama (see also Lacey in Creeber 2001: 3).

Through the character types they portray, television plays often relate to the lives of the audiences they are intended for. Generally, realism in art attempts to represent real life, so one effect is that feelings of familiarity are evoked. In Bennett's television plays, characters display a recognisable register of speech, although he comments: 'But don't let anybody imagine that because Northern dialogue is natural, that it's not extremely artificial. It seems to me more mannered and peculiar and odd than restoration comedy.'[16]

Audiences always comment that they know someone who sounds like a Bennett protagonist, although the way characters speak is sometimes associated with the past. The reason for this feeling of authenticity is that it rests on meticulous linguistic observation on Bennett's part, complemented by lifelong actual experience of the type of character he is portraying:

> 'Salad's on a new footing now, apparently,' Mam said, looking at her copy of *Ideal Home*. 'It doesn't just have to be lettuce and tomato and a slice of boiled egg. They eat celery with apple now and you can put raisins in if you want. All the boundaries are coming down.' (*TT*: 66)

Bennett's television plays are set in a recognisable period, and often a recognisable location. Representations of the North had great significance in the rise of social/domestic realism (see also Lacey 1995: 78 and 80). Character and place are nearly always connected (Lay 2002: 8–9). With few exceptions, Bennett's exterior locations show the 'grimy', run-down north of England; uninspiring, darkly-coloured inner cities, wrecked by 1960s progressive architecture. The local industries had already collapsed or were on the brink of doing so in the 1970s, the sooty remnants were still visible on the buildings, with areas brutally cut up by ring road developments. Alternatively, we are shown dull suburban environments with identical houses, but without a sense of community. Interior locations are chosen in the same 'humdrum' spirit. Alan Bennett comments that should he 'have a favourite, imaginary landscape it seems to be an empty corridor' (*Objects*: 7). The 1970s television play *Me, I'm Afraid of Virginia Woolf* shows utilitarian and drab Polytechnic interiors, with the restaurant underneath Leeds Town Hall as the canteen, all PVC, formica furniture and neon lighting:

> The place under the Town Hall was the civic restaurant for as long as I can remember. [Location for *Me*] It always seems odd to come back to Leeds and to see people having wine with their meals and eating avocado pears...I mean, I can see people eating avocado pears elsewhere and never turn a hair, but when I come back to Leeds, it seems very peculiar ... 'Avocado pear?! You want something on toast; you don't want an avocado pear! This is Leeds!' (Alan Bennett, *The South Bank Show*, 1984)

Sunset Across the Bay has a 'cuspal' visual quality, balanced between ruthless architectural progress and the world of an old couple. Consequently, exterior and interior shots show the contrast between condemned terrace houses and the high rise buildings springing up around them. Bennett's television plays generally do not idealise the present, and attempt not to idealise the past. The latter is sometimes unsuccessful, as audiences' nostalgic feelings and memories are activated through Bennett's evocation of the past, and therefore a lot of idealisation takes place in the *reception* of the works. Nelson (1997: 2–3) quotes Schroder (1992) in saying that:

> [T]he text itself has no existence, no life, and therefore no quality until it is deciphered by an individual and triggers the meaning potential carried by this individual. Whatever criteria one wishes to set up for quality, therefore, must be applied not to the text itself, but to the readings actualized by the text in the audience members.

Some of Bennett's plays could be seen to display a sense of 'moral realism'.[17] This expression seems apt as a prefix for a large number of Bennett's television plays. 'Moral realism' is not bound exclusively to northern plays, although it is most clearly extractable from them. Two of the early plays, *Green Forms* and *A Visit from Miss Prothero*, for example, insinuate clear moral statements, concerning the survival of the individual employee in a large faceless organisation. Equally, the central point of *Talking Heads* 1 and 2 reminds us that 'attention must be paid' to people with sometimes boring and sometimes troubled lives. This could easily turn to a dogmatic evocation of guilt, but all Bennett does is show details of characters' lives and their self-delusion. His language evokes pleasures of the familiar, conspiratorially drawing the audience into the work through shared references and shared language.

Linguistic familiarity and strong female characters

The specific, parochial appeal of Bennett's work is also due to his protagonists, some of whom are adapted from types of people close to him. One of the strongest connections Bennett's work has with conventions of social realism is the focus on strong women. Middle-aged or elderly women often dominate the plays. British realist television has a distinctive tradition of memorable female characters (see also Lay 2002: 16), with examples ranging from the young and underprivileged (*Cathy Come Home*) to the straight-talking, comic matriarch (Vera Duckworth in *Coronation Street*, for example).

Northern domestic realism expresses itself across a range of media. When Bennett started writing for television, the main forum for the production of realist plays with social concerns was the *Play for Today/ Wednesday Play* slot on BBC television. Domestic realism also influenced other genres, such as the series. The most notable and long-running example is the ITV series *Coronation Street*, first created in 1960, and topping the ratings nationally from 1961. Not only did it present working-class realism to a mass audience, it also included elements such as 'the stress on women and the strength of women, and the perspective of nostalgia' (Dyer et al. 1981: 4, quoted in Lacey 1995: 76; see also below). Familiarity leads to audiences' identification with protagonists whose concerns, problems and, importantly, language they shared. Bennett describes his childhood environment as one 'where women did all the talking' (*CTH*: 127), drawing a connection between his life then and the later dominance of female characters in his works. Men seldom dominate the action, nor do they do much of the talking in Bennett's television plays, just as they were generally silent in his family and his surroundings. In an environment where treats and excitement were few, small events, registers and pitch of language, as well as behavioural idiosyncrasies became the foundation of the Bennett repertory:

> Northern women aren't simply southern women who can't speak properly, they're a different species who've come down a different genetic avenue. ... Too often, northern English is thought to be standard English, delivered in a dirty dishcloth voice, with 'like' shoved on at the back 'He's gone down the pub, like'. But it's actually more complicated than that. The structure of the grammar – very often the subject of the sentence is kept until the end, so that it retains its suspense throughout, which is quite useful if you're writing comic writing – 'It's gone all hectic for me, has Harrogate' 'She's got a big nose for a baby, has their Christine' 'It's him she'll get that from, is Frank' 'Considering he's only got one arm, he's not had a bad career'. (Alan Bennett, *The South Bank Show*, 1984)

Although he always preserved the conversations he eavesdropped on as a child, often writing them down in notebooks later on, Bennett states that he only realised the linguistic and behavioural distinctiveness of northern women when he saw Denis Mitchell's documentary *Morning in the Streets* (1959). Having been educated to believe that art and northern everyday life were not combinable, Mitchell's work demonstrated that everyday lives made excellent raw material for art. Forty years later, one of the 'Alan Bennetts' in *The Lady in the Van* (*Van*: 20) refers to little old ladies as his 'niche' or his 'bread and butter'. In portraying these lives, Bennett gives a voice to those who would not normally be heard. His approach is a detailed picture of a person, sometimes not altogether flattering, which demands that attention must be paid. It does not, however, demand blind sympathy. Despite choosing the supposedly humdrum lives of 'ordinary people', and making them regionally specific, Bennett does not make dramas like *Talking Heads 1* and *2* easy to watch. Several characters are portrayed as boring; nearly all of them lie to themselves or to others, and all the plays forcefully bring home the notion of characters unhappily trapped in their own lives. The women in these plays find it difficult to adjust to linguistic and social change, mirroring the anxieties within Alan Bennett's core audience. Changes in language (politically correct speech, for example) document the instability of a world which seems to be no longer theirs. Language is seen as part of this destabilisation, and new words and trends are mocked. The new and the other are generally seen as threats.

Elderly women are often shown in scenes with their grown-up sons, whom they treat as if they were still children, asking them interfering questions about their digestive system and uttering a steady stream of suspicions and non-sequiturs. In Bennett's earlier television plays, some of the elderly northern women are presented with merciless, almost forensic precision. 'Aunty Kitty' in *Intensive Care*, for example, has only narrowly escaped strangulation, according to her brother. The following makes us understand why:

> I thought you'd have been here a bit since. I was here at 3 o'clock. You'll notice a big change. He's not like my brother. He's not the Frank I knew. I don't dislike this colour scheme. I always liked oatmeal. The doctor's black. (*Objects*: 181)

The favourite topics are dirt, disease and the lavatory, another echo of Bennett's mother: 'What memory was for Proust the lavatory is for my mam' (*Van*: 6), Bennett has remarked. Hygiene is the standard against which all things in life are measured, and there will be an intricate value system involved when judging other people, based on social distinctions Bennett's mother had established.

The middle-aged, unmarried woman is another Bennett 'type'. They are generally based on Bennett's aunties, Myra Rogerson and Kathleen Roach, who were married relatively late in their lives. They are revived in ladies such as Miss Schofield in *A Woman of No Importance*, Miss Ruddock in *A Lady of Letters* and Miss Fozzard in *Miss Fozzard Finds her Feet*.[18] These respectable ladies, employed as secretaries or shop assistants, are constantly trying to increase their status. Although people do not take much interest in them, they manage to convince themselves that they matter, and that they are a cut above the rest. This attitude expresses itself in a mannered way of speaking, exaggerated in construction and using words that seem heightened and betray social pretence: Miss Fozzard says that her disabled brother 'broadcasts the entire contents of his bladder down the stairs' (*CTH*: 147). Miss Schofield 'frequents a table' or 'concludes her coffee' (*CTH*: 14). Like most of Bennett's northern characters, these women are trapped in restrictive lives which can only be made bearable through shielding themselves from obvious truths and through editing their uneventful reality. They are built up convincingly as characters to whom nothing is more important than respectability, and we see the stifling nature of this ambition.

Despite frequent subversion and merciless precision in their portrayal, Bennett's women are generally seen to be affectionate and accurate takes on familiar characters.

Critics have argued[19] that there are three developments that hamper the intended effects of social realism: the neglect of the political in favour of the private, the increasing influence of autobiography, and a tendency to recreate the past through the eyes of the protagonist:

> [T]he move from public to private, political to personal, narrows the vision to such an extent that the wider structural inequalities not just regionally or nationally, but globally, are lost from the frame. (Clifford and King 2002)

These criteria can be applied to Alan Bennett to a certain extent. So, are a parochial approach and social realism in fact incompatible? Some of Bennett's texts explore the subjectivities of their central protagonists through a recreation of the past. In this respect it could be argued that they offer a nostalgic alternative to, for example, the heritage film in British cinema. Looking back instead of considering the contemporary settings from a highly individuated perspective can be seen as further undermining a sense of the 'public' (Lay 2002: 19). However, it is debatable whether Bennett neglects the political in favour of the personal. Scarr (1996) argues that Bennett's political argumentation actually becomes valid through its application to the individual, and its effect on the playwright himself. Certainly his writing lacks *direct* aggression and unmistakable links to contemporary party politics. Bennett's underlying anger at, for example, Margaret Thatcher's re-election expresses itself in statements like 'Governments come and go. Or don't go' (HMQ in *A Question of Attribution*). But generally, these references are not topical, and his plays show inarticulate characters trying to cope with difficulties brought on by governments or bureaucracies. The helplessness of silenced characters can, of course, be read as political, but is generally not seen in this way, as the characteristics linked with Alan Bennett probably prevent an unbiased reception.

I would argue that Bennett's early works are influenced by social realism, without insisting on linearity of timelines, and occasionally employing techniques such as the flashback or flashforward, or the voice-over. *Intensive Care* (1982) contains a dream section that can easily be interpreted as the protagonist's subconscious recreation of his childhood relationship with his parents, brought on by his father's imminent death. *Me, I'm Afraid of Virginia Woolf* (1978) has a voice-over commentary, a narrator, who validates and contextualises the actions of Hopkins, the protagonist, and also verbalises what he thinks, but cannot say:

Wendy: I think when one is married
Narrator: [voice-over] She meant 'we'.
Wendy: And I don't mean 'we' ...

(*Me:* 120)

This is one of Bennett's first departures from the diegetic mode. In a move away from seamless realism,[20] the text is opened up to self-referentiality, a device used in nearly all Bennett's later works. If an increasing autobiographical influence and a tendency to draw from the past can be seen to hamper 'proper' realism, then Bennett has certainly been moving away from the convention since the 1990s. *Talking Heads 1* in 1988 constitutes a definite formal departure from previous works. Realism has not been abandoned, but shows less connection with the social realist conventions in which his earlier works could be seen. The increasingly autobiographical works that follow *Talking Heads 1* take up this momentum of a modified realism, and the convention becomes one that is juxtaposed with others. This leads to hybrid forms, such as *The Lady in the Van*, where the dialogue is still written in realist fashion, but the boundaries of the diegetic scenario are nonetheless challenged through non-realist interventions. While the stage play *The Lady in the Van* has been accepted as a departure from Bennett's well-established style, earlier works that did not meet the audience's expectations of the playwright failed critically and commercially. *The Old Crowd* (1978) and *Enjoy* (a stage play, 1980) are examples of this.

With his considerable generic and formal range, Bennett is not a writer who can easily be categorised. Although he acknowledges that he has a 'constituency' (*The South Bank Show*, October 2005), he has always tried to avoid labelling. Moving towards the contextualisation of his television plays, however, it is suggested that works of the 1970s and early 1980s are more easily placed in the loose category of 'provincial realism' rather than 'social realism'. Bennett's work does not show the politicised campaign-play style of many the television dramas of the 1960s and 1970s. With their personalised narratives, their interaction with specific places or landscapes, his television plays are deliberately low-key and uneventful social miniatures. They do not generally have a tight dramaturgy or an intricate plot. Social issues and political concerns are clear, but generally only through the eye of a character, who is not the spokesperson for social change, but an example of what might happen if change is not achieved.

Excursus: theatre and film

This present study is published in *The Television Series*, and so it is a reasonable expectation that this first chapter should deal with contexts and critical approaches specific to television. However, Bennett's prolific and varied output (television, stage, feature films, autobiographical prose and essays) means that this is not a straightforward matter. While all of his works in their specific media have distinctive styles and registers, they cannot just be seen as discrete categories. A study on Bennett's television work can therefore not exclude these other forms and media and the impact they are seen to have.

Works for theatre

Bennett's first play, *Forty Years On* (1968), is a history play, a school play, a play in a play, a series of sketches – a mixture of genres that suggests the tension between Bennett's careers of historian, playwright and comic performer. *Forty Years On* is set in an English Public School, Albion House, 'a rough metaphor for England' (*WH*: 314). It draws on a broad range of literary styles and parodies and features historical figures, including Max Beerbohm, Bertrand Russell and Lady Ottoline Morrell. History and literary biography still feature in Bennett's stage work to date, with his latest play, *The History Boys* (2004), examining how history is taught and examined in schools.

It is widely agreed (Turner 1997, Eyre 2000, Dick 1999) that there is a divide in Bennett's work: stage plays are predominantly set in southern environments, and the ideas expressed are not directly connected to Bennett's Yorkshire roots, but located more in those surroundings he inhabited after he 'moved south'. With the exception of the northern stage play *Enjoy* (1980), all texts originally written for the stage[21] represent Bennett's 'southern', educated voice. As he has always had the ability to write in different registers and different genres within the same period, there is no such thing as a typical Bennett play for the stage – Richard Eyre (2000: 326) comments that 'In theatre, he's moved from form to form, never quite settling.' Bennett's voice is as recognisable in his works for the stage as it is in other media, but generically almost every play is an exploration of a different dramatic convention. In the stage works that followed *Forty Years On*, Bennett employed a wide range of forms with no discernible evolution, and subjects covering an equally wide range. In some cases, it is possible to trace areas of interest or unresolved questions as the source of a play in Bennett's published diaries, *Writing Home*. The plays, *Getting On* (1971) and *The Old Country* (1977), roughly fit into 1970s conventions of realism (although *not* working-class realism),[22] and explore ideas relating to public discussions of the time – the disappointment of the left with the Labour Party, and the question of what constitutes treachery of one's country. *Habeas Corpus* (1973) is Bennett's attempt 'to write a farce without the paraphernalia of farce' (*Plays 1* 1996: 17), exploring questions surrounding the permissive society and combining music hall songs with slapstick farce routines. Alec Guinness, who starred in *Habeas Corpus*' first production, describes the resulting formal pastiche:

> I suspect he [Bennett] would be a bit tetchy if I described the play as a farce but it has all the ingredients of a farce. But it's also like a kind of restoration play, some of it goes into doggerel verse and rhyming couplets. It is unlike anything I've ever been connected with before. The form is rather odd, but it is very funny indeed in places. (Guinness 1994: 221)

Habeas Corpus has been described as Bennett's 'dramatic riposte to the saucy seaside postcards of Donald McGill. Thus we have fake breasts, lost trousers, randy vicars, randy doctors, and desperate – and, yes, randy – housewives.'[23]

Enjoy (1980) builds on realist conventions, only to turn them into a play that has touches of absurdist drama (see also O'Mealy 2001: 34; Turner 1997: 14–16). *Enjoy* differs from Bennett's other stage works in that it is set in the North of England amongst seemingly ordinary people. Looking for conforming works outside the stage plays is only marginally helpful, because *Enjoy* is also different from all Bennett's previous northern television plays. It bewildered audiences and critics in 1980 because the absurdist plot and Bennett's acerbic criticism of the environment he came from were unexpected (and seen as out of character) and, for audiences and critics, unwelcome. *Enjoy* satirises northern realism and sees the familiar 'Bennettian' templates of ordinary folk exposed as mere performers, trying to be as 'typical' as possible. *Enjoy* deconstructs northern notions of nostalgia from an insiders' perspective, with almost Ortonesque ruthlessness.[24]

The absurdist influence in *Enjoy* is also detectable in Bennett's next play, *Kafka's Dick* (1986). It shares farcical conventions with *Habeas Corpus* and *Enjoy*, but combines them with biographically inspired drama, although it is not 'factual' authenticity Bennett is pursuing in his exploration of Franz Kafka.[25] The play is thus a stylised biography of a writer, with a sceptical message about the dangers of biography.

It is interesting to see how Bennett's three farcical plays– *Habeas Corpus*, *Enjoy* and *Kafka's Dick* – differ from each other through their added generic ingredients: elements as diverse as music hall, northern realism or black comedy and absurdist conventions.

Both *The Madness of George III* (1991) and *The Wind in the Willows* (1992) were commissioned or supported in production by the National Theatre. *George III* is a history play, which can be read as both a parable on contemporary British politics and a study in family psychology. *The Wind in the Willows* is an adaptation of Kenneth Grahame's children's book for the stage, a Christmas family show with musical numbers, preserving the pastoral elements of the novel, but also making subtle contemporary and intertextual references. The weasels bear an uncanny resemblance to property sharks, while Albert, the carthorse, is a close relation of Eeyore in *Winnie-the-Pooh*. By the early 1990s, Bennett had also started transforming his works for other media: from a psychologically poignant history drama on stage, *George III* underwent a transformation to large-scale costume film.

Bennett has also written two plays about spies, *An Englishman Abroad* (1983) and *A Question of Attribution* (1991), and they are frequently programmed together on the stage as *Single Spies*. The former, however, was first written for television and then adapted for the stage, while the latter was first produced for the National Theatre and was later adapted for television. Both plays are discussed in detail in their television versions in Chapter 3.

Bennett's play *The Lady in the Van* (1999) is a formal departure from other works for the theatre. It was the first stage play after nine years of Bennett producing work mainly for the screen, and for *The London Review of Books*. *Van* veers between realism, interior autobiographical monologue, extra-diegetic narrative and detective story. It is the most formally complex of Bennett's plays. Former boundaries of North and South become blurred, personified by two characters from Bennett's two lives – 'Miss Shepherd' and 'Mam'. All Bennett's 'Mam' characters carry obvious connections with Bennett's late mother, previously rooted in northern works on ordinary people, whereas eccentrics like the deluded bag lady Miss Shepherd had inhabited the realm of the 'southern' works. The two characters in the play signify the breaking down of this threshold. *Van* also makes intriguing statements about autobiography and Bennett's ambivalence about his authorial self. The two Alan Bennett characters are presented as two aspects of the author, one showing him as a caring, self-doubting person, the other representing his inclination to exploit events and people in his life for his writing.[26] Autobiographical, biographical, realist and surrealist conventions dominate the play in turn.

In spring 2004, Bennett and Nicholas Hytner, director of three of Bennett's plays, produced a new play, *The History Boys*, at the National Theatre. Although it has been compared to Bennett's first play, *Forty Years On*, uniting Bennett's careers as historian and as playwright, it has a different focus. It examines questions about history, and, almost more importantly, on the function and value of education. Conflicting positions are personified by three teachers. Hector represents the old school idea of an inspirational teacher, driven by the ideal of passing on knowledge. Mrs Lintott stands for the factual, date-based approach to teaching, although not without sarcastic references to history: 'Can you, for a moment, imagine how dispiriting it is to teach five centuries of masculine ineptitude?' (*History Boys*: 84). Irwin, brought in to increase the number of students gaining entry to Oxford and Cambridge, is focused on how to achieve the best possible exam results, and values presentation over content. Bennett aspires to Hector's approach, but admits he became good at the technique Irwin promotes at school and at university, seeing exams as a strategic and editorial exercise rather than the communication of knowledge. *The History Boys* became the National Theatre's most commercially successful play ever, and, after several seasons, went first on a national and then on an international tour, all to highly enthusiastic reviews. In 2005, Bennett and Hytner adapted the play for the screen (partly financed by FilmFour), and it was shot with its original cast. The *History Boys* film was released in October 2006, after the stage play finished its run on Broadway. In June 2006, the play won 6 Tonys, an achievement only equalled by Arthur Miller. Bennett, although reportedly touched and excited by the play's success, commented the morning after the Tony ceremony:

It is very gratifying, but it does not help when you are writing the next one. (Alan Bennett on *This Morning*, Radio 4, 12 June 2006)

Film

It would seem that Bennett's work in feature films started later than that for stage and television. However, in 1984 (Hassan et al. 1984: 121), he commented that he had written four films, and none of them had been produced up to that point. Bennett's first script, *The Vicar's Wife*, for Ned Sherrin, then at Columbia, was written as early as 1966, so this in fact pre-dates his first stage play by a few years, and is simultaneous with *On the Margin* for television. Bennett also adapted Evelyn Waugh's *A Handful of Dust* for John Schlesinger (1973), which proved too expensive to make and was thus abandoned. His adaptation of his own television play (in collaboration with Lindsay Anderson) *The Old Crowd*, for the Swedish Film Institute, fell victim to 'a boardroom revolution'.

Bennett's three scripts that have been released as feature films (*A Private Function*, Malcolm Mowbray, 1984, *Prick Up Your Ears*, Stephen Frears, 1987 and *The Madness of King George*, Nicholas Hytner, 1994) differ considerably, and display formal diversity and stylistic variety, similar to the generic range of the stage works. Did Bennett the auteur, present in nearly all his texts, have to give up his status to the film directors with whom he collaborated? Traditionally, the auteurist primacy is the writers' in works for stage and television, and belongs to the director within film. However, in all three films, Bennett's voice is always identifiable through his distinctive rhythm of speech and style. Visually and dramaturgically, the films demonstrate the three directors' diversity of style and approach. Bennett's competence as a historian and (particularly in the case of *The Madness of King George*) as an art historian is evident in all three films, demonstrated not only by the precision of his research, but also by his description of visual detail in the published scripts.

A Private Function is a film comedy about an illegal pig. Set in post-war Britain in 1947, it is a story jointly conceived by Bennett and his director Malcolm Mowbray. During the post-war years, Mowbray's in-laws secretly raised and killed a pig, and used their own bathroom to scald it. Bennett brought to the story memories of his father's work as a butcher during rationing. He did not have fond nostalgic feelings about this time: 'the weekly worry that his allotted supply would not be enough to cover the requirements of his registered customers eventually landed him in hospital with a duodenal ulcer' (*Private Function*: 53).

A Private Function can be classed both as a comedy with elements of farce and as a period film, accurately reproducing the context of post-war

Britain on the eve of the royal wedding in 1947. Visually, *A Private Function* may have qualities associated with heritage film aesthetics,[27] but overall it has more in common with the Ealing Comedies of the late 1940s and early 1950s. This is consistent with its subject matter: a 'small' man comes up against the provincial powers and, through his wife's hunger for social status, is driven to crime and subversion. *A Private Function* is shot with a lot of attention to period detail, incorporating newsreel footage, for example. It illustrates the context of post-war food deprivation and the battle for social status. The emphasis seems to be on the satirical portrayal of societal hierarchy and social aspirations in a small northern town. Joyce Chilvers (Maggie Smith), the fiercely aspirational wife of a nice-but-dull chiropodist (Michael Palin), concentrates these aspirations:

> Virtually every single line that Maggie Smith delivers is a classic – 'Don't bring feet to the table Gilbert' – and her character is a rich source of all the ridiculous snobbery that is the property of a certain kind of Yorkshire woman. She's like a cross between Lucrezia Borgia and Margaret Thatcher and she manages to be simultaneously terrifying and oddly attractive. (Sutton 2003)

For Bennett and Mowbray, the production process was hampered by interference from the producers 'to the general detriment of the film':

> Scenes were cut without consultation, the budget was slashed, the score made jokier: all the usual weary litany of complaints film-makers have about 'the money'. One of the producers was Denis O'Brien, the other George Harrison, and I never worked with either of them again. Experience in the world of entertainment is simply a list of people you would be happy to find yourself working with and another list of those you never want to see again; with luck the first list is longer than the second. (*Private Function*: viii–ix)

None of these problems have ever occurred in Bennett's television work, which shows the shrewdness of his collaborators, notably producer Innes Lloyd, but also makes a statement about television before it was perceived to be ruled entirely by monetary considerations. By the time commercialism had a stronger footing, Bennett was in a position to resist the kinds of pressures he and his directors encountered on *Prick Up Your Ears* and *A Private Function*:

> The boss of Chrysalis thought he was getting another *Cage aux Folles*. (Bennett 1984: 121)

Bennett's adaptation of John Lahr's Orton biography, *Prick Up Your Ears*, was scripted in 1981 but not produced until 1986, and then in a very modified form to its previous drafts. This film was Bennett's first large-screen collaboration with Stephen Frears, and also the last of a significant number of other collaborations with the director. Lahr's biography of the same title was based on Orton's diaries, also edited by Lahr. Frears comments that he sees himself largely as the interpreter of a writer's work:

> I'm useless unless the script is very good ... I like them [the writers] there the whole time. It's just one big conversation.[28]

Prick Up Your Ears was released in 1987. Critics commented on the strong central performances from Gary Oldman (Orton) and Alfred Molina (Halliwell), and on the film as a candid depiction of Britain's gay subculture in the 1950s and 1960s. It was generally well received, though some critics found the modern-day framing narrative distracting, and claimed the film had little to say about Orton's artistic achievements.[29] It approaches biography with a similar poetic licence to that of *102 Boulevard Haussmann*, the 1991 television play about Marcel Proust. The known facts are included accurately, but unknown periods of Orton and Halliwell's life together are written into the film. Duncan Petrie (1992) and Helga Bechman disagree about the film as part of the biopic genre, Bechmann commenting that the film does not conform to the half-documentary, realist characteristics of the biopic (see also Bechmann 1997: 53). If this is a biographical film, it is a shared one, as it is as much Kenneth Halliwell's film as Joe Orton's. At first a guiding influence, Halliwell had increasingly lived in Orton's shadow as the playwright became more successful in the early 1960s, not able to appear as his partner, but also sidelined. Kenneth Halliwell battered Orton to death and then took an overdose in August 1967. Characteristically, Bennett found himself more interested in the murderer Halliwell. Stephen Frears acknowledges that his inspiration might have come from surrounding artists whose first marriages were dissolving:

> Frears: Orton was such a fashionable thing, that to work out that Halliwell deserved the sympathy, because Orton was so attractive, seems to me an extraordinary piece of thinking.
>
> McKechnie: Bennett put Halliwell in the role of the first wife, who'd supported the husband through the rough times, and then found she was dumped once success had been established.
>
> Frears: Yes, of course he would have known about all that. Peter Cook's first wife was wonderful, she was a sort of art student. So the notion of becoming successful – because Alan had seen all that with Peter ... and Orton was as glamorous and successful as Peter. So Alan would have instinctively sympathised. He was seeing it acted out in front of him, especially with Peter.
>
> (Interview with Stephen Frears)

There is a lot of revelatory period detail in *Prick Up Your Ears*, from interiors and clothing to provincial versus metropolitan settings. It is not London that is portrayed as depraved, as Bechmann also argues (1997: 53), it is Orton's home town of Leicester in its provincial rigidity and backward-looking ways. The turning point of the Festival of Britain in 1950 is also included in the film, which is also the story of a sexual awakening and the initially difficult assertion of homosexuality in the 1950s and 1960s.

Bennett uses the device of including a narrator. The film is framed by Peggy Ramsay, Orton's agent, and a famous London literary figure, telling the story leading up to the murder. It is John Lahr, Orton's editor and biographer, and his wife she is talking to, and the Lahr's relationship is presented to mirror that of Orton and Halliwell. Ramsay reinforces this by ignoring Anthea Lahr, and treating her almost like a servant.

Prick Up Your Ears can be grouped with Bennett's works on other writers (Kafka, Larkin and Proust), and the implications and thematic recurrences are discussed in Chapter 3.

The Madness of King George is adapted from Bennett's stage play, *The Madness of George III*. Turner calls it a tragi-comedy (1997: 86); it could be termed a royal revisionist biopic, or categorised as a costume or period film with certain heritage conventions, or as a historical film based on 'factual' sources, as well as a case study of mental illness. Like *Private Function* and *Prick Up Your Ears*, it is very faithful to the visual reproduction of the period it is set in, drawing from eighteenth-century portraits, landscape paintings and caricatures (Hogarth and Gainsborough being the most likely inspirations). *King George* stays within its diegetic confines visually, but textual links are made with contemporary politics and royalty create an extra-diegetic innuendo with a 'knowing' audience.

Commenting on the final scenes of the film, Bennett hopes they would have 'rung a bell' with sociologist Erving Goffman, 'whose analysis of the presentation of self and its breakdown in the twentieth century seem just as appropriate to this deranged monarch from the eighteenth century' (*WH*: 391–392). Bennett's interest in exploring Goffman's theses on behaviour as performance[30] in practice is represented particularly well in *King George* (also pointed out by Games 2001: 2). *King George* can also be aligned with Bennett's two plays on the Cambridge Spies,[31] where complex issues around the notion of being and seeming are explored. The distinction between private and public persona is particularly poignant in Bennett's depiction of the King as head of state in all his icongraphic and symbolic power losing his ability to deliver the performance expected of him. Adopting Bennett's simile of the mask bearing his own face, the removal of the King's behavioural mask equals insanity for those around him, as his demeanour no longer matches his function and his status. The 'head' of state is reduced to a gibbering wreck who cannot control his language, behaviour or bowels. There is a disjuncture in the 'expected consistency between manner and appearance' (Goffman 1990: 35). In *King George*, when the King is at the height of his crisis, a new doctor whose methods are non-traditional is brought to Windsor. Dr Willis's approach to the King's alarmingly unrestrained behaviour is that he must be artificially restrained until he remembers how to behave himself. The King is seized and strapped into a restraining chair, an episode that could serve as a metaphor for the royal condition within constitutional monarchy and parliamentary democracy, showing the loss of regal power. The scene is reminiscent of a coronation, where the moment that symbolises ultimate power is perverted to a moment that signifies complete loss of free will, speech and human dignity. Throne and crown are replaced by restraining chair and gagging device. As the mouthpiece of the restraining apparatus is fastened, a chorus simultaneously bursts out in fortissimo with the first line of the coronation anthem, 'Zadok the Priest'.

Nigel Hawthorne's performance carries all these points about role and persona, and also illuminates them further through the intertextual connection with *King Lear* and his madness, which George III is known to have read while he was recuperating. When the King has recovered and is congratulated on being more himself, George III replies that he has always been himself, but has only now remembered how to *seem* himself. (*King George*: 65). This remark shows the King's realisation of his own royal behaviour as a performance, which is dominated by the necessity for self-restraint. Once the King has learned again how to 'seem', he no longer needs the restraining chair. This exposes the tension between the flawless picture of regal power the nation sees and the private agony of a man stripped of all control and dignity.

The film was a collaboration between Bennett and director Nicholas Hytner, who had already developed the stage play together. They refer to the film as grounded in a non-competitive merging of ideas (see also Wu 2000), which can be interpreted as a 'sharing' of the auteurist supremacy. It was Hytner's first work for the large screen, and he and Bennett were accused of thinking mainly of pandering to an American audience in their adaptation of the stage play (see also O'Mealy 1999). But what is, with a note of British arrogance, deemed an Americanisation, was merely seen as an acknowledgement of the different needs of different media by Hytner and Bennett:

With George III, it immediately became apparent that you could either do everything, and make it the biggest pile of scenery ever seen on the London stage, or do nothing – so we did nothing. [The film version] was everything. Yes. Because that's what films are. (Hytner in Wu 2000: 101)

There are certain elements which Bennett's stage plays and films have in common, but there is no sense of arriving at a winning formula, as there is in Bennett's television work: with the format of *Talking Heads*, Bennett created a form considered highly suitable to his voice as a television writer. Here, the formal development is directed towards increasing simplicity, whereas in stage works there is a sense of Bennett taking on as many conventions as will fit into any one play. Many of Bennett's contemporaries (Ayckbourn, Pinter, Hare, for example) have forms they will return to for many of their plays. Bennett has one of the most distinctive voices among British playwrights, but a formally and generically diverse repertory. Bennett is perhaps comparable to Michael Frayn (with whom he studied Russian at Cambridge in the 1950s), who not only writes in many different forms for the stage, but also produces other genres, such as prose fiction. Tom Stoppard is another contemporary who has an identifiable voice, but no fixed form or genre, and who produces work for stage, film and television. Bennett and Stoppard are also similar in that they regularly portray 'real' historical characters, often writers, in their works, but make no claim for the authenticity of their portrayal. *Travesties* (Stoppard, 1972) imagines a scenario where Joyce meets Tristan Tzara meets Lenin meets the characters from *The Importance of Being Earnest*. Bennett's *Kafka's Dick* sees Franz Kafka and Max Brod invade a Leeds suburban household, mixing the farcical plot with themes from Kafka's novels. Stoppard's *The Coast of Utopia* (2002) examines the history of Russian revolutionaries; Bennett's *The Madness of George III* unfolds against the historical background of the American War of Independence, and the transition from a nominal to a democratically functional English parliament.

Conclusion

The scholarship boy has been equipped for hurdle-jumping, so he merely thinks of getting on, but somehow not in the world's way ... He has left his class, at least in spirit, by being in certain ways unusual, and he is still unusual in another class, too tense and overwound. (Hoggart, quoted *The History Boys*: xxii)

Alan Bennett uses this quotation in the introduction to *The History Boys*. It explains the dilemma of the scholarship boy, destined to leave his original environment, but not guaranteed to fit into the new social and academic sphere. Far from wanting to transfer this notion to Bennett himself, it is nonetheless suggested that he has solved this conflict rather successfully by investigating it in his works. Rather than inhabiting no man's land – not part of the home environment, but outside the one aspired to as well – Bennett belongs to both. He can write from one perspective and give the impression of feeling excluded from the other:

> The fact is, northern writers like to have it both ways. They set their achievements against the squalor of their origins and gain points for transcendence, while at the same time asserting that northern life is richer and, in some undefined way, truer and more honest than a life of southern comfort. 'Look, we have come through,' is the message, but I can't quite see why a childhood in the industrial north is less conducive to writing or whatever, than a childhood in Petersfield or Wimbledon or wherever. I mean it's quite true if you're born in Barnsley and you set your sights on becoming Virginia Woolf, it's not going to be roses all the way. [Laughter][32]

'Virginia Woolf in Barnsley' is a comic juxtaposition, but also a fitting transition to Chapter 2, which explores the world of Bennett's northern characters through comedy, bathos and, crucially, compassion.

Notes

1 There are several academic and popular sources on *Beyond the Fringe*, notably Roger Wilmut (*From Fringe to Flying Circus*, London: Methuen, 1980) and Humphrey Carpenter (*That Was Satire That Was*, London: Victor Gollancz, 2001).
2 'In a Manner of Speaking' (*WH*: ix).
3 Interview with Alan Bennett at the National Film Theatre, 1984, www.screenonline.org.uk/audio/id/1115595/index.html.
4 In critical literature, this encounter between Bennett's mother and T.S. Eliot is given great significance as the source of creative tension in Bennett's writing, for example Daphne Turner (*In a Manner of Speaking*, London: Faber & Faber, 1997: 148), Peter Wolfe (*Understanding Alan Bennett*, Columbia: University of South Carolina Press, 1999: 12), Delia Dick (*Talking Heads: York Notes*, London: Pearson Education, 1999: 6).
5 According to Cook (*Dennis Potter. A Life on Screen*, 2nd edn, Manchester: Manchester University Press, 1998: 27), there is a distinction between realism and naturalism, in that naturalism 'eventually came to be perceived as a passive form. People were felt to be stuck where they were ..., with no possibility of changing their social lot'. Realism, most functional when defined in contradiction to something else, consequently emerged as a form where intervention and change was a possibility' (Raymond Williams, 'Realism and Non-Naturalism 1', *The Official Programme of the Edinburgh International Television Festival 1977*: 30).
6 'In addition, "Working Class Realism" was as much a critical as it was a creative

moment, denoting public language, a set of reference points and an interpretative framework, in which these texts were discussed and positioned in relation to wider debates about post-war change. In this sense, it can be compared to the moment of anger, with which it clearly had affinities' (Lacey, *British Realist Theatre: The New Wave in its Context 1956–1965*, London: Routledge, 1995: 72).

7 This is a reworked version of a sketch from the comedy series *On the Margin* (1966), so Bennett was aware of the ambivalence his 'northerness' held for him from an early stage in his career.

8 Bruce Robbins (2006) '"Martial Art" Review of Science and Reflectivity, Pierre Bourdieu', in *London Review of Books*, vol. 8, no. 8: 18.

9 'I've written many television plays about the North; most of them set in the present and more often than not, they are drawn from my memories of the past' (Alan Bennett, *The South Bank Show*, October 2005).

10 The influence of Bennett's childhood and the surrounding northern women of his family have also been discussed in works such as Turner (*In a Manner of Speaking*, 1997), Wolfe (*Understanding Alan Bennett*, 1999) and O'Mealy (*Alan Bennett: A Critical Introduction*, London: Routledge, 2001).

11 See also *WH*: 5, 'The Treachery of Books'.

12 As defined by the *Oxford English Dictionary*, provincial implies 'Having the manners or speech of a province or "the provinces"; exhibiting the character, especially the narrowness of view or interest, associated with or attributed to inhabitants of "the provinces"; wanting the culture or polish of the capital' (*OED Online*).

13 'Solcher auf ein historisches Phaenomen eingegrenzten Diagnose scheint das in der Literaturkritik lange allgemein verbreitete Vorurteil zu entprechen, Regionalismus und Moderne schlössen einander grundsaetzlich aus' (Mecklenburg, *Erzählte Provinz: Regionalismus und Moderne im Roman*. Königstein: Athenaeum, 1986: 7).

14 'I was, however, at one with Bennett in his wish to get out of the place. This was one of the few emotions common to sensitive Leeds teenagers. The most powerful encouragement to do so in the Classical Sixth at Leeds Grammar School came from our teachers – who told us that if we didn't work harder we would 'end up at Leeds University.' Reader's letter from Chris Price (2006) *London Review of Books*, vol. 22, no. 22 , accessed 2 December 2004, www.lrb.co.uk/v22/n22/letters.html#35.

15 Andy Medhurst, Keynote address at interdisciplinary conference 'Other(ing) England', July 2001, University of Buckinghamshire and Chilterns.

16 Alan Bennett, interview at the National Film Theatre, 1984, www.screenonline.org.uk/audio/id/1115595/index.html.

17 'From the documentary movement, through free cinema, to the mid-1990s, British social realist texts have been propelled to varying degrees by a mission, ideal or goal. Within the text this can, in Andrew Higson's view, manifest itself as a kind of "moral realism"' (Lay, *British Social Realism: From Documentary to Brit Grit*, London: Wallflower Press, 2002: 10).

18 These three monologues are all published in *The Complete Talking Heads*. All three characters are played by Patricia Routledge in their televised versions. She is also well known for playing Hyacinth Bucket ('Bouquet') in the comedy series *Keeping Up Appearances* (BBC1). Obsessed with status and status symbols, this character has similar pretensions to Routledge's three *Talking Heads* protagonists.

19 See Lay (*British Social Realism*, 2002: 14–19) for a summary of critical views on realist representation.

20 Samantha Lay (*British Social Realism*, 2002: 8) sees television drama in its earlier days as utilising a 'kind' of realism which did not draw attention to the illu-

sionist techniques it employed to produce a 'reality effect', calling this 'seamless realism'.

21 *Talking Heads*, for example, was originally written for television, and first transferred to the stage four years after it was broadcast.

22 See also Chapter 2.

23 *Evening Standard*, www.thisislondon.co.uk/theatre/articles/23240163?source=Evening%20Standard&ct=5.

24 There are certain elements in *Enjoy* that resemble the 1982 television play *Say Something Happened*. Although this television play is written in a style more naturalistic than *Enjoy*, the narrative of a social worker coming to 'assess' Mam and Dad makes for parallels, as does the *Talking Heads* monologue *A Cream Cracker Under the Settee* in 1988. Bennett also points this out in his introduction to the volume *Rolling Home* (xii).

25 Bennett's extensive research on Kafka also generated a television play, *The Insurance Man*, discussed in Chapter 3. The stage play *Kafka's Dick* is also discussed in this context.

26 When *The Lady in the Van* was previewing at the Queen's Theatre in November 1999, one of the two Alan Bennett actors (Nicholas Farrell) could not appear, and the understudy was not ready to go on. The part of Alan Bennett was therefore read by Alan Bennett himself.

27 For a detailed overview on the continuing discussion on the (often derogatorily applied) label 'heritage film', see Monk ('The British heritage-film debate revisited', in C. Monk and A. Sargeant (eds) (2002) *British Historical Cinema*, British Popular Cinema Series, London: Routledge, 2002).

28 Stephen Frears, *This Morning*, BBC1, 6 November 2002.

29 British Film Institute, www.screenonline.org.uk/people/id/469201/index.html.

30 See also Chapter 4 for more context on the influence of Goffman on Bennett's works.

31 *An Englishman Abroad* and *A Question of Attribution*, see Chapter 3.

32 www.screenonline.org.uk/audio/id/1115595/index.html.

1 Doris and Doreen (*Green Forms*, 1979). 'I wouldn't like to think she's been made redundant, she's very nicely spoken.' Patricia Routledge and Prunella Scales

2 *Afternoon Off* (1979). Korean waiter Lee (Henry Man) looking for a girl in hostile Hartlepool

3 *One Fine Day* (1979). Estate Agent Philips (Dave Allen) looking out from his top floor hideout

4 *An Englishman Abroad* (1983). 'For in spite of all temptations to belong to other nations, he remains an Englishman.' Burgess (Alan Bates) shows off his new clothes to an indifferent Moscow

5 *Talking Heads 1: Bed Among the Lentils* (1988). Maggie Smith as Susan

6 *Talking Heads 2: Nights in the Garden of Spain* (1998). Penelope Wilton as Rosemary

7 *Talking Heads 2: Miss Fozzard Finds Her Feet* (1998). Patricia Routledge as Miss Fozzard

8 *Talking Heads 2: Waiting for the Telegram* (1998). Thora Hird as Violet

9 *Telling Tales* (2000). Alan Bennett

'Fair to cloudy in mid-town
Morecambe': from single play
to season of plays

2

A Day Out (1972)
Sunset Across the Bay (1975)
A Little Outing (1977)
Six Plays (1978/79):
    Doris and Doreen (later *Green Forms*) (1978)
    A Visit from Miss Prothero (1978)
    Me, I'm Afraid of Virginia Woolf (1978)
    Afternoon Off (1979)
    All Day on the Sands (1979)
    The Old Crowd (1979)
Objects of Affection (five plays, 1982):
    Intensive Care (1982)
    Our Winnie (1982)
    A Woman of No Importance (1982)
    Rolling Home (1982)
    Say Something Happened (1982)

> Hi, all you leisure lovers. Eight o'clock, the temperature is 52 degrees and it's fair to cloudy in mid-town Morecambe. This is your Miramar host, Percy Cattley, saying hello again and welcome to another fun-packed day.
> (*All Day*, in *Rolling Home*: 30)

Bennett started writing television plays in the early 1970s, a time when the majority of commissions were still single plays. One of the programming slots for plays by different authors, *Play for Today*, often opened up public debate about the issues of social and material inequality in society. Although he had two plays produced in this slot, Bennett did not fit easily into its canon of left-leaning, sometimes explicitly political plays. Even in its early stages, Bennett's television writing is already distinctive in its unapologetic parochialism. It is made more so by the contributions of his collaborating directors, cinematographers and producers; the two most important contributors being Stephen Frears and Innes Lloyd. Success with audiences meant that seasons of his plays were being produced by the late 1970s. This chapter documents Bennett's development from single play to season of plays, inherent thematic strands and formal tendencies. It also outlines the context of television drama in which Bennett's plays came into existence.

Trends in British television drama

> We got a [television] set rather late – about 1964. I used to watch the early *Plays for Today* and sometimes the weekly and twice weekly plays they had on, so I was obviously nurtured.[1]

While Alan Bennett and his family were still listening to the 'wireless' in the 1950s and early 1960s, on television most plays were studio productions of classic plays or adaptations of novels. The 1960s saw a shift in emphasis with the emergence of plays written specifically for television. Television drama originated from theatrical conventions of the period, and its propagators then started to develop new, television-specific plays for a wider audience.[2] The initiative of Sydney Newman, the Head of Drama (1963–67), as supervisor and producer established the first regular slot for television drama on ITV: *Armchair Theatre*, which started in 1958 and was considered a pioneering drama strand. The BBC's weekly drama slot, *The Wednesday Play* (1964–70) and its successor, *Play for Today* (1970–84), featured new plays by contemporary playwrights and developed a reputation for innovation and controversy. Two of Bennett's single plays were produced in the *Play for Today* slot: *Sunset Across the Bay* (1975) and *Intensive Care* (1982).[3]

In the early days of the genre, the 'Golden Age' of television drama, as it is sometimes referred to, the single play was the main form of production. Although topics were diverse, the slots in which single plays were commissioned quickly gained a reputation for confronting societal and social issues of some controversy. Contents and themes can be linked to conventions of social realism, whereas the style often has characteristics of theatrical realism. This stands in contrast to what Hayward (quoted in Lay 2002: 8) terms 'seamless realism', a realism that does not draw attention to its own illusion.[4]

In comparison with the series, the single play places fewer obligations on the writer; there is no need to continue a storyline, or to write in order to serve the strengths of actors already involved in the series, or to cater to predetermined environments. In the early days of the genre at least, a playwright of a single play was not affected by precedent, as a single play could be looked at in isolation and offered a prime canvas for developing talents, as has been argued by critics and television practitioners of that period, such as the writer Alan Plater:

> What we had in the 'Golden Age' was what Denis Norden once called 'a place to be lousy in', a quiet, underpopulated, underpublicised corner where you could learn the trade in gentle stages without metropolitan controllers breathing down the producer's neck, and without, praise be, smartarse postmodernist critics from the Groucho Club saying we should have our fingers broken. (Plater in Bignell et al. 2000: 71)

The single play in its earlier stages offered stylistic and thematic innovations, but also a fair amount of mediocre work. Its reputation for quality and innovation is based on a fairly small number of plays (see also Cooke 2003: 92). It must, however, be acknowledged that there were more opportunities for emerging writing talents, and more willingness to invest in 'one off' single plays, particularly by the BBC, through its trainee scheme. Those critical of the gradual disappearance of the single play (see, for example, Bignell 2000) therefore mourn the decrease in opportunity and variety more than the loss of quality.

> I had no idea how to write a TV play. I had no notion how to do it, I just wrote bits of dialogue and farmed them out among the characters. Stephen Frears made it [A Day Out] work, as it were, but he didn't know how to do it either, because it was also his first television play. One learnt as one went along. One of the joys of TV in those days – you were allowed to learn, you were allowed to make mistakes. ... TV was a kind of play pen.[5]

In the next phase of evolution, plays were often produced in seasons, a platform for authors who had acquired a certain level of success. Through the natural selection process of the single play, commissioners of drama spotted television authors with potential and audience appeal. Their work would then be showcased in a season, loosely programmed sequentially. The plays were often not directly linked with each other, but were connected through the stylistic and thematic characteristics of one writer, sometimes from different stages of his or her career. 'Seasons' are not exclusive to television: in the theatre or in art-house cinemas, seasons will often be programmed to give the audience a sense of continuity and coherence. In television, seasons enable the audience to gain a wider impression of one writer's work and voice, and links are thus often made between the work and the life of an artist. Dennis Potter's 1976 season of three plays (*Brimstone and Treacle*, *Where Adam Stood*, *Double Dare*) serves as an example. Potter stated that it was 'not a formal trilogy', but conceded that all three plays 'occupy the same territory' and should therefore be seen together (Cook 1998: 92). Which is why, when *Brimstone and Treacle* was banned by BBC executives three weeks before its transmission, Potter did his utmost to prevent the screening of the other two plays.

The example of Dennis Potter shows how a television auteur's career developed alongside changing formats, something that is also true of Alan Bennett. Potter was one of the writers regularly contributing single plays for the *Play for Today* slot, but production slowed down in the 1970s, and after 1979, Potter ceased to contribute to the single play strand. Frustrated that a 'generation of second-rate bureaucrats' was 'leading the BBC down from the heights' (Cook 1998: 100), Potter predicted the decline of the single play: the hated bureaucrats were not only prioritising money over creativity and innovation, but were also imposing their, in Potter's eyes, narrow moral parameters on television drama. He predicted that everything would be produced on film, transforming the television play into a director's medium (Cook 1998: 100).

The season does not necessarily demand a link between the works shown, whereas the mini-series (and its 'successor', the long-running drama series) is a story told in instalments. Mini-series might also see different plots emerging around a number of connected characters, but continuing plots and formally unifying criteria generally have to be adhered to. Throughout the 1970s and 1980s, the series increasingly became the favoured format among commissioners of television drama.[6] This had economic reasons, but also documented a tendency towards less experimentation, and a general move towards 'the reassuring predictability of the drama series [which] could quickly build up a large and loyal audience' (Creeber 2001: 12). This audience made drama series more cost-effective than single plays, and more certain to achieve high ratings.

When Alan Bennett started writing for television, his name was already associated with satire (*Beyond the Fringe*) and comedy (*On the Margin*), and he had also acted in a number of television productions.[7] He bypassed the two most common development paths of television writers: one of them, often referred to as the 'nursery school', was the BBC directing trainee scheme; the other was generally through theatre.[8] Later, it became the practice for writers to learn their craft by working as part of teams on long-running serials. As a writer, Bennett has never worked collaboratively on any produced work.[9]

Television drama in its earlier days, especially work produced in *The Wednesday Play* and *Play for Today* slots, was seen as a 'natural symbol for social commentators who wish to criticise the apparent 'dumbing down' of contemporary television, presenting it (somewhat nostalgically) as representative of a 'Golden Age' when television was, in their view, still interested in challenging its audience's views and expectations' (Creeber 2001: 9). Critics such as Robin Nelson (1997) and John Caughie (2000) point out that it is inappropriate to idealise the 'Golden Age'. Plays such as *Cathy Come Home* (Ken Loach, 1966) exemplify the values attached to television drama of that age. Its significance to television drama (and its critical assessment, which some comment on as exaggerated) is comparable to that of *Look Back in Anger* for post-war British theatre in 1956. Caughie (2000) argues that the single play in the style of social realism was a descendant of the theatre of the Angry Young Men, via the 'bypass' of the short-lived New Wave in British cinema, 1959–63. After the dispersion of its leading figures, the politicised, realist mission was carried on through television drama. Ken Loach's plays, for instance, combine the accessible (both through seeing familiar character types and through the medium of television) and the political and constituted, as Barry Hanson states, 'a line in the sand'. Hanson describes *Cathy Come Home*, a story about social workers taking a child away from a homeless young mother, as 'the first dramatic political statement on television in terms of form and content ... The previous major political statement on television had been the Coronation of Elizabeth II in 1953'(Bignell 2000: 59).

> [T]he impact of *Up the Junction* and *Cathy Come Home* may have had as much to do with the way they were taken up in public and press discourses within a particular historical moment as it had to do with their form. (MacMurraugh-Kavanagh, quoted in Caughie 2000: 108)

It is only natural that, in following theatrical conventions, especially those post-1956, the format of the single play should have had such an important position in the production of television drama for so long.

> The economic 'wind of change' was felt sharply during the 1970s at the BBC. As inflation began slowly to outstrip the Corporation's fixed revenue and the licence fee fell more and more out of phase with costs – from being an other-worldly institution where vulgar things like money were somehow slightly sordid considerations compared with the fondly-paraded 'enrichment' of the cultural life of the nation – we slipped inexorably into the era of 'cost effective' television. Slowly accountancy, rather than 'creativity', became the most important talent. Nowhere was this more important than in the single play. (Gardner and Wyver, quoted in Cooke 2003: 96)

The political and cultural climate during the 1980s was a decisive factor in the decline of the single television play. The BBC was a particular target of the monetarist conservative policies. The single play had established itself as a vehicle for asking awkward social questions, not always welcomed by funding bodies, in their turn dependent on government approval. As the television market became more competitive, potential ratings dominated other considerations, such as innovation and the inclusion of politically and socially relevant material. The series and the long-running serial offered a far more cost-effective way of building up and maintaining audiences.[10] Consequently, new serials were launched in the 1980s, most notably *Eastenders* in 1985, the first ratings competition for *Coronation Street* since its launch in 1960. Within this developing trend, there were big differences in format and quality. The mini-series, for example, is associated with the higher end of the market, and can almost be seen as 'the next best thing' for those hankering back to the 'Golden Age'. Alan Bleasdale's *Boys from the Blackstuff* is an example of a critically acclaimed mini-series, with episodes that are, although populated by the same inventory of characters, finite narratives. Dennis Potter's series *The Singing Detective* is another influential example.

Until fairly recently, the single play had become a rarity in programming schedules. If single plays are commissioned and produced, the traditions of social realism are often reinvoked: in the 2002 BBC1 production *The Stretford Wives* (Peter Webber, 2002), style and content fit into this tradition. A tale of three working-class sisters, it shows northern women constantly abused and let down by men and battling through a life that has never offered them any opportunities. Similar to productions like *A Taste of Honey* (Tony Richardson, 1961), establishing shots are of industrial surroundings and shabby back-to-back terraces, action taking place in the rain or the dark. In a self-referential reminder of 1960s kitchen-sink drama, Rita Tushingham, who played the pregnant daughter of a semi-whore in *A Taste of Honey*, is cast as the mother of the three sisters in *The Stretford Wives*.

At the beginning of the twenty-first century, there seems to be a modest 'comeback' of the single play in a variety of conventions. Many of these plays are written in the tradition of social intervention.[11] Directors who have not worked in television drama for a long time have contributed new work. Stephen Frears and Peter Morgan's 2003 dramatisation of Tony Blair and Gordon Brown's *Deal* for Channel 4 can be seen as an example of this. Slots such as *The Afternoon Play* on BBC1 have revived the single play slot, although it cannot be said that they are as issue-based and politically vocal as their 1960s and 1970s ancestors. Cooke (2003: 138) sums up the reasons for the decline in play production as 'aesthetic, economic, political'.[12] The sheer range of channels, starting with the launch of Channel 4 in 1982, followed by Channel 5 in 1997, the digital age and its specialisation, as well as an expansion of types of programme (reality television, for example) are contributing factors to the contemporary rarity of single television plays.

This short overview demonstrates a certain evolution – single play to series – and certain hierarchies of cultural value. The 'radical' single play carries the notion of cultural seriousness, and is seen as the 'the respectable end of television' (Caughie 2000: 2) for its 'high culture' origins. The series, on the other hand, is perceived as a crowd-pleasing, commercially driven enterprise, although the mini-series is seen to have higher creative integrity.

Alan Bennett's development within the medium of television roughly fits into this evolution, starting with single plays and ending with the mini-series. He is also a typical example of the author as auteur, of the writer 'as the one and only originator of the television play' (Self 1984: 70).

Bennett as a television auteur

It can safely be said that television drama has developed from theatrical origins, and, accordingly, the writer is still very much the auteur, seen as the 'hallmark' of a television play, whereas the director is perceived as the 'realiser' of the text.[13] It is generally the writer whose name will be used to sell the plays to the public and who will be measured against previous work. It is no coincidence that *The Television Series* (Manchester University Press) focuses mainly on writers. They might sometimes take on multiple functions, such as producer or director, but it is still the writer who is seen to be at the helm of television production.[14] Lindsay Anderson has expressed discontent with television drama being 'traditionally and emphatically a writer's rather than a director's medium' (Preface to *The Old Crowd, Writer:* 163).

> [T]he television playwright very much came to be regarded as the 'artist' and was given relative creative freedom by the institution to pick his or her theme and express an 'idea' (though always subject to ultimate veto from senior management, in terms of constantly shifting guidelines of public taste, decency or offence). (Cook 1998: 4)

It is a characteristic of auteurism that the creative products of one auteur often prompt the audience's 'desire to relate ... themes to the individual's autobiography' (Ros Coward in Stam and Miller 2000: 12). It is an established way of reading the creator of a novel, a poem, a stage play or a short story. Although attempts might be made to divorce author and text, readers and critics seem to gravitate naturally towards personalised readings, that is, they measure the life against the work and seek connections.

> Yet despite recognising the text before them as a 'fabric of quotations' (Barthes 1968: 53), these readers and viewers still blithely persist in talking

about authors (writers, film-makers, scriptwriters), attributing the work to those named, special individuals. Consequently, a gap arises between theories of authorship and those pre-theoretical, intuitive notions of authorship that underlie common usage. (Cardwell 2005: 10)

Within the field of television, Dennis Potter and Alan Bennett are perhaps the strongest examples for the connection between biography and auteurism, but writers like Jimmy McGovern and Stephen Poliakoff are also read in the contexts of their lives and often their origins.[15] The concept of auteurism offers a key to the understanding of Bennett's development. Originally applied to film, auteurism rests on the notion of a work of art being creatively headed by a 'single maker', and this is the way Bennett's work, especially for television, has come to be perceived. Although this study argues for Bennett as an auteur in all the genres and media he writes for, this status is most evident within his work for television.

As both the creative and increasingly the biographical centre of his television works, Alan Bennett has a recognisable and distinctive voice and develops recurring themes and preoccupations. This nurtures familiarity, leading to biographical curiosity on the part of the audience. These characteristics are present from the very early stages of Bennett's television work. He started out as the writer, with Stephen Frears and Innes Lloyd taking the roles of director and producer. Bennett is said to have exerted control over the treatment of his script and pronunciation, and to have made changes during production where needed. He would also occasionally take on small parts, such as appearing in a tea party and playing croquet in A Day Out. In 1982, he took on the main part in Intensive Care, was the protagonist of A Chip in the Sugar, and also directed Bed Among the Lentils (both in the Talking Heads 1 series, 1988). Bennett's latest two works for television, Talking Heads 2 (1998) and Telling Tales (2000), have been produced by Slow Motion, the company he and Mark Shivas founded. Bennett and Shivas are joint executive directors of the production company, Shivas taking the role of producer and Bennett that of executive producer within the production process. In Telling Tales, Bennett's roles therefore include that of the writer, subject (the monologues are about his early life), performer, and executive producer. The increase in Bennett's artistic control (together with reduction of forms, as will be seen) has meant more restricted possibilities for his collaborators. In his television career, Bennett started out by being 'just' the writer, and has since acquired numerous other roles, making him what Tony Garnett (Bignell et al. 2000: 14) calls 'the power centre' of his plays, in terms of decision making and creativity. It could be said that Bennett has used his creative control to produce works that suit his dramatic style. His increasing involvement does not exclude collaborative artistic product, but does suggest that he has strong ideas about how he wants his work to be presented.

Bennett's use of form and genre is highly individual. In order to consider his particular generic and formal 'hallmarks', one must dispense with the idea of pure genres. Within literature, work is classified and labelled in retrospect by a critical establishment. Within popular writing and film and television production, where writing is commissioned, a particular genre and its requirements have more importance. However, due to his popularity and the marketability of his name, Alan Bennett's work is not aligned with a generic matrix. In an unobtrusive way, Bennett has produced formally innovative works during his career: he has, for example, made a significant contribution to the form of the monologue, has injected autobiographical content into forms not traditionally associated with life writing, and has made innovative contributions to the genres of history play (*The Madness of George III*) and the 'biopic' (*The Insurance Man,* the spy plays), proving the 'connectability' of histories past and contemporary. An erudite writer, he eludes formal conventions in his writing, both in terms of genres and the media for which he produces. Bennett's persona has emerged as the centre of his works, and the genres he creates increasingly serve as vehicles for his presentation of himself. This can backfire, as the following excerpt from a review shows:

> In the end, for all the talk of real speech patterns and real lives, we are taken only to Bennettland, where the past elbows its way into the present, where people say 'As a rule, I steer clear of suede'. (Parker 1998: 11)

Apart from being ridiculed as domestic and old-fashioned, Bennett also gets labelled as a 'jack of all trades', meaning he is often associated with another area, such as stage or comedy. Within the British media there is a tendency to pigeonhole, and this is problematic with Bennett as his command of genre and media is prodigious.

Bennett was never part of the inner circle of writers relevant to the most prestigious slots for television drama, *The Wednesday Play* and later *Play for Today*. The two plays he did contribute would not have been regarded as typical products for these slots. Bennett emerged towards the end of the 'Golden Age' of the television play in the 1960s and early 1970s. His texts do not fit in with the type of plays Creeber (2001: 9) calls 'agitational television and the dramatic airing of topical issues'. Bennett's characters are generally low key and often inarticulate. He can probably make greater claims to realism than any of his contemporaries, however, when it comes to reproducing the minutiae of real people's speech. The issues he is pursuing emerge on the margin of his stories, and are often subtextual.

Bennett and the single play

> The first two television plays that I wrote, *A Day Out* and *Sunset Across the Bay*, were done on location and on film, and to this day I don't know whether to call them plays or films. They were only television films, it's true, and in those days people working in feature film were quite condescending about television ... but when I did eventually graduate to writing the occasional feature film there didn't seem to be all that much difference anyway. (*Private Function*: viii)

A Day Out (Stephen Frears, LWT, 24 December 1972), *Sunset Across the Bay* (Stephen Frears, LWT, 20 February 1975) and *A Little Outing* (Brian Tufano, BBC TV, 20 October 1977) are Bennett's early single plays for television. All three feature the lives of unremarkable people in their environment. The plays are filmed on location, and do not follow the conventions of studio-based television plays, with artificial lighting and box sets (see also Cook 1998: 5). Bennett's earlier, more naturalistic works for television are more story- than plot-dominated,[16] often mimetic[17] and chronological in nature. *Sunset Across the Bay* (1975), for example, imitates real life, and also seems to occur in real time in its slow pace. Events follow on from each other: Dad retires, he and Mam move to Morecambe, they find it difficult to overcome their isolation, they enjoy a visit from their son, Dad dies suddenly, Mam's future is left open. But beyond the chronology of the story, the plot weaves causalities about the lifelong wish to escape, but being disappointed by the reality when this change does occur.

Bennett's early plays do not draw particularly strongly on trends introduced by the likes of Ken Loach and Troy Kennedy Martin. It could be said that Bennett and Frears, both new to television drama, side-stepped the mode of production that was earning the most critical and popular attention in the early 1970s. This is possibly due to their relative outsider status, not being part of the coveted 'nursery school' of young talent at the BBC. Frears was asked to direct Bennett's first television play after just having directed his first feature film, *Gumshoe* (1971), and previously having assisted Karel Reisz and Lindsay Anderson. *A Day Out* started both Bennett's and Frears' television careers:

> And I remember going to the BBC to see about the job on a Monday, and my film [*Gumshoe*] had opened on the Friday to the most incredible reviews. And when I appeared at the BBC – and I didn't really know

much – they said 'what would you like?' They couldn't believe that this man who'd had these wonderful reviews wanted to make television drama and of course it turned out to be exactly the right thing to do. It's how I learnt my job. (Interview with Stephen Frears)

A Day Out

A Day Out is set in 1911 and is inspired by an old group photo of a cycling club. Originally called *There and Back to See How Far It Is* (WH: 418), it tells the story of a Halifax cyclists' outing to Fountains Abbey. Bennett wrote the play in 1969, but it took three years to be commissioned:

> Frears: A woman called Irene Shubik turned down *A Day Out*, saying it didn't really go anywhere, and Bennett responded that it went to Fountains Abbey and back. [laughter]
>
> (Interview with Stephen Frears)

Filmed in Halifax, the village of Hebden Bridge and at Fountains Abbey, *A Day Out* is as much, if not more, about the landscape as it is about the people native to it. All the characters going on the trip are introduced at the beginning of their day, and so we first see them in their home environments, and then see how differently they behave when within the all-male cycling fraternity. Of Mr Shorter, for example, Bennett remarks that 'We see him setting off on his bicycle, very upright, very neat, and the further he gets away from his wife, the more self-assured and self-satisfied he becomes' (*A Day Out*, in *Me*: 6). This gives us an insight into the private and the public faces of these characters, and gives a foreboding of the way Bennett will integrate the two faces of his characters in later material. The cycling club has its own social ranks, its pecking order – age, respectability, affluence and class being some of the factors. These come into play during the outing: landscape and architectural interests are given attention, but generally under the guidance of the chairman, Mr Shuttleworth. However, the audience gradually realises that the West Yorkshire pastoral idyll is deceptive:

> Shuttleworth: I can remember when all that were fields. It's where my grandma lived.
> Ackroyd: There's going to be nought left o't'country if they're not careful. When I were little you could stand on t'steps o't'Corn Exchange and see t'moors. Nowadays there's nought but soot and smoke and streets and streets.
> Boothroyd: Ay, but there's all this. It'll be a long time before they build up England.
>
> (*A Day Out*, in *Me*: 10)

The characters refer to the apparent stability of the surroundings, which has tinges of tragic irony for the audience, who know how much this landscape will change during World War I and the furious pace of industrialisation (see also Turner 1997: 9). Bennett acts as 'sympathetic historian' (O'Mealy 2001: 21) to the members of the cycling club. This foreboding, a knowledge to which the audience alone is privy, carries the film.

Bennett wrote *A Day Out* in West Yorkshire idiom, something he did not do in subsequent scripts. While most of his television plays are set in Yorkshire, Bennett realised that the detail of the idiom was not something that needed prescribing as closely as he did in *A Day Out*. It could be left to the actors, with occasional corrections from the writer on location. Bennett jokily compares his function on set to that of 'the props man or the make up girl, who dash onto the set just before a take to tweak a doyley into position or powder a nose. And it was at moments like this, getting an actor to repeat "My bum's numb" for the seventeenth time, that I began to wonder if this was a proper profession for an adult person' (Introduction, *Me*: x).

Bennett comments that the delay in the making of *A Day Out* made him forget 'the impulse that had made me write it or whether I had any other intention than to write a story' (*WH*: 418). Stephen Frears comments on the impressionist quality of Bennett's early plays for television:

> Frears: Do you mean they are slight? Yes, they were. You mean, slight as narratives?
> McKechnie: Yes. Is the emphasis more on interaction?
> Frears: Interaction – that wasn't a word that had been invented in those days. ... I know he [Bennett] wrote some work, and he was surprised how robust the characters were. ... So I don't quite know where the emphasis lay, except that he'd had these little ideas for scenes, inspired by a photograph of a men's cycling club. There were these little exchanges, that was really all. The surprise was how things turned out, started turning out underneath, more complicated. ... But not a great deal of interaction between the characters ...
> McKechnie: Observation?
> Frears: Yes, observation, and a sort of mode, and a sort of selection, a sort of selected taste. Things he [Bennett] chose to pick out.
> (Interview with Stephen Frears)

Despite its loose-knit narrative and its rejection of overtly political tones, *A Day Out* offers insight into issues of class – as Turner (1997: 11) remarks: '...everyone has a place and knows it'. Bookish cycling club member Cross encounters Florence, a girl from a wealthy, upper-class family. She invites him to join her family for tea and croquet. Cross is shy due to his club-foot, and made to feel uncomfortable by the family, and so flees as soon as he can. A bolder member of the group, Edgar, has meanwhile persuaded a 'Pretty Girl', Connie, to follow him down to a secluded spot by the river. Here, he mechanically undoes her buttons, and then just as mechanically feels her body, neither of them looking at the other, the whole scene sulkily commented on by her friend, 'Plain Girl', who is waiting only a little distance away.

Both *A Day Out* and *Sunset Across the Bay* feature their characters' failure to articulate feelings and generally to express themselves. Dialogue becomes secondary in these two plays; at the centre is the relationship between a figure and a landscape.[18] This might be seen as another departure from contemporary television plays. In both plays, the landscape and the social setting have a crucial part in the narrative, and the texts would become meaningless if shot in the studio.

Sunset Across the Bay

In *Sunset Across the Bay*, Bennett and Frears accentuate the contrast between the two landscapes of the play, Leeds and Morecambe. Mam and Dad's retirement from 'mucky old Leeds' to a flat in Morecambe turns out to increase their displacement in a world that has already ceased to be theirs, confirming Bennett's statement that the home town he so extensively writes about no longer exists. The camera follows Dad (Harry Markham) on his last day at work, as he carries home his retirement present, an inscribed toaster.

> *Montage of journey home. Crossing railway sidings with his tea-can. A bridge. A recreation ground. An underpass under a new road. A half-derelict street on the edge of a demolition area. (Sunset, in Me: 35)*

These are the directions in the published version of *Sunset*. In the play as it was produced, we see Leeds and its changing face to a voice-over from Dad, describing the cityscape 'then and now', almost like a northern Betjeman. This sequence momentarily gives Mam and Dad's story the character of a documentary. It seems as though Bennett and Frears have the need to document what they present as the destruction of an urban environment. The changes Leeds is seen to be undergoing are linked back to Mam and Dad (and others like them) losing their habitat. It seems far-fetched to compare Mam and Dad's story to that of the *Boys from the Blackstuff*, Alan Bleasdale's memorable manifestation of the effects of 1980s politics on individual lives. The role Leeds plays in *Sunset*, however, is similar to the way Liverpool is shown in Bleasdale's drama serial five years later, as Pawling and Perkins (quoted in Cooke 2003: 133) point out:

> The 'subject' of the drama was not simply the 'Boys', but Liverpool itself as a city under intense pressure. So the location shots of the derelict docks or the demolition of the Tate and Lyle refinery in 'George's Last Ride', were not just signifiers of a generalised backcloth of dereliction, but acted as specific records of the concrete destruction of people's working lives at a particular moment in time. This, then, was no dramatic recreation for visual effect, but actuality footage of Liverpool's devastation as it occurred, brick by brick.

Despite their environment disappearing around them, Mam and Dad seem self-sufficient and happy in each others' company. A scene shows them at night in bed, just their heads visible in the light falling into their bedroom through the window. The conversation ranges from remembering Empire Day (and Mam singing the song to prove it), their courtship ('It was my teeth you fell for', says Mam) and, after twenty-seven years, noticing a crack in the ceiling that looks like a man smoking a pipe. On their journey towards their new life in Morecambe, conversation revolves around the lavatory on the coach. Lavatories, along with dirt and disease, are the dominant topics of conversation in the Yorkshire women Bennett so frequently (and essentially lovingly) portrays.[19] So, after Mam has braved the novelty lavatory, she is proud of her courage and encourages Dad to sample it. When he doesn't want to go, she remarks he has 'no spirit of adventure' (*Sunset*, in *Me*: 43).

Once in Morecambe, open, sparse frames and long silences dominate the style of *Sunset*. The retirement Mam and Dad have been looking forward to for a long time now apparently destabilises the comfortable routine of their life together . Not natural 'mixers' socially, their isolation makes them dependent on each other, bringing about tension and differences:

> Mam: You've got to make an effort. Join in. That woman next to me was ever so nice.
> Dad: I don't care. Three months ago I was doing a responsible job and now I'm fit for nowt but clapping my hands with a roomful of daft old lasses.
> Mam: It wasn't at all like that.
> Dad: I had six men under me. I'm not soft in the head.
>
> (*Sunset*, in *Me*: 55)

Another feature of the play's visual style is the relatively still position of the camera. Frames are often set up, then Mam or Dad's voice might be heard, and only then do they walk into the frame. It is rare that the camera tracks along. These static frames could be seen to express the rigidity of the situation – either Mam and Dad adjust to their environment, or they are left out of the frame.

After going to a matinee at the cinema one afternoon, Mam and Dad are walking along the promenade. Dad is not feeling well, and after he fails to come back from the toilet, Mam asks a passer by to go in and find out what has happened. The final section of the film passes with very few words, and hardly any visible emotion: Dad is taken to hospital, and later dies. Mam goes to see his body, and is then seen in a shot from behind, walking along a hospital corridor on her way out. After sending a telegram to their son in Australia, Mam is seen walking along the beach, watched by a character described as 'Boring Woman', who has previously tried to engage Mam in conversation about her deceased husband. Mam returns the woman's wave, but strides on purposefully along the beach, and out of the frame. Whereas the narrative has been fairly unambivalent in its attribution of sympathies and opinions, in the sequence after Dad's discovery in the public toilet this is no longer the case. The camera observes, and takes note in an entirely unsentimental way. Mam shows no outward emotion. This is an ambiguous final image to the film, as it might mean an increase in Mam's isolation, but might also mean a sense of liberation after her and Dad's unhappy venture into retirement.

Sunset has significance as Bennett's first play with an autobiographical subtext:

> In some way the couple are not unlike my parents ... I had to consider these similarities when I was writing because my parents had not long retired ... Unlike the couple, though, their retirement was very happy, if marred by illness, and in 1974, when I had written the play but it had not yet been filmed, my father had a heart attack and died, leaving my mother in much the same position as the widow in the film. (Introduction, *Me*: xi)

Bennett had a feeling of 'involuntary prediction ...; having written my father's death I had helped to occasion it' (Introduction, *Me*: xii). The normal assumption of an autobiographically interested audience would be that the play was modelled on life, rather than life resembling the plays' plot, as Bennett describes it here. One also has to balance *Sunset's* parallels with his parents' retirement and his father's death with his mother's reaction after she had watched the play:

> 'They're from Leeds,' she said, 'and we're from Leeds, but that's as far as it went. Mind you, it was grand seeing Morecambe.' (Introduction in *Me*: xii)

A Little Outing

Sunset introduces the recurring theme of the redundancy of an out-of-date generation in Bennett's works. This theme and the deterioration of old age also feature in Bennett's next play, his first for the BBC: *A Little Outing* (1977). Brian Tufano, cameraman on *Sunset*, is the director. Its script has never been published, nor has the play been mentioned or contextualised by Alan Bennett in any other publication. Tufano himself said that the idea to have him direct came from producer Innes Lloyd. As he wanted to work on material about old people, he thought Bennett 'was the best writer on that particular subject' (Badder 1978: 75). His only objective was that the photography should be 'unobtrusive, should go along either parallel with or secondary to the narrative' (Badder 1978: 75). *A Little Outing* features a family – parents and grown-up son – going to see the grandfather in an old people's home. Concerns and topics are again autobiographically filtered, this time through Bennett's mother's long descent into dementia in mental hospitals and nursing homes. There is a forensic and almost documentary account of her earlier spells in hospital in *Untold Stories*, the core autobiographical piece of his 2005 volume of the same name. But plays like *A Little Outing*, *Rolling Home*, *Intensive Care*, and, very much later, *Waiting for the Telegram* (*Talking Heads 2*, 1998) and the radio play *The Last of the Sun* (2003) return to the themes of institutional problems around caring for old people, and their families' way of coping with their guilt.

> Dad: I hope I die, that's all
> Mam: Anyway, Jeff will look after us, won't he? ...
> Dad: You have children, then once you've got them started off, it's your parents you've got to look after. There's never a clean slate.
>
> (*A Little Outing*)[20]

In direct comparison, Bennett was at this time spending a lot of time visiting his mother during her spells in mental hospitals, and for about fifteen years, from the mid-1970s to the early 1990s, his mother was in a nursing home. Here, he would watch the nurses taking possession of, and infantilising a former individual, even if it was with the best intentions. In *Untold Stories* (118–19), Bennett comments how the loud and cheerful demeanour of the nurses would reach his deteriorating mother, whereas the 'tasteful' and heartfelt sentiments of her son, whom she no longer recognised, went unnoticed. He objected to them calling her 'Lily', when her name was 'Lillian'.

In *A Little Outing*, a similar situation occurs. The carers, although cheerful and generally competent, are obviously not aware of the former life of a person in their care:

'I wish they wouldn't keep calling him Joey – his name's Joe.' 'Makes him sound like a budgie.' (*A Little Outing*)

A Little Outing is similar to *A Day Out* in its unspectacular 'there and back' structure, and it is up to the viewer to pick up things that are either familiar or relevant according to their own experiences. For some this might be the familiar scenario of a visit to see an ageing parent or grandparent; for some this might be the constant banter of the mother about the classification of things, be it her other son's new car ('Doreen and Raymond's car is walnut'), or be it about the frequency of buses ('The service is *that* spasmodic'). For others, this familiarity might be captured by well-known expressions ('I'm Champion', as the friendly, but confused granddad repeatedly insists), or Mam and Dad's exchanges over the dinner table.

Bennett returned to writing single plays in the 1980s. Both *The Insurance Man* and *102 Boulevard Haussmann* are very different from their 1970s predecessors, as will be demonstrated in Chapter 3.

Bennett and the season of television plays

As already established above, seasons enable the audience to gain a wider impression of one writer's work and voice, but they are normally not open to newcomers, but to auteurs who have already acquired some distinction. Bennett was already a 'name' in the late 1970s, the time of his first season of television plays, if not yet the 'brand' he has since become.

Six plays

Bennett's first season of television plays, *Six Plays*, was produced for LWT in 1978/79 by himself and his main collaborator, Stephen Frears, producing and directing the majority of the plays. Lindsay Anderson, Giles Foster and Piers Haggard directed one play each.[21]

Incorporating the three earlier single plays discussed above, two new editions of Bennett's television plays were published in 2003 with new introductions. They appeared in a different order to the original ones, under the new titles *Me, I'm Afraid of Virginia Woolf* and *Rolling Home*.

Although later united and published with *Green Forms*, *A Visit from Miss Prothero* was broadcast nearly a year earlier than *Six Plays*, on (BBC TV, 11 January 1978; shot in studio, on tape). There are many different orders that can be applied to the two seasons of Bennett television plays in 1978/79 and 1982: the writing order, the production order, the broadcast order and the publication orders, of which there are several, and they intermingle. Alan Bennett confirms the writing order as that of the 2003 volumes *Me* and *Rolling Home*: 'Roughly, I think, yes. I tend to have one or two things on the go but the 2003 order is about right.' (Letter to K. McKechnie, September 2006)

This writing order reads as follows:

A Visit from Miss Prothero
Me, I'm Afraid of Virginia Woolf
Green Forms (Doris and Doreen)
The Old Crowd
Afternoon Off
(*Our Winnie* – broadcast in the *Objects of Affection* season in 1982, see below)
All Day on the Sands
One Fine Day

The 1978/79 broadcasting order, then, for *Six Plays* was as follows: [22]

Me, I'm Afraid of Virginia Woolf (2 December 1978); shot on film and on tape on location and in studio.
Doris and Doreen (later published as *Green Forms*) (16 December 1978); shot on tape in studio.
The Old Crowd (27 January 1979); shot on tape in studio.
Afternoon Off (3 February 1979); shot on film (location).
One Fine Day (17 February 1979); shot on film (location and studio).
All Day on the Sands (24 February 1979); shot on film (location and studio).

The *Six Plays* season had mixed reviews, the general critical tenor harsher in tone than it would probably be now. Some of the critics (and it is assumed the public reaction reflected this to some extent) showed preference for the recognisable, the familiar Bennett. Expectations were also geared to Bennett as a writer of humorous material, and critics expressed irritation at Bennett seemingly keeping it in check 'as if he had decided it was time to give a little more weight to his work and persuade us to take him a bit more seriously' (Knight 1979). Despite some stereotyping, critics were commenting on Bennett's use of unspectacular and non-dynamic storylines and characters, but conceding that he had the ability to make the boredom of his characters watchable:

Daft, but all clever stuff!

It was holidaytime in Bennettland at the weekend. ...

Most writers would be pushed to scrape even a short sketch out of such flimsy material, but dear old Bennett managed to make it last. (Murray 1979)

Some critical voices were very unforgiving, particularly with regard to *The Old Crowd*. The following comments, however, relate to the series as a whole:

> LWT last Saturday completed the near impossible. TV companies all too often put on a one-off stinker, but for a company to put on a series of six in succession is really something. It can only show peculiar judgement.

> Someone once said that if a monkey banged away on a typewriter for long enough it would by the law of average, write a book. This collection must have been the result. The one good thing to be said about it is that it gave work to a lot of actors, although some of them probably regretted it. (Afton 1979)

In the 1970s, Bennett was well known for satire, comedy and West End plays. The critics and the public took their time to accept another one of his voices in the television plays. Bennett, however, regarded and regards his northern voice as the inner voice he hears most clearly.

As mentioned above, the plays *Miss Prothero* and *Doris and Doreen* were originally separated, as the former was broadcast nearly a year before the latter. The plays, however, have a natural affinity in setting, through their characters, and another connection through the casting of Patricia Routledge in both plays. Together, the plays almost constitute a mini-season, although their plots and characters are not directly linked. The two plays could be part of an episodically constructed film, with characters existing close to each other, without mutual awareness, but with similar social and professional backgrounds. *Doris and Doreen* was re-named *Green Forms* and published with *Miss Prothero* as a double bill, *Office Suite*, by Samuel French in 1981. Bennett's introduction includes an almost Darwinist explanation as to the evolution of the middle-aged or elderly northern lady:

> Northern women are another species. Like the Galapagos turtles (whom some of them resemble) they have developed own characteristics and attitudes. Hopes are doomed to be dashed, expectations not to be realised because that's the way God, who certainly speaks with a Southern accent, has arranged things. (*Office Suite*: 2)

Stylistically, the two short plays later conform to the studio-shot, dialogue-dominated format of many contemporary single plays, referred to above. Doris, Doreen, Mr Dodsworth and Miss Prothero are the ancestors of the characters whose 'dull lives' Bennett later examined under a magnifying glass in *Talking Heads*. These texts do not conform to politicised, 'agitational' demands of the single play, because they make their point indirectly.

Doris and Doreen

Doris and Doreen (*Green Forms*) raises the threat of redundancy, but
has a firm focus on the long-established office routine and daily eccentricities of two middle-aged ladies. Apart from green and pink forms,
conversations quickly switch between the washbasin plug ('nicked' by
Personnel), fellow workers ('You'd think having one arm would make
somebody nicer') and family:

> Doris: I don't talk about mother.
> Doreen: You do.
> Doris: I don't.
> Doreen: Listen. She spent half the night on the commode. How do
>   I know that? It wasn't in the *Yorkshire Post*. You think you've got a
>   mother monopoly, you. Other people have mothers. Clifford has a
>   mother.
> Doris: Clifford's mother hasn't got a plastic hip.
> Doreen: He wouldn't broadcast it if she had. ... And what about me?
>   I'm not strong. But of course we never talk about that. Because I'm a
>   Grade 4, semi-skilled, ancillary worker. Semi-skilfully clearing up all
>   this skilful Grade 3 mess. You've done it on me, Doris.
>
> (*Green Forms* in *Me*: 153)

Most of Bennett's characters are constantly battling the insignificance
with which the world regards them, but Doris and Doreen are addition-
ally threatened with redundancy. The cosy and sometimes petty office
microcosm of these northern women in sensible shoes will not exist for
much longer.

A Visit from Miss Prothero

A Visit from Miss Prothero is the portrait of a woman turned bitter
because her surroundings deny her any significance. She uses her frustration to ensure that other people are as miserable as she is. This is of
course caused by a work environment, which mirrors a society in which
the individual is powerless and unimportant. Bennett returns to this
theme time and again in his television work, often with the focus on an
'unfashionable', and eventually redundant, generation. Miss Prothero
owes her voice to Bennett's aunties, particularly 'Aunty Kathleen':

> 'I've half a dozen people who are always begging me to pop in,' says Miss
> Prothero, 'one of them a chiropodist.' A character in an early play, hers is
> the unmistakable voice of Aunty Kath. (*US*: 86)

This voice is heard in many other female protagonists in Bennett's
works, their speech peppered with his aunties' expressions, such as 'If

you follow me, Lillian ...', 'As it transpired, Walter ...', 'Ready to wend my way, if you take my meaning ...' (*US*: 87).

The plays' narratives in the *Six Plays* season are not related as such, and they do not depend on each other for understanding, but they show unity through environment, style and through the similarity of their protagonists. Four of the plays combine qualities of location-shot drama of the earlier plays with domesticity and 'humdrum' realism. Behind the ordinary façade lurk twisted tales of human repression and isolation. Characters sometimes speak in a heightened style, which can border on the parodic, and features non-sequiturs, ensuring dialogue is often comic even when the content is not. This is not seen as a departure from the realist style of the plays, but as a confirmation of a particular northern idiom. Bennett, for example, has mentioned that his father, a butcher and wary of pretence, would never say 'I'll find out', but 'I'll ascertain'.[23] Some characters are prone to self-deception, of which the viewer is made aware, but the protagonist appears not to be. This theme becomes a significant part of the *Talking Heads* formula a decade later.

In 1985, over six years after the plays were first broadcast, five of the original *Six Plays* season were published in the volume *The Writer in Disguise* (Order: *Me, I'm Afraid of Virginia Woolf*, *All Day on the Sands*, *One Fine Day*, *The Old Crowd*, with an introduction by Lindsay Anderson, and *Afternoon Off*). Bennett refers to the plays' autobiographical subtext in the title, *The Writer in Disguise*. In the volume's introduction, Bennett 'officially' acknowledges parallels between himself and some of his male protagonists. So, through declaring them as a disguised version of himself, he partly comes out of his 'authorial' disguise, as Daphne Turner (1997: 110) also points out. Bennett describes the characters thus:

> Passive, dejected, at odds with themselves, they are that old friend, the Writer in Disguise. A doleful presence, whatever his get-up, he slips apologetically in and out of scenes being heartfelt, while the rest of the cast, who are invariably more fun (and more fun to write, too), get on with the business of living. (*Writer*: 9)

These protagonists are versions of the Bennett persona, and essentially variations on the same character. The *Writer* characters are trapped in unfulfilling lives for want of confidence, company or charisma. Although, as protagonists, they are central to the action, they do not move it, but are passively moved along by it. They are outsiders and observers of the ease with which others master 'living', unable to participate in everyday life and to belong. If at all, these characters can only be themselves when nobody is watching. In public, they attempt to perform a self they feel is expected of them. As a writer who portrays other people's lives, Bennett similarly sees himself as unable to participate in life, as this comparison between himself and the protagonist of *Intensive Care* shows:

> I deliberately write myself out of my own work. In this case, though, Gavin hasn't been able to find anyone else to play the part, so here I am. It is a hard job because I have written myself very few lines, something I regularly do with the central character. Supporting parts I don't find difficult, either to invent or to supply with dialogue; the central character is a blank, a puzzle, and one which I hope the actor will solve for me. But now the actor is me and I don't know what to do. (*WH*: 167)

The loneliness of the observer makes the writer successful, and also has a part in the construction of the central character, the Bennett persona, which is always 'being a spectator on the sidelines' rather than 'being a player in the game' (Brissett and Edgley 1990: 40). Bennett also links his characters' escapist impulses with his own wish to escape, and with his frustration at the inability to perform in a way that allows him to feel at ease. His trapped protagonists[24] are central to stories over which they have no control. They do not act, they react:

> There was a lot to laugh at in *Afternoon Off*, perhaps because there were so many people quietly drowning. (Banks Smith 1979a)

Afternoon Off

Afternoon Off is a melancholic and evocative play that deals with being on the outside, looking in. It does so in front of an equally melancholic and evocative backdrop of industrial desolation and small-town mentality. Initially planned in Harrogate, Stephen Frears decided, on seeing Hartlepool on the east coast, that he had found his perfect location. He was:

> ... fascinated by the contrast of someone waterskiing across the bay ... and the men picking up coal on the beach. And it had this long street, in the western town. ... Hartlepool is a sort of poetic place, it's bleak ...
> (Interview with Stephen Frears)

The protagonist, a Korean waiter called Lee, only has a few words, but his inoffensive presence prompts people to utter racist, stereotyping diatribes, or the kind of stream of consciousness that does not really say anything. Lee is in turn taken for Chinese, Japanese, Korean, Hawaiian and is habitually called 'Ghengis' by his colleagues at the hotel. *Afternoon Off*, like many Bennett plays, positions a lone figure in a particular landscape. Lee's search for a girl called Iris, who allegedly likes oriental types, or so he has been told, turns into a confused journey full of misunderstandings. Looking for the shop in which she works, Lee walks down a deserted high street, a row of forbidding houses, which seem to come from nowhere and go nowhere. In his wanderings, he enters locations such as a shoe shop, where he is treated with suspicion and coldness; a factory where he experiences the confrontational jingoism of the workers; a hospital where he gives the chocolates intended for 'Iris' to an incoherent old lady of the same name, who asks him whether he is 'one of those Japs' (*Afternoon Off*, in *Me*: 238). Another patient, after talking about her 'darkie vicar', comments that it will 'take more than a Dairy Box to erase the memory of Pearl Harbour' (*Afternoon Off*, in *Me*: 239).

In the most stunning scene of the play, Lee, still in search of 'Iris', follows the sound of music through a run down building. The song he is hearing is 'Pedro the Fisherman', and we see it performed by two music hall professionals, all teeth and smiles, frilly shirt and bouffant hair, on a stage that has seen better days. When it comes to the chorus, we hear whistling, and then the camera slowly tracks along an audience of old ladies, all of them in coats and hats, handbags on their laps, contentedly whistling along to 'Pedro the Fisherman'. The building is so cold we can see their breath. Lee stands in the wings, and, having misunderstood a gesture by one of the performers as a cue, walks onto the stage, very much to the entertainers' confusion, and to applause from the old ladies. This is a funny and sad scene of displacement, isolation and misunderstanding, so many of which permeate the unspectacular northern landscapes of these plays.

In 2005, Bennett looked back on *Afternoon Off* as an early indication that the monologue was to become his most renowned genre:

> ... a scene in a café and a long speech by Anna Massey. Stephanie Cole plays the other part, but it's hardly a conversation as she only has one line with Anna doing all the talking. And I realise, as I haven't until now, that I was writing monologues long before I specifically tried to, only in the earlier plays they were just long (long) speeches. *Afternoon Off* has several, because the leading figure is a Chinese waiter with very little English so everybody talks at him. ('Diary', *LRB* 2006: 36)

One Fine Day

Like *Afternoon Off*, *One Fine Day* is a study of a man's loneliness and isolation while in the company of others. Bennett remarks: 'The play is a flight from clutter, both materially and emotionally' (*Rolling Home*: x). It is a play where most of the action happens in silence, and the words that are spoken emphasise the meaninglessness of the domestic and professional worlds that Phillips, the protagonist, inhabits. Beside this personal narrative, the play is also an exploration of jargon and the pretence that accompanies it: the embellishing language of estate agents is examined both critically and parodically. Meetings take place in a high-rise office with large windows, against the architecture for which the firm is partly responsible: a city motorway, new concrete blocks, housing estates. The camera then pans to a model of a new development by the office window, promising more anonymous and cheap housing. When our attention is turned to the estate agents' meeting in progress, the euphemistic and misleading way of speaking has already been juxtaposed with the grim evidence of what this language is trying to sell.

Philips (Dave Allen), the protagonist and the firm's second-in-line to a noisily jovial Robert Stephens, is seen as standing outside the action from the beginning of the play. When he is shown alone, he is accompanied by music from Puccini operas: *Manon Lescaut, Tosca, La Bohème* and *Madame Butterfly*. The title of the play is adapted from the most famous aria from *Madame Butterfly*: 'Un bel dì – One Fine Day.'[25] The Puccini extracts are diegetic when listened to in Philips' car or on the headphones, or extradiegetic, a soundtrack to the alternative world Philips starts creating for himself. He is shown as feeling alienation at home and isolation at work. The impression that Dave Allen gives in a minimalist performance is that of a not unfriendly, but detached and essentially uninterested onlooker. His actions are never explained or psychologically framed, and some are difficult to understand. While driving through a small road in woodlands, Phillips accidentally runs over a hedgehog, stops the car, looks at it through the back mirror, and then reverses back over it, pausing to look at the dead animal again before driving on.

Challenged by a young ambitious colleague who has his boss's ear at work, Philips comes home to find his family 'invaded' by his son's adolescent relationship with a girl, Jennifer, who communicates only through her boyfriend. When his wife goes away for a few days, Philips feels driven out of his 'occupied' home, coinciding with his marginalisation at work. This is the point at which his secret other life begins, with an attraction to the empty, vast space of Sunley House, a long-term worry for the firm, which has failed to sell:

> A liking for bare stages and empty sets partly explains the unrented office block which is the setting for *One Fine Day*. ... I found it [the building which was the location for Sunley House], particularly on summer evenings, a setting as compelling and evocative as Fountains Abbey had been in *A Day Out*. (*Rolling Home*: x)

The thrill of being in the empty, unfinished building without anyone knowing is increased by Philip's discovery of a roof garden opposite the building. He can observe without being seen, and discovers a young couple with a baby who seem to be blissfully happy in their secluded garden on the top of an anonymous building. Philips hears bursts of romantic Puccini when watching them, whereas at home, he hears Puccini loudly on his headphones to avoid communication.

The idyll cannot last. The young upstart colleague, having decided that the quickest way to promotion is to push the sale of Sunley House, realises that someone is in the building, and sets up traps to catch the 'squatter'. Philips, sunbathing on the roof, manages to hide from a security man, but is trapped on the roof when his access door is locked. His only escape route is to winch himself down in a window cleaner's pulley. In an extraordinary scene, and to full-volume Puccini (*Madama Butterfly*), Philips descends at the side of the building, finally getting stuck about halfway down. With determination, he crashes the pulley against the glass window front again and again, until it breaks. This sequence is shot in slow motion, with startling angles from both above the pulley, and from inside the building. Finally, Phillips has escaped. The damage he has left also spells the downfall for his young competitive colleague, Ryecroft, as he is becoming obsessed with surprising the suspected squatter and is spending nights in Sunley House to catch him out. When the high-profile Japanese clients he has courted come to view the building, they first find the smashed window, and then Ryecroft asleep on Phillip's put-u-up, disgracing the chairman and the firm. This occurrence restores Philips to his former status within the firm. His alienation within his home is also resolved through a short, low-key confrontation with his son about whether his new girlfriend can stay the night ('Dad?!' – 'No.').

The play has a final sound collage where all jargon catchphrases and overlapping secretaries' conversations echo around the busy workplace:

> 'Guess where I'm heading – Harlesden, a chemist with potential for a client with imagination.'
> 'Sugar and a splash of maraschino.'
> 'He's threatening to take me to a topless steak house.'
> (*One Fine Day*, in *Rolling Home*: 96)

> Frears: And all those girls I used to find in Mike Leigh films, girls at shoe shops. In the one with Dave Allen, there was a lot about cocktails, one girl doing this long thing about how to do cocktails. You'd meet these girls, people like Mary Maddox [who plays the secretary Avril in *One Fine Day*], and they were so wonderful, you just wanted them to be in somewhere. They were just so funny.
> (Interview with Stephen Frears)

The final 'coda' about cocktail, client visits and topless steak houses characterises the play as having as much a musical as a narrative structure. Through its visual style, *One Fine Day* also alerts us to the unexpected beauty of things that we might normally consider non-descript or ugly.

All Day on the Sands

> There is a seeping sadness in Alan Bennett like leaky wellies and the saddest words of tongue or pen are, for him, holiday, half-holiday, afternoon off, retirement. He is never so desolate as when he is enjoying himself. (Banks Smith 1979b)

All Day on the Sands is an impressionist play about family seaside holidays, and about families who are 'cross because they [are] not happy', as Bennett remarks in the introduction (*Rolling Home*: x). As the other plays in the season, *All Day* makes poignant comments about language. *Afternoon Off* unmasks racial, commonplace prejudice, whereas *All Day on the Sands* offers a concentration of clichéd northern speech. We have already been introduced to Mr Cattley, the Miramar's owner, at the beginning of this chapter. His convivial talk, almost like the host of a music hall revue, is strictly reserved for his 'on stage' (i.e. tannoy) persona:

> Mr Catley: The service of breakfast will shortly be commencing in the Portofino Room. Top of this morning's menu are kippers, fresh in from Fleetwood, the best Pouton-le-Fylde can do in the way of bacon plus free-range eggs and your choice of starters ... [In the doorway we see Colin looking up inside the shaft of the dumb waiter.] Leave that alone unless you want decapitating.
>
> (*All Day*, in *Me*: 30)

Bennett and Frears present a play that has even less of a narrative than *Afternoon Off* or *One Fine Day*. The dramatic climax of *All Day* is the discovery that a young boy, Colin, has dropped his sister's sandal onto an adjoining roof, and the furious telling off he receives from his father. It is similar to *A Day Out* and *Sunset* and *Afternoon Off*, in that it shows figures in an environment and focuses closely on their behaviour under these specific circumstances: looking for a girl in a hostile town, isolating oneself and craving anonymity in anonymous buildings and, in *All Day*, a family together, but alone anyway, on a windy Lancashire beach.

Of course, there is a social subtext to the play. *All Day* is a play about children's frustrated expectations, mirroring Bennett's attitude as a child, that 'we had already seen the best'. The family in *All Day* is under strain because 'Dad' has just been made redundant. This, apart from the economic implications of having to settle for Morecambe instead of a Spanish holiday, also hurts his pride, and is therefore not to be talked about. The unmentionable segregates the family even more, and, frustrated in their own company, arguments occur. It is interesting to compare *All Day* to *Sunset*, as it deals with specific problems of the protagonists – redundancy and the trials of a boarding house holiday for one family; the feeling of redundancy that can come with retirement for the other. Morecambe, beautiful as it may look in some of the shots, provides the appropriately atmospheric backdrop for both of these stories that can feel defeating and claustrophobic, despite the vastness of the bay with its uninterrupted views.

The Old Crowd

The Old Crowd, directed by Lindsay Anderson, the script edited by Anderson and Bennett together, stands apart in the *Six Plays* season.

> But to be abused and the play vilified was for me a novel experience which I was surprised to find wasn't entirely disagreeable. If I haven't written anything like it since it's not because I learned my lesson, just that nothing similar has occurred. (Introduction, *Me*: xiii)

As Bennett and Frears commented in an edition of *The South Bank Show* (1979), the play has 'no plot, no beginning, no end'[26] and its style seems to parody Brechtian conventions on the one hand, and to draw from surrealist imagery on the other. Bennett's starting point, he comments, was the image of an empty house with the sound of a piano tuner, and the contemporary strike of lorry drivers, which partly explains the empty space in which *The Old Crowd* is set. The threat in the play is not tangible, and obscure references are made to viruses spreading, vandals roaming the streets, and places turning into ghost cities. The contrast between this suggested anarchic exterior (the camera never leaves the house) and the exaggerated traditional demeanour of people inside the house is intriguing. *The Old Crowd* is a play of many disjunctures; one of them being the clash between the familiar Bennett idiom and its lack of connected content. While Bennett's other plays of the period are hardly heavy on narrative complexity, it seems that *The Old Crowd* tries to avoid any associations with linearity altogether. Visually, the style of Buñuel is referenced through an eye operation seen on a television screen, and other surreal juxtapositions include a pink marigold glove casually fished out of a food terrine at the start of a meal.

The play also has an extensive symbolist inventory: the theme of cracks emerges at fissures in the play: a crack in the ceiling, getting bigger as we look on; a woman doing her make up in a cracked mirror. This could be read as the invasion of the external state constantly referred to in the text, the near-apocalypse threatening to invade the strained normality of the house. But it could also simply be read as an interest in showing images of disintegration and disjuncture. Indeed, these images are probably the biggest visual 'thread' in *The Old Crowd*. Semiotically, it alienates the viewer to see people sitting on chairs too low for the dinner table, or to see servants carrying terrines on their heads, or brandishing knives. Critics were divided on whether this alienation was applied in Brechtian terms, through the juxtaposition of conventional and entirely unexpected behaviour and the resulting disruption of the narrative flow. This happens all through *The Old Crowd*, and we are also reminded of the fact that we are seeing a film by catching regular glimpses of the crew on the studio set. One shot is particularly stunning: the 'slaves' hang up a large mirror, and we see the cameraman filming them in the mirror as soon as it is on the wall. For the filming, Stephen Frears 'appeared' as the play's director, despite really being its producer.

Bennett and Anderson integrate many themes and references in *The Old Crowd*, but the play seems to incorporate slightly too many conventions. In addition, there is a sense of old school acting indulgence. Anderson assembled a cast of fine actors he had worked with before, such as Rachel Roberts, Jill Bennett, Valentine Dyall and John Moffatt. While this old-fashioned quality was no doubt intended (licensed over-acting?), it seems that the cast and the production team, while having a wonderful time, were also enjoying a private joke to which the viewers are not privy. Bennett recalls this:

> He [Anderson] believes in the creative power of mischief. At one point I suggest that Jill Bennett should say a line in a different way. 'Oh yes. Tell her that. I've just told her to do the opposite. Now she won't know what to do.' (Introduction, *Writer*: 15)

The play suffers from problems with pace and offers heightened performances that can be seen to have a demonstrative detachment, trying to teach the viewer a lesson in alienation. Nevertheless, *The Old Crowd* is a highly intriguing text, precisely because it does not offer a clear interpretational route, and because of its multiple stylistic references. The critics were either baffled or acerbic in reaction to the play.

> Most worrying, though, was Bennett's evident belief that the widespread dislike of both critics and public for *The Old Crowd* is a reliable signal to him that this is the direction his future work should take: 'To some extent the hullaballoo confirms me in what I want to do'. Fair enough that Bennett should ignore the critics – but against that, critics have always been extremely kind to him. They're likely not to be expressing malice or hatred of experimentalism, but a sharp interest in their future

pleasure, which isn't a despicable motive. Bennett might beware the obstinately beguiling syllogism which goes 'many significant works of art cause a hullaballoo; *The Old Crowd* caused a hullaballoo, therefore ...' (Barnes, 1979)

The public reaction can be attributed to confusion, expecting a typical Bennett product and seeing something that seems to ridicule these expectations. The hostile reactions were largely aimed at Bennett specifically, and at times quite personal. The play might have been deemed avant-garde and 'different', as its director Lindsay Anderson certainly had radical credibility. The audience and critics, however, demanded the Bennett style they were familiar with, and saw Anderson as a 'corrupting' influence on the author.

Anderson was keen to stress the political possibilities of the text, as well as its potential reference points to the state of British public services in the late 1970s:

> [S]even hundred 'pickets' mass daily against policemen with truncheons and riot shields to prevent one man going to work – emotion on both sides, inflamed by omnipresent television cameras ... In which the robbing, battering and raping of old ladies as they totter home through inner-city streets, their pensions in their purses, has become commonplace ... In which ambulances fail to arrive, trains fail to run, 'essential services' prove a luxury. (Anderson in 'Introduction to *The Old Crowd*', *Me*: 170)

In a footnote to Anderson's abrasive and emotional introduction, Bennett differs in his perception, not having intended *The Old Crowd* to be 'a tract for the times', although he concedes that it could be read like that, since it was broadcast during a lorry drivers' strike.

Julian Barnes took the opportunity to comment on Bennett and Frears' appearance on *The South Bank Show* the night after *The Old Crowd* was broadcast:

> The day after, the *South Bank Show* (incidentally LWT)[27] had a rather unadversarial Bragg letting Bennett and his producer Frears meander away about how nice it was to work with each other and how super it was to work with Lindsay Anderson. (Barnes 1979)

Frears comments:

> Frears: But we were very, very good. We defended it [*The Old Crowd*]. I remember Lindsay saying we were brilliant. We just said 'Oh! It was absolutely wonderful, wasn't it?' – Never even questioning, never even contemplating the fact ... It's a brilliant tactic. I didn't know it at the time. But I remember Lindsay saying that's the only tactic, 'Crisis? – What Crisis? Oh! It was absolutely wonderful!'
> (Interview with Stephen Frears)

The case of *The Old Crowd* and its critical reception is significant for a number of reasons: Bennett enjoyed the controversy, and stated he wanted to go down the experimental and collaborative route more often in his writing. He did not, however, produce other texts that have the experimental and unexpected (or even unfinished) quality of *The Old Crowd*. Instead, Bennett's approach to presenting his audience with confrontational content has since been a 'Trojan Horse' one. Bennett 'smuggles' controversial material into the text, at first obscured by familiarity: typical old ladies from Bennettland unexpectedly talk about sex (*Waiting for the Telegram*), William Pitt the Younger shows glimpses of Thatcherism (*The Madness of George III*); or nice bright schoolboys discuss why being touched up by a teacher is not the end of the world (*The History Boys*).

Objects of Affection

Bennett returned to the BBC for the making of his next season of television plays, six plays broadcast in the *Playhouse* slot, and published as *Objects of Affection* in 1982.[28] He has never been 'faithful' to any one commissioning agency and seemed to make his choices according to who offered the best conditions. In the introduction to *Objects*, Bennett denies that there is a strong thematic connection between the plays in this season ('Repetitions, yes; preoccupation, certainly; but not a theme', *Objects*: 7). Similar to the preceding season in 1979, characters are predominantly middle-aged or elderly, they are disillusioned and disappointed by their inability to 'live!'. Some of the plays deal with alienation and the breakdown of loyalties within a family. Meaning is normally not placed within the characters' speech, which is proof of their difficulty in expressing themselves, but within the subtext of reactions, silences and visual signifiers.

It is worth noting at this point that geographical locations gradually become less important in Bennett's television plays. Where the countryside (West Yorkshire) and particular urban environments (Morecambe, Leeds, Halifax) were very important in early single plays and in the first season of plays, Bennett seems to concentrate more on foregrounding his characters in their domestic environments. These are not necessarily exciting locations, and so plays are set in back-to-backs (*Marks, Say Something Happened*), hospitals or homes for elderly (*Rolling Home, Intensive Care*), and generally non-descript buildings and corridors, be they in office blocks or schools. Bennett comments, realising the parochial look and settings of his plays:

The number of ladies in little costumes in these plays must be well above the national average (though vicars in civvies come hard on their heels). If I have a favourite, imaginary landscape it seems to be an empty corridor. These are not comfortable facts for a writer in middle life to have to face. (*Objects*: 7)

In earlier plays, a view of the building site that is Leeds townscape is juxtaposed with Morecambe Bay, forming a crucial part of the narrative. In this season, the locations are less specific, although still very identifiably northern English. The tendency towards the reduction of locations is taken to its conclusion in *Talking Heads*, where we see only the immediate surroundings of the characters who are telling their story. In *Objects*, there is also a tendency to focus on institutions, not just for their visual qualities, but for the duality they can expose: 'I'm interested in their double lives – the way there's an official public life going on, and at the same time a quite separate underground existence which belongs to the people inside the closed world'.[29]

The plays in the season were all produced by Innes Lloyd and broadcast in the following order:

> *Intensive Care*, Director Gavin Millar (BBC TV, 9 November 1982; *Play for Today*)
> Playhouse:
> *Our Winnie*, Director Malcolm Mowbray (BBC TV, 12 November 1982)
> *A Woman of No Importance*, Director Giles Foster (BBC TV, 19 November 1982)
> *Rolling Home*, Director Piers Haggard (BBC TV, 3 December 1982)
> *Marks*, Director Piers Haggard (BBC TV, 10 December 1982)
> *Say Something Happened*, Director Giles Foster (BBC TV, 17 December 1982)

Again, Bennett's writing order, confirmed in the 2003 new volumes, differs from this, in that *Our Winnie* seems to have been written earlier than most of the other plays, followed by *Marks*, *Say Something Happened*, *Rolling Home* and *Intensive Care*.[30]

Intensive Care

Alan Bennett's *Intensive Care* was a fine script to work with, but its acute combination of tragedy and farce was not one to commend it to international audiences, or to the producers who must guess their taste. It was also strongly regional, accurate, funny, affectionate about Bennett's neck of the south Yorkshire [sic] woods. But I don't believe it was the apparent parochialism which would have been a disqualifier. It was its refusal to confront small subjects with big capital letters – Love, War, Sacrifice – or give easy answers. It was about death, jealousy, sexual identity, parents, children, about whom and which it made desperately funny jokes. (Gavin Millar in Bennett 1984: 120)

Intensive Care is not technically part of the *Objects* season, as it was produced as a *Play for Today*. It was, however, broadcast three days before the season started (after that, the other plays were broadcast in a weekly slot) and has close stylistic and thematic links with the other plays. Indeed, it also has connections with the 1978/79 season of plays, as the protagonist, Midgley, is another writer in disguise, another inarticulate, middle-aged male, intimidated by his surroundings and frustrated by the blandness of his life. This time, he is played by Bennett himself.

Intensive Care takes Bennett's ongoing interest in parent–child relationships to its final stage, with the exploration of the death of a parent, set in a typical Bennett location: a hospital. When Midgley is called to the hospital, where his father is hovering close to death after a stroke and subsequent fall, he is determined to behave according to expectation, and to be there when his father dies. This plan is 'complicated' by his father's unexpected resilience (although he remains in a coma), and by an unexpected opportunity for Midgley to act on his unfulfilled desire to 'live'. In keeping with Bennett characters, liberation is often a sexual one. Midgley's realisation that his father had a glamorous lady friend whom he kept secret gives him the impulse to do something entirely uncharacteristic: he asks the night nurse (Julie Walters) to go to bed with him. She agrees and, for once, Midgley feels that he is behaving like other people who master the art of 'living'. It is of course during this that his father, who has been clinging on to life for a few days, dies.

Bennett created this character without planning to play him himself, meaning that he himself had to find a way of filling the void that he often describes his protagonists as 'a blank, a puzzle, and one which I hope the actor will solve for me' (*WH*: 167). Bennett speaks the dialogue he has written and plays a character that resembles his public persona. This contributes to the confusion between character and author and leads to assumptions of autobiographical material as the inspiration for the plot. In *Intensive Care*, it is not just silent and morose character Midgley going to bed with the night nurse, it is Alan Bennett and Julie Walters in a sex scene. Bennett explains in the introduction that the inspiration for this scene was an event in the life of M.K. Gandhi who was sleeping with his wife while his father died in the next room. *Intensive Care*, in Bennett's own low-key style, juxtaposes Eros and Thanatos in the unlikely settings of Airedale Hospital near Keighley, West Yorkshire.

Our Winnie

Our Winnie shows female Bennett characters in their microcosm, their natural habitat: suburban roads, bus stops, cemeteries.

> Cora: We haven't done so bad today. We've been interviewed vis-à-vis the bus service. We've come into contact with the younger generation and we've had our photograph taken.
>
> (*Our Winnie*, in *Rolling Home*: 20–1)

Minutiae of daily life are heightened, attention from others is considered a success, which lends these ladies' lives meaning and importance. Cora and Ida are sisters, and Cora has a daughter, Winnie, who is in her thirties. In twenty-first century language, she has 'special needs', but for Cora and Ida she is simply 'not right'. However, their relationship with Winnie is full of affection, but Cora's perspective on her daughter's disability is still one that includes the feelings of shame and failure:

> Cora: Once we knew for certain, I didn't go out. Didn't go anywhere. I didn't take her out. Dad had it all to do. Dad and you. The housework. The shopping. Everything. It was long enough before I came round. Still, life has to go on. I suppose. Folks stare. They look at her and they don't realise. Then they do realise, and they look away. You don't want them to stare and you don't want them to look away either.
> Ida: It's a good job there's love.
>
> (*Our Winnie*, in *Rolling Home*: 21)

Our Winnie is Bennett's first text that is about exploitation for art's sake. This becomes a very big theme in later plays, and is one of the central issues in his autobiographical writing. The continuing theme is set up in this play when an art student takes a photo of Winnie, pretending to do it just to please her, and assuring her mother that there is no film in the camera. As Winnie has been upset by being excluded from the photo with her mother and aunty, and thus consents to being photographed as a consolation, the question of whether she is exploited is not a straightforward one. It is, however, clear that the art student is prepared to be devious to get the picture she wants. In the final shot, we see the photo in an exhibition, decorated with what looks like a prize ribbon. Bennett here introduces the fundamental question under which circumstances it is acceptable to use real people in art. While he explores this concept in general terms, in *Our Winnie* he also compares a photo and a drawing, and the resulting question why a drawing seems to be less of an ethical problem than a photo. This is a theme that surfaces in an entirely different context in the spy play *A Question of Attribution* (see Chapter 3).

Our Winnie shows a straightforward case of exploitation, with the not very likeable art student tricking Winnie's mother into letting her take photographs and, if an excuse were necessary, presumably telling herself she is an artist or a professional and sheltering behind the privileges such designations are thought to confer. What writers tell themselves I'm not sure (which is presumably why I keep writing about it).

(*Our Winnie*, in *Rolling Home*: vii)

Marks

Marks, thematically in keeping with the rest of the season, deals with frustrated expectations and isolation in families. It is, however, stylistically very different from the others in the season. It is not filmed in the straightforward, provincial realist style of the other plays in the season, instead leaning on symbolist and leitmotif imagery. The visual direction and production design foreground symbolic aspects, showing a preoccupation with mirrors and eyes. The play opens with a close up of two eyes, then moving in even closer into showing just one eye, and then the eyeball. This sets off a swirling shot of almost psychedelic associations, before arriving in a scene which shows a christening in 'normal' suburban surroundings. While the juxtaposition is intriguing, and the device communicates someone looking back in time, it certainly makes for a stark contrast between realism and more experimental visual styles, one that Bennett was not comfortable with:

Marks was slightly skewed in production because, though a naturalistic play, it was designed and shot in an almost experimental fashion with strong colours, jagged outlines and none of the understated working-class interiors I was used to and comfortable with. It was a deliberate experiment by the director and the designer, perhaps, though, reflecting a lack of confidence in the interest of the text. I went along with it, though I thought it confusing and unhelpful. ... In my experience – and this applies to stage and television – authors are seldom given much credit for visual sense, the setting one carries in one's head when writing not being thought to be of much relevance when it comes to the design. To my mind, though, it's as pertinent as the words themselves. (Introduction, *Rolling Home*: x–xi)

Marks focuses on the problematic relationship between a single mother and an adolescent son. Marjory's daughter Margaret has failed to fulfil her mother's expectations by getting pregnant and 'having' to marry, and so the younger son, Les, is the focus of ambitions and hopes for his mother, who interferes uncomfortably with normal teenage issues. The son's attempts to both distance himself from his overpowering mother and to reassure her of his love at the same time culminate in him having a 'Mother' tattoo done to please her (he calls her 'Mam', but thinks that 'Mother' sounds more classy). This, although it carries his mother's name, is the separating device that brands him a failure in her eyes:

> Les: I haven't done anything. I did it for you.
> Marjory: For me? But there was no need to do anything for me. You were lovely. You were perfect. You didn't have to do anything for me. You were mine as you were. You were perfect. Now you're not perfect. ... It'll never come off. You're stuck with it. It's indelible, is that. It's like a bruise. A bloody great ornamental bruise. It's like my varicose veins, that's blue. Is that what you wanted?
>
> (*Marks* in *Rolling Home*: 125)

The play starts with a flashback, and returns to the frame narrative, where a grown-up Les, who is homosexual, is showing a lover his tattoo. While not conclusive, this scene offers a link between Les' sexual orientation and his mother's stifling love.

Rolling Home

Rolling Home was also directed by Piers Haggard, but bears little stylistic resemblance to *Marks*, and has a close visual affinity with other 'hospital' plays, such as *Intensive Care* and *A Little Outing* in 1977. It is another opportunity for Bennett to explore the implications of care for the elderly, and the resulting institutionalisation and estrangement:

> We shot the film in a derelict hospital in Richmond [North Yorkshire], one of several of such institutions I filmed in at this time (with another in *Intensive Care*), the availability and decrepitude of such locations I suppose saying something about what was happening to the NHS in the seventies and eighties.
>
> (Introduction, *Rolling Home*: xii)

The protagonist, Mr Wyman ('Joey' to his favourite nurse, 'Dad' to his two daughters), is a long-term patient in a hospital. His daughters, one a 'career girl', one a housewife and mother, use their visits as a continuing competition for their father's attention and their own rivalry. Professional achievements and the grandchildren's latest endeavours such as diving and rock climbing are relentlessly presented to their completely indifferent and apathetic parent. Despite being confined to an uneventful existence, 'Dad' is not interested in the distraction these family visits might offer, wiping his face in disgust after his daughter has kissed him goodbye, and telling the male nurse to not ever have children. The only thing old Mr Wyman is interested in is what might be behind a wall he looks out onto from his ward window. Nurse Donald makes up a lovely little scenario for him, also reflecting his own desire to get married and find a house with his fiancée:

> Donald: It's a house. A really nice little house. Two up, two down. Porch, path up to the door. Honeysuckle. There's a little garden. Flowers. Apple tree. And a vegetable patch. It's ideal. ... A couple. They just got married.

(Rolling Home: 171)

It is natural to sympathise with Mr Wyman in the awkward family visit scenes. However, in poorly suppressed arguments between the sisters, it transpires that Dad might have abused his (long dead) wife.

Bennett's statement about the decline of the NHS and general quality of care for the old and infirm is not a dogmatic one, as he shows staff who are kind, committed and funny. One hilariously 'orchestrated' scene begins with a wheelchair race along a hospital corridor, given a voice-over by one of the male nurses. Then, the familiar scene of an 'event' for the elderly unfolds. The exaggeratedly chirpy and often patronising tone of the female 'animateur' is mingled with the sounds of old people shouting answers to quiz games and, in one case, obscenities. One confused old lady contributes the high-pitched call of 'I'm not here!' to the general cacophony at regular intervals. Bennett includes such scenes in *Sunset Across the Bay*: Mam and Dad sit in a circle of elderly people, encouraged to sing 'I'm H-A-P-P-Y! – referred to by Bennett as 'the geriatric Horst Wessel, that sad and mendacious anthem'. In *Afternoon Off*, the old ladies whistle along to 'Pedro the Fisherman'. The results are in all three cases hilariously funny and depressing at the same time. Bennett's inventory for these scenes becomes apparent only when *Untold Stories* is published – with characters, or some of their eccentricities, taken from mental wards and care homes, where his mother lived (latterly simply existed) for nearly fifteen years of her life.

Intensive Care presented us with the consequences of 'living', that is, of giving in to one's sexual desires. There is a similar sense in *Rolling Home*, where Mr Wyman's male nurse, Donald, has sex with his fiancée during his night shifts. The inevitability of discovery strikes the viewer early on in the play, and when it happens, it is not just the shock and the lovers' shame of being caught that is chilling. While Donald and Jenny are making love on the floor in the staff room, Mr Wyman, Joey, has left his bed to see the idyllic scenario behind a brick wall that Donald, after constant questioning, has told him about. With tragic inevitability, Mr Wyman has fallen into the river close to the hospital and died. His escape from the ward and subsequent death from hypothermia has a strong parallel with Bennett's Aunty Kathleen's death in 1974. Suffering from dementia, she had wandered out of the hospital and was found dead, by Bennett, in the woods near a motorway (see also *US*: 86).

> Molly: I don't know what all that was about, him wanting to know what was on the other side.
>
> Val: He knew what was on the other side. I've told him a time or two. Just staring and staring and not talking. I got fed up of it. I said 'I don't know what there's to stare at. There's a wall. And a canal, and beyond it's the cemetery.
>
> (*Rolling Home*: 182)

Say Something Happened

The protagonists in the play *Say Something Happened* are familiar ones: an elderly couple, not natural 'mixers', and suspicious of the intrusions of the outside world. They receive a visit from a social worker, sent to 'assess' their needs. Inexperienced and only superficially trained, her professional jargon soon reveals a deeply insecure young woman. The assumptions about old people are attacked by Mam, when she turns the tables on 'June':

> Mam: A bedsitter? Child of a broken home, living in a bedsitter in one of the inner city areas: you're the one that's at risk. You want to get yourself on a register. Coming round telling us. Isolated. We like being isolated. We're like that. It's the same as the radio now, every programme you turn on, it's folks ringing up. And they make out you're all friends. Everybody friends. Well we're not friends. We've got each other and that's enough.
>
> (*Say Something Happened*, in *Rolling Home*: 42)

Roles are then reversed as June becomes tearful at not doing her job properly and is reassured by 'Mam' and 'Dad', who are nonetheless enjoying the visit. They talk extensively about their daughter, Margaret, and her 'jetsetting' career as a personal secretary. There are some strong parallels in the way Mam and Dad refer to their daughter to the stage play *Enjoy*, where the daughter turns out not to be a personal secretary, but a prostitute. The social worker in *Enjoy*, on the other hand, turns out to be the couple's son after a sex change. The surprises in *Say Something Happened* are on a smaller scale; nevertheless, while Dad is out of the room, Mam hurriedly confesses that they also have a son who is 'not right', and to whom they never refer.

Alan Bennett saw stronger connections between *Say Something Happened* and *A Cream Cracker under the Settee* (*TH 1*). In the monologue, there is a stillborn son to whom nobody ever refers, compared to a disabled son in *Say Something Happened*. Also, Doris in *Cream*

Cracker experiences the isolation that the social worker June warns of so urgently in *Say Something Happened*:

> And though no one has ever compared the two plays, I did feel I was perhaps repeating myself. Not that a television audience minds that, or a theatrical audience either; as in other areas of human endeavour, it pays to repeat yourself: the public always like to know what they are getting. (Introduction, *Rolling Home*: xii)

Conclusion

> [H]ow fitting it is, how appropriate, how excusable to use one's own family background, parents, relatives and such as a resource, a memory bank from which to draw material. (*Rolling Home*: vii)

As the content of Bennett's work, always biographically *inspired*, moved closer towards autobiographical material, Bennett's involvement in the production process also increases. These two overall linear developments are complemented by a third: that of ongoing reduction of form, which is not mirrored by Bennett's works for the stage. Plays such as *A Day Out* (1972) are 'group portraits', plays in the late 1970s and 1980s tend to be 'family portraits'. Within the season of *Objects*, Bennett arrived at the form of the 'portrait' of a single person: the monologue. *A Woman of No Importance* was the first television monologue Bennett wrote, and, although content and characters underwent changes in subsequent monologues, he has essentially kept to a similar form and structure in the two *Talking Heads* series. The monologue developed into the dominant form in Bennett's television work in the late 1980s.

Bennett has worked with many 'writer's directors'. Because his voice is so distinctive, their considerable influence has not received much attention (except in the case of *Old Crowd*, because Lindsay Anderson's 'auteurship' was to some critics more recognisable than Bennett's). The collaborative relationship with directors does not just mean that Bennett is involved in the production process, but also that directors influence the making of a televisual text to quite a great extent. Bennett claims he does not think in terms of aesthetics or technical aspects while writing, although associative images often provide a starting point, as they also prompt changes in direction during shooting. The homogenous quality of the plays in both seasons discussed (*Old Crowd* and *Marks* perhaps excluded) is proof of the ability of his directors to respond 'filmographically' to the demands of Bennett's simple, yet complex plays.

Bennett's television plays from the 1970s and early 1980s have a distinctly televisual quality. In a collection of articles addressing the state of British film, and the question of whether 'British cinema is alive and well and on television' (Hassan et al. 1984: 116), Bennett explains his different perceptions of writing for cinema and television:

> In terms of writing I don't think one can talk of feature films and TV films in the same breath, and it's not simply a question of scale or scope. It seems to me to have something to do with the space between the audience and the screen. On television, one does not have to raise one's voice. The relationship with the audience is intimate, the tone conversational. ... There has to be more air in a film. (Bennett 1984: 121)

There are television plays that are more adaptable to the large screen than others, surfacing mainly in the 1980s (see Chapter 3). Bennett partly assigns this to topic and setting, remarking that:

> upper classes and espionage are always dear to English hearts, more so certainly than the touching stories of sudden incontinence north of the Trent in which I generally specialise. ... My scripts, where the infantry is recruited from aunties and wheelchairs make up the armoured division, are not ready-made movie material. (Bennett in Hassan et al. 1984: 121)

Notes

1 Alan Bennett on *Front Row Special*, 4 October 2005, BBC Radio 4.
2 For a detailed account on the early age of television drama, see Bignell et al. (*British Television Drama: Past, Present and Future*, Basingstoke: Palgrave, 2000) and Caughie (*Television Drama – Realism, Modernism, and British Culture*, Oxford: Oxford University Press, 2000).
3 303 *Plays for Today* were broadcast between October 1970 and August 1984; an average of 21 plays per year: 101 were shot on film, 202 were electronically recorded (see Cooke, *The Television Drama Book*, London: British Film Institute, 2003: 92).
4 Some of the functions of social realism: 'To represent social experience that has hitherto been largely underrepresented within dominant forms of post-war drama is to validate that experience, to argue that it is worthy of interest in itself and to remedy a significant absence' (Lacey, *British Realist Theatre: The New Wave in its Context 1956–1965*, London: Routledge, 1995: 74). For a general discussion of realism and possible definitions, see Lacey (*ibid.*), Chapter 3 'Realism, Class and Culture', pp. 63 ff.
5 Alan Bennett on *Front Row Special*, 4 October 2005, BBC Radio 4.
6 The term 'series' refers to those shows whose characteristics and settings are recycled, but the story concludes in each individual episode. By contrast, in a 'serial' the story and discourse do not come to a conclusion during an episode, and the threads are picked up again after a hiatus. A series is thus similar to an anthology of short stories, while a serial is like a serialised Victorian novel (see also Creeber 2001: 35).
7 Bennett appeared as an actor in *My Father Knew Lloyd George* (Jack Gold, 1965) and *Alice in Wonderland* (Jonathan Miller, 1966), for example.
8 Ken Loach, in a television documentary, commented that he first applied as assis-

tant floor manager at the BBC and got turned down, and then applied to the director training scheme and was accepted.

9 This cannot be said categorically, of course. Bennett worked with Lindsay Anderson and Stephen Frears on scripts, and will have done so with all his collaborators. He has not, however, written television work as part of a group of writers, nor contributed to any long-running serial.

10 See also Brandt (*British Television Drama in the 1980s*, Cambridge: Cambridge University Press, 1993 15) and Self (*Television Drama: An Introduction*, Basingstoke: Macmillan, 1984: 3).

11 *May 3*, BBC1, April 2004, for example, a play about a young woman suffering from multiple personality disorder as a result of childhood abuse.

12 'Aesthetically, the single play had been converging with the TV/cinema film since the 1960s as a consequence of the shift between electronic studio recording to location shooting on 16 mm film' (Cooke *Television Drama Book*, 2003: 138); 'Economics – the cost of producing single plays in the new era of 'cost effectiveness' – is probably a more significant factor in charting the demise of the television play. ... In a period of recession, when budgets were being cut, the single play began to seem like a luxury the television companies could no longer afford' (ibid.: 139); 'In the more reactionary climate of Thatcherism a loss of editorial freedom had political consequences and it became increasingly difficult for radical or progressive drama to get commissioned in the 1980s and virtually impossible after *Play for Today* ended in 1984' (ibid.: 140–1).

13 There are exceptions, not just among directors: drama adapted by Andrew Davies is announced with his name as a heading, for example (although one might still argue for the adaptor as the writer, and the author of the source text also features prominently).

14 'If a film has a single maker, then it is much easier to accept it as 'Art'. That acceptance also makes it worthy of academic and critical study. Is it too cynical to suggest that critics who advance the auteur theory do so out of a vested interest. For similar reasons there is a desire to preserve the status of the writer as the one and only originator of the television play' (Self, *Television Drama*, 1984: 70).

15 'Many [critics] harbour the Romantic ideology of the primacy of authorial 'originality' and 'vision', emphasizing individual style and artistic "self-expression". In this tradition the artist (in any medium) is seen as breaking the mould of convention' (Chandler, 'An introduction to genre theory', 2000: 9).

16 The story is the actual sequence of events as they happen, whereas the 'plot' is those events as they are edited, ordered, packaged and presented in what we recognise as a narrative [a version of the story, not to be taken literally] ... story is determined by chronology and plot is determined by consequence or causality' (McQuillan, *The Narrative Reader*, London: Routledge, 2000: 325).

17 'The parts of a narrative which are presented in a mimetic manner are "dramatised", which is to say they are represented in a "scenic" way, with a specified setting, and making use of dialogue which contains direct speech. "Mimesis" is "slow telling", in which is done and said is "staged" for the reader, creating the illusion that we are "seeing" and "hearing" things for ourselves. By contrast, "diegesis" means "telling" or "relating". The parts of narrative which are presented in this way are given in a more "rapid" or "panoramic" or "summarising" way ... In practice, of course, writers use the two modes in tandem, moving from mimetic to diegetic, and back again, for strategic reasons' (Summary of Gennette in Barry, *Beginning Theory*, 2nd edn, Manchester: Manchester University Press, 2002: 233).

18 For further discussion of *A Day Out*, see Turner (*In a Manner of Speaking*, London: Faber & Faber, 1997: 12; particular emphasis on the pastoral) and O'Mealy (*Alan Bennett: A Critical Introduction*, London: Routledge, 2001: 21).

19 'What memory was for Proust the lavatory is for my mam' (*Van*: 6).

20 There is no copy of the text of *A Little Outing* available. The quotes have therefore been transcribed from video tape.

21 Lindsay Anderson directed *The Old Crowd* and Giles Foster directed *All Day on the Sands*. Stephen Frears was director for all other plays in the season.

22 The *Writer in Disguise* figure provides a link with *Afternoon Off, One Fine Day, Me* and *All Day* in the first edition; in the second edition this 'red thread' no longer exists.

23 *The South Bank Show*, ITV, October 2005.

24 Hopkins in *Me! I'm Afraid of Virginia Woolf*, Lee in *Afternoon Off*, Philips in *One Fine Day* (all in *The Writer in Disguise*); Midgley in *Intensive Care* (in *Objects of Affection*); Graham in *A Chip in the Sugar* (*Talking Heads* 1).

25 'Un bel di, vedremo levarsi un fil di fumo, sull estremo con fin del mare. E poi la nave appare. ...' (One fine day, we will see a plume of smoke over the far horizon at the end of the sea. And then the ship appears). Lyrics of aria from *Madama Butterfly* (Puccini).

26 This refers to the demands of drama traditionalists (voiced, for example, in letters to the *Radio Times*): 'I like a play to have a beginning, middle and end.'

27 *The Old Crowd* was also shown on ITV.

28 For other readings of plays from the *Objects* season, see Turner (*In a Manner of Speaking*, 1997, Part 3), Wolfe (*Understanding Alan Bennett*, Columbia: University of South Carolina Press, 1999, Chapter 6) and O'Mealy (*Alan Bennett: A Critical Introduction* 2001, Chapter 3).

29 Alan Bennett in 'Observation' *Radio Times*, 6–12 November 1982, p. 8.

30 It has not been possible to ascertain when exactly *A Woman of No Importance* was written, due to the simultaneity and overlap of Bennett's writing.

Spies and writers:
the devil's work?

An Englishman Abroad (1983)
A Question of Attribution (1991)
Poetry in Motion (1990)
Me, I'm Afraid of Virginia Woolf (1979)
The Insurance Man (1986)
102 Boulevard Haussmann (1990)

So far, Alan Bennett has largely been discussed as an autobiographer in disguise. This section examines his work as a biographer, although he employs unconventional forms of life writing that do not necessarily stress veracity and historical accuracy. The spy and the writer populate the same decade of Bennett's career, from the early 1980s to the early 1990s. At this time, separation between contents specific to stage and to television is less pronounced than in the previous decade. Bennett's study of Kafka and his works, for example, resulted in two plays, one for television, one for the stage. Exploring the interface between spying and writing in Bennett's work, the chapter also shows critical approaches to the relationship a writer has with literary precursors, and applies them to Bennett's plays about writers. The relationship between life and art, art as sacrifice and the intimidating effects of literature are also discussed. Bennett demonstrates these both through his own experiences, and through developing them into topoi in his biographically inspired plays.

Spies

The spy plays (An Englishman Abroad and A Question of Attribution) seem to form a stylistic unit when presented as a double bill on stage, but the two originate in different media: An Englishman Abroad was first conceived as a television drama (1983), and then adapted for the stage to pair with *A Question of Attribution* in 1987. The latter was then adapted as a television drama. *Englishman* is quite closely based on an actual event involving the Soviet spy Guy Burgess, and therefore has a certain documentary quality. *Question* takes the case of Sir Anthony Blunt's unmasking as the fourth of the Cambridge Spies as a departure point and presents a parable pointing to the similarities between concealment in humans and forgery in art. On stage, both plays present their case in a style that could be termed realism with components of self-referentiality, at times drawing on the audience's knowledge of the Cambridge Spies and their unmasking.

Critics (Eyre 2000 and O'Mealy 2001, among others) have linked the plays on spies with the plays on writers, as all can be connected through Bennett's continuing interest in the notion of a secret self – a theme that has become more centred on his own presentation of self in his later career. As an author who has explored aspects of Englishness, Bennett also considers the concept of treachery through the spy-plays, or the plays about exile, as Bennett would prefer them to be known (to which should be added the 1977 stage play *The Old Country*). Bennett's interest in exile, spying and treachery might be linked to his status as one who has 'defected' from his native environment. His writing technique is akin to a form of spying, based, as it is, on observation and eavesdropping, while preserving his own, secret self. Much as the Bennett-persona has come to the forefront of his work in the 1990s and the early twenty-first century, in the 1980s he was still putting his thoughts on the secret self and the relationship between art and life into the mouths of his characters.

> Alan's fascinated by the idea of spying: the idea of being outside a society and at the same time within it. There's the sense that as a writer he's a spy on his own world: it's certainly one of the characteristics throughout his work. (Eyre quoted in O'Mealy 2001: 56)

Bennett's concept of an author as a spy is one of many recurrent ideas in his writing. The relationship between authorship and exploitation is another pervasive strand of this ongoing investigation, picturing the author as an outsider, observing rather than participating, and using other peoples' lives as a means of self-expression. Ideas of authorship and Bennett's autobiographical writing are inextricably linked.

> Spies and writers are secret sharers in a literal sense; they observe where often they shouldn't, and they pass along what they have seen, often to the distress of those they have observed. They work best in solitude and isolation. In Bennett's world, their loyalties are often only to themselves, rather than to any ideology. The writer expresses himself for the

sake of self-expression; the spy transgresses for the sake of transgression (O'Mealy 2001: 56).

An Englishman Abroad

Exile interests me, espionage interests me not a bit. (Bennett in *WH*: 329)

I may not be interested in espionage, but I am a glutton for gossip. (Bennett in *WH*: 330)

In 1977, Alan Bennett put his interest in patriotism, Englishness and treachery into the play *The Old Country*.[1] Many people thought that the third Cambridge spy to be unmasked, Kim Philby, was the model for the protagonist, Hilary, although Bennett had not had him in mind while writing. Many viewers also found that the play brought back memories of one of the biggest scandals of the post-war period: the defection of Guy Burgess and Donald Maclean, the first two of the Cambridge Spies to be revealed, in 1951. Among those reminiscing was the Australian actress Coral Browne, who had spent a memorable day in Moscow with Guy Burgess in 1958, when the British Shakespeare Company visited Russia with a production of *Hamlet*. Bennett was so intrigued by the strange meeting between the actress and the spy that he turned Browne's account into a play. Directed by John Schlesinger, starring Coral Browne as herself and Alan Bates as Burgess, *An Englishman Abroad* was first broadcast on BBC TV in 1983.

When the Shakespeare Company visited Moscow, Coral Browne was playing Gertrude to Michael Redgrave's Hamlet. He called her into his dressing room during a show one night to help with a drunken man who was throwing up in the basin. This man turned out to be the defected Soviet spy Guy Burgess. Despite his drunken state, and his stealing her belongings from her dressing table, she agreed to join him for lunch in his flat the next day. There, Burgess and Browne made stilted conversation about figures and episodes long past, and she measured him for some new suits from his old tailor in Savile Row. As he was not allowed to leave his flat until granted permission, they spent long hours waiting for the phone call, Burgess playing Browne his only record. This scene in an anonymous and shabby flat, Jack Buchanan's 'Who Stole my Heart Away?' playing over and over, sparked off Bennett's imagination. Funny and sad, it is at the core of the play.

During and after the war in England, Guy Burgess was at the heart of upper-class London society, outrageous, but entertaining, with a traditional background of Eton, the Navy, Cambridge, the War Office and the BBC. In 1951, he was ordered to accompany his fellow Cambridge spy Donald Maclean to Moscow, as the net was closing in on both of them.

They disappeared, and surfaced as defectors in Russia a few months later. For the remaining twelve years of his life, Burgess lived in Moscow, redundant and isolated, unable to return, but equally unable to adapt to his new environment.

If changes are made from Coral Browne's telling of the tale, Bennett has 'rearranged it for dramatic reasons' (WH: 335). He wanted the emphasis to be on the scene between Burgess and Browne in the flat, and therefore curtailed the events in the theatre during the performance of *Hamlet*. A scene in the British embassy, where Bennett introduces a pair of arrogant young employees (Alexander Walker: 'Guildenstern and Rosencrantz are well and in the Foreign Service')[2] is invented.

> I have taken a few liberties with the facts as Coral Browne told them to me. The scene in the British embassy, for instance, did not occur, but since the Shakespeare Company were warned by the British Ambassador to 'shy away from that traitor Burgess, who's always trying to get back to England' it seemed no great liberty. (WH: 333)

From the outset, *Englishman* finds a visual and aural style that juxtaposes contradictory elements. The titles run to the sound of 'Who Stole My Heart Away?', with opening shots of the heads of Stalin, Marx, Engels and Lenin. They turn out to be banners outside a theatre. The camera moves to busts of playwrights, and rests on a female attendant who could almost be mistaken for one of them in her immobility. The scene on stage of the theatre is from *Hamlet*, Act 2, Scene ii: Claudius is welcoming Rosencrantz and Guildenstern. He talks about Hamlet's recent transformation, and briefs the pair to watch him closely. As we see Guy Burgess, drunkenly slumping in his seat, we see another example of somebody transformed and constantly watched by others. Burgess leaves the auditorium to find a toilet, and the next shot sums up his ambiguous personality through another bold juxtaposition: while he urinates, he cheerfully sings a traditional hymn ('O God, our help in ages past ...'); possibly prefiguring Coral Browne's later remark to him: 'You pissed in our soup, and we drank it' (*Englishman*, in *Objects*: 245).

Bennett comments on the character of Burgess through a description of the author Yevgyeni Yevtushenko, as described by Anthony Powell:

> He exemplified that favourite type in the classical Russian novel, the buffoon: the man always playing the fool, not only for his own amusement and love of exhibitionism, but also with the object of keeping everyone in the dark as to his own inner view and intentions. (WH: 332)

Character, as Bennett remarks in the introduction to the play, is seen as something 'by which they [the English] mean the power to refrain' (WH: 332).

The motto 'Never apologise, never explain' seems to dominate the scene between Coral Browne and Guy Burgess, later sarcastically commented on by Browne: 'He popped by my dressing room last night and threw up in the basin. It was love at first sight.'³ The most poignant image from this sequence is its ending: Browne, as Gertrude, has been called back on stage after the interval. Burgess, who has pretended to be sick once more in order to be alone in the dressing room, carefully examines her belongings and steals her soap, her whisky and her face powder. Before he leaves, we see him looking at himself in the mirror, solemnly putting some of the powder on his face, as if he were preparing for a performance. The shot of his face in the mirror surrounded by light bulbs thus enforces the simile between spying and acting – the notion of pretending to be someone else at the core of both.

After having found out who Burgess is from a colleague, Coral Browne decides to accept the invitation to lunch, furtively pushed under her hotel room door. Finding Burgess' flat the next day proves almost impossible, however, and the British embassy staff are certainly no help. Bennett presents 'Toby' and 'Giles' in a flurry of mannered and clichéd splutter of Englishness: kedgeree, old boys and cricket. They refuse to give Coral the address, and prevent their bullied secretary (a 'a skivvy who is just marking time until she gets her face on the front of *Country Life*', as they describe her) from doing so. When the actress walks off angrily, watched by Toby and Giles from the embassy window, one wonders which country is applying totalitarian measures.

The core scene of the play takes place in Burgess' shabby flat. As Coral wearily climbs up the staircase, we hear Burgess reciting 'The Lady of Shallot' in his flat. Again, we experience his quality of being charming and completely insensitive to others' feelings at the same time, as Coral puts it: 'You still have charm, she said through clenched teeth' (*Englishman* in *Objects*: 241). Burgess admits to missing his homeland desperately, and condemns it at the same time. Not that he likes his Moscow surroundings much either. All the things he used to be good at, or the only things he cared about, he is now without, as they are all determined through language: seduction needs language, and so does gossip. Burgess thus joins scores of other Bennett protagonists who are characterised by not having a voice. Bennett describes Burgess as 'alert and watchful', even when he is at his most incapacitated, and he is certainly guarded and evasive when talking about his past and the reasons for his becoming a double agent. Of course, Bennett includes the question 'why?', but leaves the answer open, not even attempting to explain an ideal that has probably long since faded. Burgess does not pretend now to have pretended then. He claims his views and his reports submitted to the Foreign Office were always Marxist, but due to his always conforming 'in all the important things ('How can he be a spy? He goes to my tailor', *Englishman*, in *Objects*: 244) he got away with them. So, the initial image of Burgess as a performer is specified by him here to being merely a performer of his own self: 'If I wore a mask, it was to be exactly what I seemed' (*Englishman* in *Objects*: 243).

Burgess' character and characteristics are given much more attention than the politics of his case. We hear 'traitor', and we see an outwardly jovial man, desperate to cling on to his former persona. Burgess is a sad and forlorn figure in his threadbare suit, not able to hide the signs of drink and excess. This stresses the futility of his erstwhile mission, undertaken mainly, it seems, to outrage the establishment. His actions are only understandable in the context of their time. Public history thus moves into the background, the revolution that was hoped for has transformed to a system where, as Coral puts it, 'there's no gossip, their clothes are terrible and they can't make false teeth' (*Englishman* in *Objects*: 243). As later on in *A Question of Attribution*, statements with potential double meanings are used in *Englishman*, although more sparingly. For example, Browne suggests listening to the other side of the Jack Buchanan record, to which Burgess replies that he never listens to the other side.

While Bennett, like Coral Browne in the play and in her original tale, takes pity on the isolated and condemned ex-spy Burgess, many critics, although applauding the film's quality, were not so charitable:

> [T]he sad, shoddy, well-merited end of that abominable creature is self-exposed like a jester in tawdry finery trying to cover up the patches in his motley by a show of forced glibness. Bates really takes us on a tour round a man who has only one thing left to hang on to – his Englishness. (Walker 1983: 22)

Walker describes the shabby Savile Row suit Burgess still wears as 'tawdry finery'. It is the last remnant of his home country the redundant spy has managed to cling on to. It is this suit that he wants renewed, together with other signifiers of his past: an old Etonian tie, a bowler hat and various other accessories of his class and generation. He wants to renew his subscription to the very 'club' of Englishness he condemns as 'little', 'timid', 'tasteful' and 'nice'. The 2002 series *Cambridge Spies* (BBC TV, Tim Fywell, 2003) also makes this point: 'The British Intelligence Service works like a gentleman's club. They look after each other because they wear the same tie.'

In the following statement, Bennett puts his own ambivalent relationship with his country and the concept of patriotism into the mouth of Burgess:

You see, I can say I love London. I can say I love England. But I can't say I love my country. I don't know what that means. ... I don't want it to change. They've no business changing it. The fools. You should stop them changing it. (*Englishman* in *Objects*: 244)

In the play, Coral Browne challenges Burgess' self-conception (and Bennett adds another aspect to the relatively sympathetic way he portrays Burgess). She, of course, does not see his treachery from an exclusively English perspective, being Australian. Neither does she accept spying as a 'minor social misdemeanour' (*Englishman* in *Objects*: 244), comparable perhaps to well-known actors being caught performing lewd acts in public lavatories (a likely reference to John Gielgud). She makes a point that often features in Bennett's work: fear of embarrassment overrides everything else in English society, and thus con artists such as Burgess and the other Cambridge Spies live under the mantle of strained politeness. Nobody escapes criticism in Browne's final rounding up: Burgess is criticised for being amoral and indifferent to others, the establishment is criticised for not raising an eyebrow, and the people who have not forgiven Burgess are criticised for their petty intolerance. This diatribe is placed in the penultimate scene, where Browne, back in London, is ordering clothes for Burgess, and discretion prevails among the gents' outfitters. Remarking that the gentleman in question is 'a very long way from home – I thought he was done with', the tailor blows the dust off the dummies for Burgess' shoes. Only when ordering some pyjamas in a different shop, Coral is given to understand that, following his unmasking, Mr Burgess is not a desirable customer anymore. Her response is an impressive critique of establishment hypocrisy:

You were quite happy to satisfy this client when he was one of the most notorious buggers in London, and a drunkard into the bargain. Only then he was in the Foreign Office. ... But not any more. Oh no. And why? Because the gentleman in question has shown himself to have some principles, principles which aren't yours and, as a matter of interest, aren't mine either. But that's it as far as you're concerned. No more jamas for him. I tell you, it's pricks like you that make me understand why he went. Thank Christ I'm not English. (*Englishman* in *Objects*: 250)

The film with its superb choice of locations (Dundee and Glasgow standing in for Moscow) ends on the ambivalent image of Burgess walking across a Moscow bridge in the snow, resplendent in his new suit, coat, hat and tie, matching the misreading of a letter he had sent to Browne:

Claudius: 'Then at last my outfit will be complete, and I shall look like a real ... agent again.'

Cora: What? [She takes the letter.] No, dear. 'Then I shall look like a real gent again.'

(*Englishman* in *Objects*: 249)

And so Burgess walks through Moscow, standing out from the crowd through his clothing and his indelible Englishness, to the tune of 'He Remains an Englishman' from Gilbert and Sullivan's *HMS Pinafore*. This is a powerful image that shows, in Alexander Walker's (1983) words, that while 'clothes make the man, the man himself is as hollow as hell'. Other critics showed more compassion with the forlorn figure, still performing as himself. Ian Johnstone (1983) confessed to the final scene 'opening the tear ducts'.

Ironically, Walker sees *Englishman* as a passport home for another exile, director John Schlesinger, who, with typical English establishmentarian attitude, he comments on as having taken a few wrong steps in Hollywood previously. Critics were unanimous in their praise for Schlesinger and Nat Crosby, his director of photography. Bennett himself names *Englishman* as one of the few works he would not change.

While Bennett's views are clearly not compatible with those of the government, he comments that they were relatively mild in 1983, the year *Englishman* was produced. At the time of its transfer to the stage in 1988, the height of Thatcher's reign, Bennett had become more acerbic about the government's double standards. He expressed his frustration in an addition to the 1983 preface in 1989:

It suits governments to make treachery the crime of crimes, but the world is smaller than it was and to conceal information can be as culpable as to betray it. As I write, evidence is emerging of a nuclear accident at Windscale in 1957, the full extent of which was hidden from the public. Were politicians and civil servants responsible for this less culpable than our Cambridge villains? Because for the spies it can at least be said that they were risking their own skins, whereas the politicians were risking someone else's. The trouble with treachery nowadays is that if one does want to betray one's country there is no one satisfactory to betray it to. If there were, more people would be doing it. (*WH*: 336)

Consequently, the third of Bennett's biographical plays about spies and exiles, *A Question of Attribution*, shows Bennett's disillusionment with the spin which politicians put on crimes such as treachery, allowing them to 'bury' other public scandals, some of them a lot more damaging and life-threatening.

A Question of Attribution

> I have not enjoyed a television play so much since ... since ... oh all right,
> *An Englishman Abroad. (Financial Times* 1991)

A Question of Attribution was first written for the stage, to form the double bill *Single Spies* with *An Englishman Abroad* at the National Theatre in 1988. Alan Bennett played the part of Anthony Blunt. For the television adaptation in 1991, James Fox played the part. Bennett felt Fox was 'naturally upper-class in his appearance' and also bore some physical resemblance to Blunt. The published script of *Question* is that of the stage version; there has been no publication of the television play so far.[4]

Where *Englishman* draws parallels between spying and acting, *Question* is concerned with art and its forgeries, and juxtaposed with treachery, which can be about not being what one seems. The metaphorical richness of the territory is obvious, although it makes for a less personalised and more academic play than *Englishman*:

> [A]s Lynne Truss in *The Times* would observe, the film [*A Question of Attribution*] was a play of ideas, not psychology, dealing far less with 'Why did he do it? than with 'Why do you want to know?' (Mann 2005: 534)

The idea for the play originated around the time of Sir Anthony Blunt's unmasking in 1979. Director of the Courtauld Institute and Keeper of the Queen's Pictures, his secret identity had been known to government and MI5 since 1964, and he had been promised immunity in return for names of other spies from the period. After writing a version of an imagined conversation between Blunt and HMQ, 'both knowing and neither saying', Bennett put the fragment to one side. In 1986, however, he discovered the discussion about a picture formerly attributed to Titian, now believed to be a forgery, in an art history journal. The 'Triple Portrait' showed two men, but revealed a concealed third and later a fourth and a fifth. He thought the picture and its hidden figures made such an 'obvious metaphor I thought I'd better do it before somebody else did' (all quotes from Kim Fletcher 1991: 15).

Question takes a 'real' situation as its starting point and tells the story speculatively, in alignment with the extraordinary parallel between the fourth man on the Titian portrait and the imminent exposure of the then Sir Anthony Blunt, who had to give back his knighthood and resign from the Courtauld after his unmasking. It is a play where almost every scene has a double meaning or a hidden relevance to the themes of exposure, the secret self and forgery, in art and in life. Bennett, commenting that 'writers simply displace their uncertainties and put their opinions into the mouths of their characters', claims the play was 'a flag of distress about art.' The three voices in the play are Blunt's, the MI5 officer, or 'policeman', as Bennett refers to him, Chubb's, and HMQ's, the latter two 'bearing the burden of [Bennett's] doubts and uncertainties about art' (*US*: 465).

The play opens with Blunt being screened in a doctor's surgery. For the procedure, he is slowly turned upside down into the right position for the X-ray. His doctor is optimistic, expressing Blunt to be 'clear'. This is not the judgement he receives from the MI5 officials on his case. Chubb's boss is disgruntled about the lack of progress and Blunt's evasiveness. Guy Burgess and Donald Maclean had defected in 1951, Kim Philby was unmasked in 1963, Blunt's involvement became known in 1964, and there had been no advance in finding the 'fifth man' since then. In *Englishman*, the character Burgess comments that spying is acceptable as long as one conforms to class conventions. Here, by contrast, an MI5 officer comments 'If he [Blunt] were languishing in Wormwood Scrubs I wouldn't care, but I see him every day in the Athenaeum' (see above and note 4). Up to this point, Blunt's conformity and his professional and academic renown have protected him. But the play is set at a time when the tide had started turning, and connections have since been made between Margaret Thatcher coming into power in 1979 and Blunt's exposure soon after. The decision to name Blunt had not yet been taken, but impatience was growing. In the play, a new officer is put on the case. Chubb is different from his public school, cut-glass-vowel predecessor, in that he is plain talking and unimpressed by reverence and Blunt's reputation. And so the two unequal men embark on an endless cycle of looking at photos of Blunt's contemporaries, none of whom he seems to recognise. Chubb takes an interest in art, or might be doing so to put Blunt at his ease, and gradually the patronising and condescending Blunt responds to his enthusiasm for learning, and reveals himself as a superb teacher.

For their first encounter, Chubb makes Blunt travel to his home in Purley. Sir Anthony seems completely out of his depth in this suburban semi, almost looking as though he has accidentally been brought into shots that have nothing to do with him or his life. When he rings Chubb's doorbell, his head appears in the glass frame of the front door, visible but not recognisable. John Schlesinger and his Director of Photography, John Hooper, construct a range of symbolic shots like this one, relevant to plot and context. The text does the same, as in the next scene in the conservationist's workshop, where the restorer says to his assistant that the picture shows 'two figures and you feel there ought to be a third'. Of course, this is said with reference to the 'ex-Titian', as Blunt refers to the 'Triple Portrait', but the connection with the imminent unmasking of the Cambridge Spies is uncanny. And when the restorer reveals an ear of the 'third man' on the picture, the camera switches to a close-up of another ear: Chubb's. He is on his way to attending one of Blunt's lectures at the Courtauld. Despite being praised almost unanimously for *Question*, Bennett was criticised for simplifying this lecture scene in order to align it with art works that form another symbolic strand of the play: suffering, martyrdom, interrogation and crucifixion, as well as various similes of treachery, such as Jesus and his apostles in the garden at Gethsemane. Bennett mostly chose pictures that enforce the view of Blunt as a victim for acts he committed a long time ago, when he was young and carried away by fashionable, radical left ideals. Indeed, the unmasking of Blunt was met with a certain amount of compassion by the public. The string of juxtapositions of Blunt and images of martyrdom and crucifixion, however, disgruntled some conservative critics, just as the fictionality of the scene enraged people who had known Sir Anthony. Of course it seems unlikely that Blunt, renowned for his precision and dedication, would have extended Auden's opening stanza from the poem 'Musée des Beaux Arts' (1976): 'About suffering they were never wrong, the Old Masters/ How well they understood' to fit his own suffering. These liberties for the sake of the core theme can easily be justified, however, in a play that does not claim to be a purely biographical or documentary account on Blunt's case. *Question* playfully combines life and art, connected by the metaphor of the secret self. It is intriguing rather than indulgent that Blunt points out parallels between a picture that shows several stages of Christ's passion with his own knowledge: Christ, he remarks, is already aware of what is happening higher up the hill. We are free to compare that with Sir Anthony and his foreboding of what is about to happen to him.

In *Englishman*, Burgess attempted to explain his actions through words relating to performance, and in *Question* it is through art that Blunt tries to explain his former acts of treachery to Chubb. This starts with Blunt challenging the much-held popular conviction that fine art is simply a development towards 'getting it right', that is, photographic realism or, on another level, fact-based information. Blunt's plea to see artists in their own context, on their own terms, such as their contemporaries saw them, is of course related to the way he thinks the convictions and resulting actions of his younger years should be seen. Chubb, realising this, retaliates: "It seemed the right thing to do at the time" – that's the argument you used when you explained your behaviour in the 30s – the difference being that art has no consequences' (see note 4).

The general question of scale and perspective is also addressed in this discussion between Blunt and Chubb. Furthermore, Bennett puts some of his own feelings of inadequacy when it comes to appreciating art[5] into the mouth of Chubb:

> Chubb: ... Is it that I don't get anything out of the pictures? Or the pictures don't get anything out of me? What am I supposed to think? What am I supposed to feel?
> Blunt: What do you feel?
> Chubb: Baffled. And also knackered.

By now, we have come to expect this exchange to be underlined by another example from the ongoing Titian discovery, and the next scene indeed deals with the issue of 'scale'. We see the puzzled restorer and Blunt looking at the now exposed third man on the 'ex-Titian'. The image is 'wrong' in scale, and it looks like Titian himself is in the wrong picture. As in his first encounter with Chubb, Sir Anthony often seems to be 'in the wrong picture' throughout the play. It seems as if shots are composed in order to contrast Blunt's perceived sophistication and refinement with the way he perceives the rest of the world: vulgar and intrusive. A series of shots makes this point: Blunt in a taxi with a Tom Jones song blaring out of the radio; Blunt, ethereal and preoccupied, walking past a pair of tourists, presented as noisy and overweight; Blunt with Chubb in the National Gallery, having a room closed off to the 'intolerable' public, and Japanese tourists in particular. There is a little 'Bennettian' reminder of the superiority of ladies in sensible shoes in this gallery scene, however. Having travelled from Petersfield, as they explain, the two ladies cheerfully invade Blunt's exclusion zone and then proceed to talk about a Rubens painting of voluptuous female shapes – 'no nonsense about slimming then, Betty'. By continuously showing Blunt out of his normal context, Schlesinger, Bennett and Hooper visually make the point the character is trying to make about his past textually. How much a figure depends on its context is shown when Blunt is on his way to Buckingham Palace. Everything in this sequence – Blunt's emergence from a hairdresser's, his way past the shops he probably frequents, the monumental and regal architecture, even the extradiegetic, Handelian fanfare music – shows the man in the environment he normally inhabits.

Question mirrors *Englishman*, in that both plays evolve around a core scene between the male and the female protagonist, and use the metaphoric vocabulary to make points about the reasoning behind treachery, or forgery, as in the case of Blunt and HMQ. But first, the point made by an unnamed critic is brought home:

Despite Blunt's cut-glass vowels, the audience is surely meant to pick up on the fact that he is an intellectual and aesthetic snob far more than a social snob. (*Financial Times* 1991)

This is proved when Blunt asks his student, Philips, to identify the frame and comment on the picture they have brought to the Queen's Gallery to take the place of the 'ex-Titian'. When Philips fails to name the characteristics of the picture, Blunt asks the steward, Colin, who turns out to have been taught by Blunt and shows Philips up by knowing the wood and age of the frame, and the school to which the painting itself can be attributed. Consequently, Philips is 'downgraded' by having to hold the steps for Blunt to reach the picture. We see only Sir Anthony's legs going up the stepladder, as a Corgi runs in through the door at the far end of the room, a powerful signifier of who is following, and causing Philips and Colin to seek refuge after failing to alert Sir Anthony. It was John Schlesinger who insisted on the introductory corgi for the film version, seeing it essential to 'royal verisimilitude' (Mann 2005: 535). The ensuing conversation between HMQ and the Keeper of her Galleries is the climax in a play that is built on hidden meaning and ambiguity. Like Chubb, the Queen has a populist and simplistic view of art, but she nonetheless represents sound judgement. Also, when it comes to perfecting statements with double meanings, she reigns supreme. The stage play in 1988, of course, had been the first time a living monarch had been depicted on stage. The character HMQ had caused the Board of the National Theatre anxiety, and the threat of censoring had made Richard Eyre, its artistic director at the time, seriously consider resignation.[6] On screen, this was less of a precarious situation, as it was by then known that Bennett had presented a flattering and witty portrait of HMQ in the stage version of the play. Also, there are more examples of living monarchs on screen.[7]

Prunella Scales revived her performance as HMQ, looking uncannily like the Queen, with acutely observed mannerisms, and imitation in pitch, inflection and voice. It is ironic that in her superb capturing of the monarch, she is given the line 'I don't think one wants to be captured', referring to a remark by Sir Anthony that none of her portraits quite capture her:

HMQ: Portraits are supposed to be frightfully self-revealing, aren't they, good ones? Show what one's really like. The secret self. ... Have you had your portrait painted?
Blunt: No, Ma'am.
HMQ: So we don't know whether you have a secret self.

Just as Blunt has had to counter the arguments of Chubb on scale and context, he has to defend his views on fakes and forgeries to HMQ.

She is quite obviously intrigued by the Keeper of her Pictures, whose 'forgery' of his own life she is aware of. He says her 'ex-Titian' is wrongly attributed, she says it is a fake.

HMQ: I suppose that is part of your function, Sir Anthony, to prove that my pictures are fakes?

Blunt: Because something is not what it is said to be, Ma'am, does not mean it is a fake. It may just have been wrongly attributed.

The exchange is like a game of chess in its precision. None of HMQ's comments are explicit, but she comes across as a shrewd and witty politician. It was this scene that alleviated fears of a breach of protocol by portraying HMQ on stage. She leaves with the greeting 'Be careful how you go up the ladder, Sir Anthony. One could have a nasty fall.' She exits, quite theatrically, through a door that opens by itself, accompanied by the corgi. Blunt, agitated and perspiring, is clearly struggling with his composure as he is joined by Colin and Philips. They want to know what HMQ talked to Sir Anthony about, to which he replies 'I was talking about art, I'm not sure she was.'

The last 'act' of the film begins with Blunt alone in his office at night, smoking and pensive. Chubb walks up and down in Portman Square outside. In the next shot, Chubb and Blunt are coming up the stairs. The naming of Blunt as the fourth man is now imminent. Chubb makes one last attempt to get the name of the fifth man from Blunt, and instead of an answer, Blunt asks him whether he wants to see his X-rays. We are not sure at this point whether these are the X-rays of his lungs, with which the play started, or of the 'Triple Portrait'. They turn out to be X-rays of the 'ex-Titian', and reveal the profile of a fourth man, as yet uncovered. Blunt shows Chubb 'the rather more substantial figure of a fifth man' that lurks behind the original pair. In the end, Blunt implies, their identities do not seem to matter – 'behind them lurk other presences'.

There is a cross fade from the 'Triple Portrait' X-ray to the face of the MI5 officer in charge, looking determined. The phone rings continuously, as it does in the next scene in Blunt's office. Sir Anthony, as he will not be for much longer, is packing his books and preparing to leave his professional and private home. He seems older and slower than in previous scenes, but comes across as stoical about his situation. 'Unfortunate certainly, but not unfair', as he sums up the situation to his secretary. As Blunt starts walking towards the exit, the Handelian music from previous scenes sets in, at a slower, grave marching pace. At this moment, Blunt's student Philips runs up the stairs, whistling, but stops in his tracks when he sees the descending Blunt and staff and students' reactions. Philips, too, stops and looks at his teacher, the camera now showing the scene from above and all the way down the staircase. The secretary makes sure Blunt is presentable, the sound of the switchboard operator refusing to make comments or put callers through is heard, and everyone who is sitting stands up as Blunt reaches the front door of the Courtauld Institute. As the door slowly opens and the noise of the assembled press outside invades the building, Blunt touches his throat, and then stands still in the flashlights of the camera and the cacophony of the reporters' questions. His face lights up again and again as he is photographed, and the frame finally freezes on his lit-up, immobile face, the exposure now complete.

Question is a less personal play than *Englishman,* less of a character study, and therefore, as Mann (2005: 535) points out, less visceral. The final sequence, however, is immensely affecting, and together with all the images of torture and crucifixion, make clear Bennett's and Schlesinger's sympathy for the character of Blunt.

The critical acclaim, comparable to *Englishman,* and the awards the play won were muted by the death of Innes Lloyd shortly before transmission in October 1991. Bennett had worked with his favourite producer on most of his television plays since the early 1970s, and the loss was still felt acutely some seven years later, when Bennett dedicated the second series of *Talking Heads* to Lloyd:

> He [Lloyd] was a charming, diffident, honest and decent man. He'd been politicised recently by Thatcher, whom he'd come to hate violently – a hatred all the stronger for emerging from such a quiet, undemonstrative and apparently apolitical man. (Eyre 2003: 161)

Like some other texts by Bennett (notably *Me, I'm Afraid of Virginia Woolf*), *A Question of Attribution* offers the possibility of being read as a gay text, with double meanings attached to terms such as 'disguise' and 'unmasking' and 'secret self' at a time when Bennett was rallying against outing campaigns and intrusions into privacy by the media.

Writers

Daphne Turner, in the acknowledgements to her 1997 monograph on Bennett, thanks him for letting the book go ahead, especially 'as the better I got to know his work, the more I realized how much he disliked writing about writers' (1997: vii). Despite his apparent unease, Bennett has written three plays and a film script about the lives of other writers: the two television plays *The Insurance Man* (1985, on Kafka), and *102*

Boulevard Haussmann (1990, on Proust), and the stage play *Kafka's Dick* (1986). Bennett has also adapted John Lahr's biography of Joe Orton, *Prick Up Your Ears* for the screen. He has produced work on his own life as a writer for most of the 1990s and early twenty-first century. As he has acknowledged, in researching other writers, Bennett does not just read their works, but uses secondary literature such as biography and critical monographs to inform his own writing. Bennett has discussed the work and lives of other writers as a critic and diarist for *The London Review of Books* and as the author of several documentaries. His series on twentieth-century British poets, *Poetry in Motion*, combined biographical and literary material. Bennett's writing of the 1980s and early 1990s often constructs a discourse on the influence other writers have on him (both as author and as persona), with Kafka, Proust and Larkin as the most prominent figures.

Bennett also comments on other writers' work, literary criticism and biography from the perspective of the critic, a profession for which he has frequently expressed dislike. Responding to Steven Berkoff's statement that theatre critics are 'like worn-out old tarts', Bennett remarks:

> If only they were, the theatre would be in a better state. In fact critics are much more like dizzy girls out for the evening, just longing to be fucked and happy to be taken in by any plausible rogue ... A cheap thrill is all they want. Worn-out old tarts have at least got past that stage. (*WH*: 257)

Bennett has shown equal dislike for literary criticism:

> [F]amished for subjects, some critics don't wait for death before hacking a chunk off their chosen prey and retiring to the academic undergrowth to chew it over. (*Poetry*: 2)

Apart from implications of critics taking possession of something they are not entitled to, Bennett's comment implies that critical interpretation of an author's life and works should not be undertaken until the artist is dead. His critics and academics are savage animals, tearing flesh off an artist who is still alive. Interestingly, these principles do not lead to Bennett's own abstinence as a critic, as he has discussed both the lives and works of other writers (Philip Larkin and John Osborne, for example) while they were still alive, and has been a book reviewer of living authors in *The London Review of Books*. Despite this, Bennett's following remarks about programme notes for a play he attended show his general dislike of the trend to introduce, contextualise and interpret a work:

> [T]here is a lengthy essay on the issues purportedly touched on in the production. If it's a revival of an unpretentious domestic comedy from

the thirties there is likely to be a photomontage of the dole queues to emphasize The Other Side of the Picture, and any play that uses words (and some of them still do) is as like as not accompanied by a thumbnail sketch of the life and loves of Wittgenstein, just to put the critics in the proper frame of mind. (*WH*: 607)

Anyone researching Bennett's works for academic purposes, writing a review of a book or play, or writing a biography, will have to take into account that he or she is regarded as superfluous and essentially as a parasite.

Programme booklets of productions of Bennett's own plays demonstrate that he himself often provides introductions on the evolution and context of his works. His prefaces to his published play texts have become longer and more detailed throughout his career. Bennett states in *Telling Tales* (1999: 9) that he wants to tell his own stories, and tell them unmediated. Critics' readings of other writers' works may remind Bennett that there are many possible readings of his own texts. It sometimes seems as though he wants to be the only authorised commentator on his own texts, although he produces work about other artists, particularly writers. Is writing about writers a privilege Bennett reserves for himself? Or, in another possible reading of Turner's acknowledgement above, does he write about other writers in order to express his dislike for the practice?

So, Bennett does not like writers' works to be interpreted for them; he doesn't like biographical stereotyping, and he is anxious about the shadows cast by literary giants. In the following, several works about other writers Bennett has written, produced or starred in are examined. These are roughly divided into two categories, not generically or chronologically motivated, but grouped according to perspective. In the play *Me, I'm Afraid of Virginia Woolf* and in the documentary series *Poetry in Motion*, Bennett makes writers a central theme, but these are not predominantly biographical texts. They could be seen to be written from the perspective of the critical commentator. The two television plays *The Insurance Man* and *102 Boulevard Haussmann* are biographical texts in that they stage the lives of Franz Kafka and Marcel Proust respectively. They do so with varying levels of veracity, and offer interesting crossovers between the world of the writer, and the world of the writers' works. The stage play *Kafka's Dick* unites the perspectives of biographer and critic, as it shows the exaggerated practice of readers obsessed with biography, but also includes the person Kafka in the discourse, though with no ambition of accuracy.

Bennett as critic: *Poetry in Motion* and *Me, I'm Afraid of Virginia Woolf*

Literary appreciation based on biographical appreciation can lead to what Bennett calls 'fan clubs'. He has frequently expressed his dislike of people who are 'fans' of a writer or a book. When Bennett was beginning work on the stage adaptation of *The Wind in the Willows*, it was the fact that the book had 'fans' that almost made him go back on his decision.[8] It seems that 'fans' stand for everything Bennett hates in the way literature is incorporated into popular culture – whether it is the menu at a Bloomsbury hotel in London ('Virginia's Favourite' one of the desserts), or whether it is the hobby biographers and collectors of trivia, as described in Bennett's parody 'Say Cheese, Virginia':

> Dilys and I have been dedicated fans of Bloomsbury ever since Dilys's dandruff and my appliance finally put paid to the ballroom dancing. ... Billingham, Prestatyn, Loughborough – scarcely a town of any size that does not boast one, sometimes two, Woolf Clubs. This last Tuesday, for instance, saw us both at Garstang, a fork supper prior to Kevin Glusburn's thought-provoking paper 'Lytton Strachey: An Hitherto Unrecorded Incident in the Slipper Baths at Poulton-le-Fylde'. Need I add that Carrington fans were out in force? (*WH*: 594)

In the stage play *Kafka's Dick*, the character of Sydney is shown to be a possessive 'fan' and biographer. One can interpret his behaviour as Bennett's attack on critics and on readers craving biographical revelation. Sydney shares a profession with his hero, Franz Kafka, and, through connections forged between his life and that of the writer, assumes he has ownership of the author:

> Sydney: You wouldn't have liked his stories. Not what you'd call 'true to life'. A man turns into a cockroach. An ape lectures. Mice talk. He'd like me. We've got so much in common. He was in insurance. I'm in insurance. He had TB. I had TB. He didn't like his name. I don't like my name. I'm sure the only reason I drifted into insurance was because I was called Sydney.
>
> (*Kafka's Dick*: 12)

Bennett shows how a myth and a real person can differ, and does not play along with the biographer's and the reader's game of finding parallels between themselves and the author. In *Kafka's Dick*, Bennett punishes the character Sydney by proving his anticipation of his relationship with Kafka wrong. Kafka, scared by the haunting of his enthusiastic host, wants nothing to do with him and instead turns to Sydney's wife, Linda, who has never read any of his works: 'When did you first get the writing bug then?', she asks him (*Kafka's Dick*: 35).

Just as Bennett differentiates between readers and fans, he makes a distinction between literature and 'Literature'. The upper case encapsulates the awe he feels in the face of literature that is considered 'great', but also the sense of sarcastic defiance, because this awe makes him feel guilty and deficient for not being able to enjoy 'Literature'.

> When I was young, I used to feel that literature was a club of which I would never be a proper member as a reader, let alone a writer. It wasn't that I didn't read books, and even the 'right' books, but I always felt that the ones I read couldn't be literature if only because I had read them. It was the books I couldn't get into (and these included most poetry) that constituted literature – or, rather, Literature. (*Poetry*: 1)

Bennett reacts with mistrust to the truism that literature can transport the reader 'to another place' – he states that from a very early stage, these 'other places' simply made reality (that is, his own place) inadequate and not 'up to scratch': 'Brought up in the provinces in the forties and fifties one learned early the valuable lesson that life is generally something that happens elsewhere' (*CTH*: 39). Just as Bennett suspected there was something wrong with him, being intimidated rather than elated by 'Literature', he suspected that his environment was deficient in comparison to places described. Life (also with a capital 'L') is therefore merrily going on elsewhere, while he, feeling short-changed, ponders on his deficiencies, resenting the allure of 'Literature' and 'Life', but wanting to be part of it all the same (see *WH*: 3–13). Daphne Turner (1997: 149) points out that 'elsewhere' invariably seemed to mean 'down south'. The reassertion of provincial values in literature through John Betjeman, Philip Larkin and social realists of the 1960s had already begun when Bennett started establishing himself as a writer. However, to him, only 'Life' associated with the London scene would produce the kind of 'Literature' he aspired to produce, and going South seemed both inevitable and a rite of passage. In retrospect, Bennett comments that his own wish to escape was also anchored in his parents' lives, through books his mother read and his father's dream of living in the country (*WH*: 8). This theme of escape was mirrored in works of writers such as H.G. Wells and J.B. Priestley (*WH*: 8).[9]

The essay 'The Treachery of Books' is a reflection on Bennett's childhood, mediated from his perspective of 1990.[10] The piece is a personalised critique of the effects of 'Literature', allowing links with Harold Bloom's theories in *The Anxiety of Influence* (1975).[11] As Edward Young (cited in Bloom 1975: 27) states: 'They [the great precursors] *engross* our attention, and so prevent a due inspection of ourselves; they *prejudice* our judgement in favor of their abilities, and so lessen the sense of our own; and they *intimidate* us with this splendour of their renown.' ... Poetic influence is thus a disease of self-consciousness' (1975: 27).

Within Bloom's confines of 'strong' poets,[12] Bennett might be a debatable choice, as he seems particularly afflicted by the intimidation caused by 'the great precursors'. His development can, however, be connected to some of the models of influence suggested by Bloom. Bennett's beginnings as an author are an example of both imitation and intimidation: as a parodist of other writers and particular styles. His very first piece of writing, produced for a 'smoking-concert' at Exeter College, Oxford, later became part of *Beyond the Fringe* under the title 'Take a Pew' and was an accurate parody of a typical Anglican sermon. The revue also contained a satire and pastiche of some of Shakespeare's plays, called 'So That's the Way You Like It', a collaboration between Bennett, Cook, Moore and Miller.[13] Bennett comments, discussing his early performance and writing work with Humphrey Carpenter (2001: 29):

> Art ... begins with imitation, often in the form of parody, and it's in the process of imitating the voices of others that one comes to learn the sound of one's own.

Beyond the Fringe is generally seen as a breakthrough for the genre of the satirical revue, addressing contemporary politics and satirising public figures such as Harold MacMillan and 'great' writers.[14] *On the Margin* also included parodic imitations of other writers' voices, such as the following parody of a Betjeman poem:

> **On Going to the Excuse-me**
> Bolding Vegas, Shanks New Nisa
> The Trusty Lichfield swirls it down
> To filter beds on Ruislip Marshes
> From my loo in Kentish Town.
> The Burlington, the Rochester –
> Oh, those names of childhood loos;
> Nursie knocking at the door –
> 'Have you done your number twos?'
> ...
>
> (quoted in Wilmut 1980: 94)

It is clear that Bennett went through a period of imitating the voices of others before finding his own, although he has retained the ability to mimic other writers.

The next stage in a writer's development is described as intimidation with 'the splendour of great writers' renown', resulting in a 'lessening of [one's] own worth' (in Bloom 1975: 27). Bennett often presents himself as a literary outsider who has never managed to feel a sense of belonging to the many genres to which he contributes (although a term used to describe Betjeman might also apply to Bennett – 'deliciously apart', a side of him that relished being an outsider).[15]

T.S. Eliot's essay 'Tradition and the Individual Talent' (1999: 13) argues that writers can only develop their voice if they are aware of the trajectory that has led to their own production of literary work. Besides this literary intertextuality, Bennett describes and practises what could be called biographical intertextuality, comparing his persona with that of other writers. Bennett's initial reaction in the face of 'great' writers was that of total submission, as he describes:

> Auden's intellect was formidable and showy, and quite off-putting. As an undergraduate at Oxford in 1956, I happened to hear his inaugural lecture as Professor of Poetry ... Had I ambitions to write at that time, the lecture would have been enough to put me off. Auden listed all the accomplishments that poets and critics should properly have – a dream of Eden, an ideal landscape, favourite books, even, God help us, a passion for Icelandic sagas. If writing means passing this kind of kit inspection, I thought, one might as well forget it. (*Poetry*: 5)

Bennett expresses feelings of inferiority in comparison to other writers' lives and works. From an early stage in his career, his frustration at constantly being overtaken by more eloquent, more deprived, more audacious or politically adept writers is evident.[16] Just as 'Literature' devalues the events in his life, the towering figures of other writers devalue Bennett's own existence as a writer. The consequence seems to be self-deprecation. Stephen Frears remarks on the compulsory modesty of Bennett's generation. Bennett confirms this: 'I seem always to be saying "What am *I* doing here?" I'm not a literary person at all' (*WH*: 138). Bennett's upbringing suggests that modesty was an important virtue when he was young, and that he learned to exploit its potential in his persona. It is assumed that on some occasions, Bennett reverts to the 'safe' pose of self-deprecation, which can exempt him from critical malice. Bennett's writing confirms Young's statement above that 'Poetic influence is thus a disease of self-consciousness' (in Bloom 1975: 29).

Poetry in Motion

> The camera breaks out of the lecture room at (mostly) appropriate moments to soar over the cliffs of Hardy's Wessex, Housman's windswept Wenlock Edge, Auden's New York canyons, or among the sepia views of vanished Betjeland. But the basic content is Alan Bennett, his plain temperance manner, his unemphatic, flat, but somehow reassuring voice making poetry sound a natural mode of communication rather than an alarming state of emotional disturbance calling for specially heightened diction. (Lewis 1990: 54)

Bennett has tried to resist the label of 'literary person' for most of his career, and tries to avoid being seen as an expert on literature. Within his work for television, this is particularly evident in *Poetry in Motion* (Channel 4, 1990),[7] a documentary series on the works and lives of twentieth-century British poets, where Bennett assumes the role of 'mediator' between a popular audience and literature, which he is trying to protect from connotations of 'Literature'. The series is pitched at first-time readers or at readers without much experience of poetry or litera-ture. In his introduction, Bennett chooses a personal tone, stressing that he is not approaching his subject from a position of superiority: 'feelings of impotence and exclusion still fresh in my mind' (*Poetry*: 1). Bennett explains his choice of authors in the introduction: Thomas Hardy, A.E. Housman, John Betjeman, W.H. Auden, Louis MacNeice and Philip Larkin are among the most popular and widely read poets of the twentieth century. 'Popular' can connote 'accessible', but also 'well known'. Bennett reassures his audience that clarity does not mean simplicity, and obscurity does not always mean sophistication. He points out that the inadequacy the reader feels opposite opaque writing, such as some of W.H. Auden's 'celebrated obscurity' (*Poetry*: 57), sometimes can point to an exaggerated convolutedness of the text. Bennett alleges that Auden hated rewriting, and thus often carelessly mixed individual lines that had met friends' approval in one poem. Generally, poets such as Betjeman or Larkin, more easily understood, are met with critical snobbery (*Poetry*: 1–2).

While discussing Ernest Kris and Otto Kurz's book, *Legend, Myth and Magic in the Image of the Artist*, Bennett links himself with the 'tradition, in which the artists themselves conspire, of making a painter's begin-nings humbler and less sophisticated than in fact they were. The public liked to believe an artist had no training, that he astonished his elders, who picked out his skill when he was in lowly or unlikely circumstances' (*WH*: 138). Bennett acknowledges that he sometimes catches himself 'slightly overstating my working-class origins, taking my background down the social scale a peg or two' (*WH*: 593). He implies he does the same with his literary credentials:

> He [Larkin] is trying to appear as an artist without a past. And so am I in my piece [for the Festschrift on the occasion of Larkin's 60th birthday], claiming that I had little reading and no literary appreciation until I was in my thirties. This conveniently forgets the armfuls of books I used to take out of Headingley public library – Shaw, Anouilh, Toynbee, Christo-pher Fry. Many of the books, it's true, I took for the look of them, and lots I didn't even read, and those I did I've forgotten. Still I did read, though without knowing what I liked or was looking for, and certainly umpteen plays, but without ever thinking of becoming a playwright. This was the period from thirteen to sixteen, just before puberty, and I always wipe it from my mind. (*WH*: 139)

Bennett's recurring insistence that 'Life was happening elsewhere' has resonances of the much-quoted final line of Philip Larkin's poem, 'I Remember, I Remember': 'Nothing, like something, happens anywhere' (1988: 88). Philip Larkin has special significance in Bennett's development as both an author and as an authorial persona. 'I Remember, I Remember' can be seen as a parody of Thomas Hood's poem (1826) of the same name, which mourns lost childhood idyll and innocence. Larkin's poem stubbornly refuses to glorify the past, and grimly rejects the nostalgia poets so often express for the lost paradise of childhood. Larkin's version resembles Bennett's way of relating to his childhood, which has often resulted in the complaint that he was deprived in that he was *not* deprived, thus disadvantaged for a writing career. It is, of course, not deprivation of life's essentials, wishing for poverty and hardship; 'deprivation' in this context can be defined as a lack of formative experience, adventure and excitement. Larkin cultivates the boredom that dominated the memory of his childhood:

> 'Was that,' my friend smiles 'where you have your roots?'
> No, only where my childhood was unspent, (...) ('I Remember, I Remember', Larkin 1988: 81)

Both Larkin and Bennett have an ambivalent relationship with the past. On the one hand, they seem to understand that it is the main source for their work, but Larkin especially wishes to be free from the memory of his early years, once saying that his autobiography should start at 21 (quoted in Amis 1993: 7). While Bennett did not include his past and his origins in his earlier works, they are now the most important themes in his work. Both he and Larkin use their past, but do not want to be tied down by verisimilitude. This explains their hostile response to those interpreting their work and researching their lives. Bennett writes about experiences he claims he did not have and Larkin omits the ones he *did* have.

> Until I read Larkin – and in particular 'I Remember, I Remember' – I'd never imagined such experiences, or non-experiences, could be the stuff of poetry, still less the credentials for writing, or that anybody could write, not about the something but the nothing that happens anywhere. (*Poetry*: 89)

Bennett pays tribute to Larkin for offering a way out of the problem of ordinariness, by confirming Bennett's feelings and making him feel more comfortable with the inevitability of an unspectacular background. Reading Larkin, appreciating that a good poem about failure could be a success, might have encouraged Bennett to venture into the intimidating world of authors. Although they were not spectacular, often positively banal, his formative experiences have turned out to be the spine of his work, be it his father always wearing black shoes, and drying his face so vigorously that it squeaked (*TT*: 47), or recollections of his mother going through phases of lampshade-making or crocheting (*TT*: 35). In 'The Treachery of Books', Bennett states he recognised his own provincial and 'inadequate' childhood in Larkin's sentiments; neither Dickensian deprivation nor Blytonian bliss:

> The families I read about were not like our family. ... These families had dogs and gardens and lived in country towns equipped with thatched cottages and millstreams, where the children had adventures, saved lives, caught villains, and found treasures before coming home, tired but happy, to eat sumptuous teas of chequered tablecloths in low-beamed parlours presided over by comfortable pipe-smoking fathers and gentle aproned mothers, who were invariable referred to as Mummy and Daddy. (*WH*: 4)

Idyll or misery in his childhood would have ensured that Bennett, in his own view, was in possession of the biographical 'prerequisites' to be a writer. Bennett's constantly recurring complaint about his 'humdrum' origins also becomes functional by opening up a discourse about these authorial prerequisites. Another formative 'qualification' for authorship would have been an environment to rebel against. Larkin had this, with a Nazi-sympathising father and a mother whom he famously described as a 'bloody rambling fool' (quoted in *WH*: 548). Bennett's parents aspired to normality, and provided a friendly and unassuming environment, but not one to draw out the rebel in their son. Bennett distinguished himself from his origins through educational achievements, and was not hindered by his parents, although his successes did not seem to attract much attention. Winning a scholarship necessitated a move away from his hometown. This, however, hardly constituted a rebellion. Bennett's essays on Larkin[18] expresses admiration for the poet who speaks his mind without worrying about whom he might insult, a quality Bennett also recognises in writers like Osborne (*WH*: 489). Larkin is referred to as a reassuring and inspiring influence, although there is still an element of intimidation in some of Bennett's comments: 'Even to quote Larkin is to feel that anything I have said has been (un)said already and that his grumpy particularities far outsay my own' (*TT*: 13). Reading Larkin, the concepts of having one's cake and eating it, or of being in two minds, become apparent. Bennett comments on his tendency to, as he calls it, 'do a Larkin':

> So, while half the audience are dining at Aske with the Zetlands, I am sitting in the Little Chef at Leeming Bar having baked beans on toast. Which is what I prefer, so it isn't a grumble. But I catch myself here doing a Larkin (or being a man) – i.e. claiming I don't want something, then chuntering about not getting it. (*WH*: 273)

Bennett has found ways in which to address feelings of exclusion, inadequacy and literary impotence. His later literary spoofs can be seen as a process of literary self-empowerment. Through 'usurping' the voices of other writers, he decreases the intimidation they cause in the process. A typically 'Bennettian' stylistic measure used in *Poetry in Motion* illustrates this. Bennett juxtaposes the notion of artistry with the mundane, obviously aiming to deconstruct the sublimity of some poems (metaphorically keeping the reader's feet on the ground) by telling an anecdote about the writer before reading the poem. Thus, the reader of the poem 'In Church' will be distracted by the image of its author, Thomas Hardy, reading the lesson in church after a long bicycle ride, his bald head gently steaming while he is reading (*Poetry*: 9–10). Possibly as a reaction against what he sees as trivialisation of literature, Bennett will often juxtapose a writer and notions of literary 'immortality' with the small and parochial, creating a comic effect in the process. It is achieved by the surprise of the combination of the great name and the deliberately unglamorous characters in the same sentence. Thus, when Bennett presents his Aunty Kathleen, he describes her as very talkative and completely unable to distinguish between relevant and irrelevant information. Everything that happened to her during a day of working in a shoe shop was recounted in 'Proustian detail' (Bennett in Hunt 1993: 19). Yoking together the sublime and the everyday occurrence, the juxtaposition of Aunty Kathleen and Proust is comically incongruous and full of bathos. Proust seems to be a particular favourite: in *Me, I'm Afraid of Virginia Woolf*, the protagonist sarcastically combines Proust's surname with his own hated first name to demonstrate its inadequacy. 'Trevor Proust' is an example of this juxtaposition at its simplest. Not only does this approach show comic skill, it also demonstrates Bennett's ability to align big ideas and small lives. Thus, in transferring Proustian or Kafkaesque moments to ordinary people, something 'Bennettian' is created. He uses classic authors to show his own ineptness at behaving in a way appropriate to a writer, as when he describes his feelings at helping Miss Shepherd, his eccentric lodger, with her car:

> Though catch E.M. Forster taking time off from writing *Howard's End* in order to fit an Exide battery into a clapped-out three-wheeler. (*Van*: 54)

This raises the question of the associations 'great' authors evoke. They are used to impress in conversation, and there is a common unspoken agreement of what the mere mentioning of a writer's name signifies. The authors that often appear in Bennett's works can almost be seen as benchmarks, amalgamating the simplified contents of their works, their lives and their meaning to the individual who is writing or talking about them. People use the term 'Kafkaesque' even if they have not read Kafka, and seem to understand what 'Proustian' means without having read *A la recherche du temps perdu*. This is an attempt to display cultural capital, or to prove that one is not afraid of Virginia Woolf.

Me, I'm Afraid of Virginia Woolf

The 1979 television play *Me, I'm Afraid of Virginia Woolf* is an exemplary text to further the discussion on the presence of other authors in Bennett's plays.[19] Answering the question raised in Edward Albee's play *Who's Afraid of Virginia Woolf?* (1962), the play has a diffident protagonist, Trevor Hopkins. Chris Dunkley (of the *Independent*) feels that for most of the play, 'the text was actually contradicting its 'irresistible yet suspect' title: the one thing that didn't seem to frighten Trevor Hopkins was the safely dead Virginia Woolf' (quoted in Silver 1999: 152).

Hopkins, a polytechnic lecturer who hates his first name ('You're in the outside lane before even the pistol goes ... Lenin, Stalin, where would they be if they'd been called Trevor?', *Me*: 100), is played by Neville Smith. Stephen Frears has suggested that Smith was specifically cast for his physical and professional likeness to Bennett. Hopkins is accompanied by a voice-over, spoken by Bennett himself. This voice says what Hopkins really thinks, providing two levels of action, text and subtext: Hopkins' interaction with the outside world, and his 'inner' reactions, as communicated to the viewer by Bennett's commentating voice. Even though Bennett had not formulated the framework of *The Writer in Disguise* when the play was produced (see Chapter 2), Frears refers to the character Trevor Hopkins as the 'writer', and emphasises the deliberate closeness to Bennett, which makes the parallel with the 1999 text *The Lady in the Van* even more pointed:

> Frears Neville was a writer and an actor, and so he could play a writer in a way that actors quite often can't.
>
> (Interview with Stephen Frears)

Smith, in his role as Trevor, and in a way also in his role as Bennett, personifies sentiments Bennett regularly expresses: '*la condition anglaise*'- embarrassment, coupled with feelings of displacement and isolation, or not belonging. Hopkins is a lecturer, and is a passive, yet resentful presence. He has the analytical ability to see his shortcomings, but lacks the courage or initiative to change anything about his unsatisfactory situation. The play's visual style supports the impression of a hostile and uninspiring world through the drab, lacklustre surroundings, either dark or lit in unforgiving neon light. This is particularly true of the conversation Trevor has with his mother (Thora Hird) in the canteen. She has come to see him at work to catch a glimpse of the woman she thinks he is involved with. A baffling range of topics is discussed, ranging from the ketchup bottle being 'a mecca for germs', first names, the value of 'being educated' and a disagreement about what constitutes lesbianism:

> Mrs Hopkins: It's only women and other women. Like me and Mrs Goodall. ... Having tea in Marshall and Snelgrove's.
> Hopkins: Having tea in Marshall and Snelgrove's isn't lesbianism.
> Mrs Hopkins: It's only liking being with other women.
> Hopkins: Not in Marshall and Snelgrove.
> Mrs Hopkins: Well, where?
> Hopkins: Bed. [Long outraged pause] You brought the subject up.
> Mrs Hopkins: Well? So. Anyway I've been in bed with other women.
> Hopkins: Who?
> Mrs Hopkins: Your Aunty Phyllis for a start.
>
> (*Me*: 102)

Hopkins teaches an evening class of mature students of mixed abilities.[20] In the farcical classroom scene, a picture of Virginia Woolf, anonymously decorated with a 'large pair of tits and a moustache' (*Me*: 106), is more than just a bit of fun. Brenda Silver points out the iconic status of Virginia Woolf in the play:

> Rather than being a countercultural icon, she [Woolf] becomes a sign of legitimate or official culture, and if not totally of the system, her suspect status resides more in her incarnation of Art, with a capital A, than in social rebellion. When combined with her class privilege, this designation would seem to render her work and perhaps her life alien if not meaningless to most of Hopkins' students. (Silver 1999: 153–4)

The conflict between 'Art' and life (Silver spells 'Art' with a capital 'A', as Bennett does 'Life' and 'Literature') are shown in Hopkins' classroom through the icon of Virginia Woolf. She stands for sacrificing personal happiness for 'Literature' and for the literary intimidation implied in Albee's title, something that is easily felt when Hopkins tries to explain the Bloomsbury Group's upper-class radical intellectual approaches in a drab classroom on a murky evening in the provincial heart of 1970s northern England. Woolf's presence throughout the text, in the title, on the vandalised picture and in the form of a book which Hopkins carries around, creates a constant subtextual significance. There are subtle references to Woolf's ambivalent sexuality through Hopkins' sexual indifference, and his lack of courage to admit that he is unhappy as a heterosexual. His response to his mother's enquiry whether he is 'one of those' is 'Mam. I'm nothing, Mam' (*Me*: 102). Hopkins' mother's dominance can be demonstrated within this small sentence, which has 'Mam' in it twice. 'I'm nothing' also means that Hopkins' feeling of infe-riority prevents him from having a choice of sexual orientation, having instead to 'make do' with whoever will put up with him. The voice-over explains this: 'he wanted someone who didn't want him, he had such a low opinion of himself that if someone wanted him that must mean that they weren't worth having' (*Me*: 123). Trevor Hopkins, the writer in disguise, and Bennett are shown to have similarities. Bennett commented on his sexuality in response to Ian McKellen's question at a National Theatre event against Clause 28. Asked whether he was homosexual, Bennett replied that that was 'like asking a man crawling across a desert whether he preferred Malvern or Perrier' (Carpenter 2000: 25–5).

Trevor Hopkins loathes his partner, Wendy, a grotesque Yoga teacher, who gets muesli in her hair and reels off esoteric clichés. She is merci-lessly deconstructed, mainly by the voice-over, as in this scene, where Wendy and Trevor are preparing to have sex:

Wendy: As I see it the body is the basic syntax in the grammar of humanism.
Narrator: [Voice over] Why did they have to wade through this every time? Other people got foreplay. All he got was *The Joys of Yoga*.
Wendy: Where are you going?
Hopkins: The lav.

(*Me*: 122)

This scene between Wendy and Trevor is a study in the loneliness ill-suited couples can experience in each other's company, and shows that Trevor is resigned to the fact that he cannot express his true thoughts or feelings. He thus conforms to the demands of his 'pale life' (*Me*: 124) where 'literature wasn't much help' (*Me*: 93). Hopkins is deeply frustrated, bemoaning his lack of a meaningful existence, so often a theme in Bennett's plays from the period. There is one student who symbolises everything that Hopkins would love to be, had he the courage. Skinner ('Hopkins hated Skinner and longed to be him', *Me*: 109) symbolises the exciting choices, the breaking free that Hopkins longs for. 'Coming out' thus acquires a double meaning. One of them obviously refers to Hopkins potentially moving from the 'nothing' that has until now defined his sexuality.[21] Another reading of 'coming out' might be the urge to escape an existence constructed solely around the avoidance of embarrassment. Hopkins wishes to participate in what

Bennett always describes as 'Living!',[22] Skinner expresses interest in Hopkins throughout the play, and finally gets a smile back from him as the credits roll. This suggests Hopkins might be ready to pursue the life that has happened elsewhere until now. There is no textual indication of this, but his moment of hope is extradiegetically accompanied by the song 'I'm in Love with a Wonderful Guy' (Rogers and Hammerstein). According to Stephen Frears, Bennett had chosen the song purely for its music, obviously unaware of the lyrics.

> Frears: Oh, of course, *Virginia Woolf* had all the gay stuff in it; and it had Derek Thompson in it; and there's all that stuff with *South Pacific* in it. Alan wrote that as music, and then I said 'Wait 'till you see the lyrics!' [Laughter] That was just a sort of accident – I had the sound-track of the film, and I couldn't believe what I was hearing.
>
> (Interview with Stephen Frears)

The song (from *South Pacific*) has very 'camp' lyrics and provides a very powerful subtext to the scene, linking the two men, who are affection-ately smiling at each other, in freeze-frame, to the upbeat lines: 'I'm as trite and as gay as a daisy in May/A cliché coming true!/I'm bromidic and bright as a moon-happy night/Pouring light on the dew!' (*Me: 126*)

Just as Hopkins admires Skinner's boldness with a mixture of envy and attraction, Bennett admires other writers for their boldness. Skinner is dismissive of 'Literature' as a template for a happy life, and as a manual for proper living. It is Skinner himself, not his views on writers, who ultimately offers the possibility of change in Hopkins' timid and frustrated life. Pointedly, it is Skinner who consigns the defaced portrait of Virginia Woolf to the wastepaper basket and who, in an almost sermon-like speech, delivers a verdict on the value of writers sacrificing their lives to art:

> Skinner: It's council property. Well, love. Was it worth it? Look at the figures. Ten novels, five nervous breakdowns, no kids, one suicide. And this is where it's landed you, sweetheart: a further education class in the Mechanics' Institute, Halifax, on a wet Tuesday night in 1978. Let me introduce you, Virginia, old love. Here it is. Posterity. (*Puts her in the waste paper basket*) You're sure you don't fancy that pint?
>
> (*Me: 117*)

Through consigning Virginia Woolf to the wastepaper basket, Bennett drastically expresses the need to knock the myths surrounding great writers. One might interpret this as something he would personally like to do, but daren't, and thus gives the desired action to one of his characters. This is mirrored in the play, as lecturer Hopkins secretly applauds the symbolic dismissal of Woolf, but would not have the courage to actually say this, or commit such an act of iconoclasm himself. As Bennett has so often pointed out (WH: xi), the ability to 'live!' or to mix easily does not come as a side-effect of being educated, but is a matter of personality and temperament. The fact that the lives of the writers discussed in Hopkins' evening class suggest unhappy, sometimes unfulfilled lives manifests Skinner's point: writing is not necessarily 'worth it', and comes across as sacrificing 'life!' for a pale replacement of the real thing. This is also underlined by a glimpse caught of another class next door to Hopkins'. The teacher is a bully, and the subject is mechanical drawing, but the class is portrayed with a sense of purpose – enhancing the participants' qualifications:

> Young, unemployed persons, the latest underprivileged group to be clasped to the dry bosom of the Welfare State. Creatures sunk in the trough of ignorance, lasciviousness, foolishness and despair. And from which there is one thing and one thing only that can deliver them, Hopkins. Literature, Hopkins? No. Virginia Woolf? No. Art? No. The one thing that will deliver them is their Higher National Certificate. But we shall not achieve it like this, my friend. Goodnight. (*He pushes Hopkins out into the corridor*) (*Me*: 111)

The play warns of the dangers of seeking answers or refuge in literature, when literature is so obviously linked with dysfunctional lives. Virginia Woolf committed suicide, E.M. Forster 'wasn't exactly Clint Eastwood' (*Me*: 109), and Trevor Hopkins is trapped in Halifax, and with a partner of the 'wrong' gender who replaces foreplay with Yoga (*Me*: 122). Does the play therefore really tell us that learning and intellectual achievement are a waste of time because their worth cannot be measured?

The production of *Me* was driven by two men for whom knowledge, or 'cleverness', as they both seem to call it, *had* provided a career: Stephen Frears and Alan Bennett embarked on their television careers together in the early 1970s, and, although not part of the BBC's graduate take up of 'clever' Cambridge trainees, they fared well, did not have to make big compromises, and prioritised having an enjoyable time during production, 'larking about':

> Frears: ... the whole BBC was like a public school, so larking about was part of it, trying to somehow get away with it. So, a lot of it in *Virginia Woolf* relates to that. There's a rather wonderful maths master who launches these attacks on art; we got immense pleasure from that, and from all the jokes. ... So, being an artist was just an invitation to be pelted with abuse!

> (Interview with Stephen Frears)

The critics who distil an earnest message from the classroom scenes in *Me* should be aware of the tongue-in-cheek quality of the work, and the nature of the jokes, some of them seemingly a way of getting back at pretentious contemporaries who succumbed to 'the myth of the artist's life'. Bennett attacks the idealisation of 'Literature', and texts like *Me* show that education and 'Literature' do not necessarily offer solutions, and will automatically enhance people's lives. In this context, concepts of liberation through education sound cynical. It seems as though Bennett does not want his educational achievements to come between him and his audience, for fear of distancing himself from his readers, or of being accused of 'showing off', as he was by his father when he was a child. When Bennett was young and a gifted pupil, his 'swotting', as his parents called his reading, writing and revising, made him aspirational. Bennett states (*WH*: 8) that education does not change someone's personality and temperament, but does not deny the opportunities that come from it, and notably its impact on his own life:

> For Tony Harrison and for me, literature – or, at any rate, education – meant liberation. (*Poetry* 2: 19)

Other writers: biographical approaches

In the twentieth century, biography and autobiography developed into hugely popular literary genres. Readers will therefore often have biographical knowledge of an author before reading his or her works, and will often read work with the objective of comparing life with art, and finding parallels. The beliefs on the author's presence in the text, relatively stable since the Romantic age, were questioned in the 1960s by post-structuralist critics.[23] In retrospect, however, despite declaring the independence of the text from its author, post-structuralism has not managed to damage significantly the importance of the life within the work within popular and academic perception. Works such as Sean Burke's *The Death and Return of the Author* (1992) document this by pointing out that autobiography and biography have become the subject of critical theory. The author is therefore restored as a central focus of interest to the text in a climate of growing critical interest in the construction of self. The confusion between persona and person is not merely a post-modern phenomenon. Tomasevskij sums up the construction of an authorial persona:

> The literary work plays on the potential reality of the author's subjective outpourings and confessions. Thus the biography that is useful to the literary historian is not the author's curriculum vitae or the investigator's

account of his life. What the literary historian really needs is the biographical legend created by the author himself. Only such a legend is a *literary
fact*. (Tomasevskij in Burke 1995: 89)

The emergence of the author-persona in the Romantic age lays the
foundation for making connections between a work and its author. The
meaning of a text is normally constructed by a reader with biographical
knowledge of the author. Bennett's works and their reception show
him as a writer whose life is inscribed in his writing. The audience's
reception of Bennett's works is very heavily influenced by his public
persona. Bennett, however, sees the connection between life and art as
ambivalent:

> That fictional characters are not drawn directly from life is a truism.
> Evelyn Waugh's epigraph to *Brideshead Revisited* puts it succinctly: 'I am
> not I; thou are not he or she; they are not they.' But such a straightfor-
> ward disavowal is misleading, because characters are taken from life: it's
> just that they are seldom yanked out of it quite so unceremoniously as
> the public imagines. (*CTH*: 121)

Bennett discourages the idea that art can be seen as an accurate reflection on the life of its creator by promoting the separation of biography
and literary product. He also puts this principle into the mouths of his
characters, such as Marcel Proust in *102 Boulevard Haussmann*. When
the servant, Céleste, asks whether she features in his book, Prousts's
reply is a close paraphrase to Waugh's statement above:

> Proust: There is a servant certainly. But you are not she and I am not he.
> You can say anything, you see, as long as you don't say I.
>
> (*Haussmann*, in *Me*: 226)

Life will always provide the material for art, but art will then probably
depart from 'what really happened'. Bennett questions whether it helps
the reader's understanding to know the exact nature of the connection between life and art. Authors 'dislike being asked what their work
means' (*Poetry*: 3), but can also be uncomfortable with readers making
their own conclusions. The reader's satisfaction of finding a possible
connection, and thus 'personalising' a literary work, has to be taken into
account, though:

> And some knowledge of a poet's life must add to the pleasure and under-
> standing of his or her poetry. What the poet is afraid of is that the life
> will somehow invalidate the art (cries of 'He's insincere!' 'She's incon-
> sistent!'). But you can enjoy literary biography while at the same time
> recognising that the literary works, once written, have an independent
> existence, regardless of the circumstances in which they were produced.
> (*Poetry*: 4)

In this statement, Bennett can be seen to assume a position of compromise in the debate about the relationship between a writer's life and work.[24] He tolerates biographical curiosity, but discourages its dominance, resenting the fact that works are read to find out more about an author's life, rather than the other way round. Nevertheless, Bennett himself often constructs his biographical works from what is known about a writer's life. He often seems to concentrate on conceived ideas and stereotypes of a writer, as in the case of Kafka and Proust, and then furnishes the resulting 'life' with a framework of intricate references to the writer's work. Bennett's two Kafka plays, for example, can be read as paraphrases to key works by Franz Kafka. *102 Boulevard Haussmann*, the television play about Marcel Proust's home life, shows life inside the famous cork-lined room. The plays all indulge stereotypes of isolation and sacrifice for art's sake, as well as illustrating their relentlessness in pursuit of material and inspiration. All Bennett's works on other writers explore ideas around the myth of the artist's life. They abound with ideas, but also, quite openly, with contradictions and conflicts; on the one hand, Bennett wants to protect his life from being seen as material for his works; on the other hand, he expresses considerable anxiety at the prospect of his texts being read in a way he does not intend them to be read. This implies the wish to own not only the text, but also its meanings and interpretations.

Bennett as a biographer: Proust, Kafka and Larkin

Just as Bennett's autobiographical material has to be defined through convention rather than through genre, Bennett's works that can be associated with biography do not follow established ways of life writing. It is a truism that biography reveals at least as much about its writer as it does about its subject, but Bennett often relates other writers' lives back to his own. He may examine a writer's life as a potential benchmark for a 'typical' artist's life, as a vehicle for the development of an idea, or may compare it with his own identity as a writer. Furthermore, Bennett develops the theme of the writer as an observing outsider, showing the inevitability of authorial sacrifice and suffering through the example of writers like Kafka, Proust and Larkin:

> I hate Berkoff's take on Kafka: manic and melodramatic. Alan's Kafka was a realist, a poet of common sense, a visionary of the detail of daily life. He chipped away at the Kafka seam and extracted mountains of material, which he melted down into *Kafka's Dick* and *The Insurance Man*. (Eyre 2003: 91)

Immersing himself in Kafka's works, Bennett discovered the ability to see through the author's and his protagonist's eyes. His transfers of Kafkaesque scenarios to present day (and often his own) circumstances are evidence of this. Sometimes they are snippets of dialogue or imagined short sequences of film that capture the concept, such as Bennett imagining a hospital patient choosing *The Trial* from the book trolley: 'The verdict doesn't come all at one. The proceedings gradually merge into the verdict It *is* his story' (Introduction, *Kafka Plays*: xxii).

Presumably through his experience as biographer, reader and critic of Kafka, Bennett explores these three roles in his two plays on the writer. Their at times differing, at times conforming aims are juxtaposed with those of the writer. This, of course, is the perspective with which Bennett probably identifies most, although it would be a generalisation to say that he speaks through the character of Kafka:

> I am reading a book on Kafka. It is a library book, and someone has marked a passage in the margin with a long, wavering line. I pay the passage special attention without finding it particularly rewarding. As I turn the page the line moves. It is a long, dark hair. (*WH*: 131)

This long, dark hair is a reminder that literary interpretation can be subjective, haphazard and irreconcilable with the authorial intention.

Bennett demonstrates one of the strategies of coping with 'great precursors', shown in *The Insurance Man*: comparative biography, or connecting biography. Eyre (2003: 91) remarks that Bennett distilled two distinctly different plays from his wealth of material. His other strategy is evidenced in *Kafka's Dick* (1986). It is based on playing with clichés, satirising, transposing, asking 'what if?' What if, indeed, a tortoise turned into Kafka in a suburban living room? But not before somebody had accidentally urinated on it, and this someone was his friend, executor and, most crucially, his biographer, Max Brod? Franz Kafka has suddenly appeared in a house in a Leeds suburb in the 1980s, unaware of his posthumous fame. In the course of the action, he finds out he is a household name, due to his friend Max Brod's 'betrayal' by failing to burn all of Kafka's work after his death. Could one, therefore, link Brod's urination with the casual idiom of 'pissing on somebody'? Looking at some of the other issues in the play – penis size, castration angst, eating disorders – means that one probably could. Kafka's sudden confrontation with literary immortality (an *adjective* is named after him!) is not a happy one.

Kafka's Dick raises questions about clichés about an artist's origins, biographical myth and the benefits of deprivation. The title sums up the play's disillusioned thesis on biography: readers do not want information about a writer's work, they want a shortcut to the reason for a writer's troubles, preferably a gossipy one. The play explores the bogus thesis of Kafka being sensitive about the size of his penis, which creates the necessary 'creative tension' for a 'troubled genius' and many other stereotypes relating to the 'myth of the artist's life' (*Kafka*: 64). In *Kafka's Dick*, Bennett makes the point that biographical investigation is undertaken the wrong way round. Instead of looking at the artist's life for explanations of his work, the works are explored to produce more information on the artist's life, or, more extremely, the size of his penis. *Kafka's Dick* can be read as a demonstration of biographical unreliability, and an invitation to be playful with others' lives, as long as it is understood that 'truth' cannot be a criterion. The play also communicates the pleasure, of reader and biographer alike, in gossip, and the overpowering wish to make connections between one's own life and that of the object of investigation. Bennett demonstrates this in the following diary entry:

> To read Kafka is to become aware of coincidence. ... In my play Kafka is metamorphosed from a tortoise and is also sensitive about the size of his cock. So to find here, by the west door, a mosaic of a cock fighting a tortoise feels not quite an accident. (*WH*: 208)

Bennett seems to include his own ambivalence about conventions of life writing and literary criticism in the play. Although *Kafka's Dick* can superficially be seen as an anti-biographical play, it is after all a play about a writer's life, and, parodic in tone, embarks on the biographical speculations Bennett has been shown to hate.

The other key issue of the play is the role of the artist's parents and of upbringing; relating to Bennett's tongue-in-cheek theory that deprivation is beneficial for a writer's career:

> Hermann K: ... a good father is a father you forget. ... bad fathers are never forgotten. They jump out of the wardrobe. They hide under the bed. They come on as policemen. Sons never get rid of them. So long as my son's famous, I'm famous. I figure in all the biographies, I get invited to all the parties. I'm a bad father, so I'm, in the text.
>
> (*Kafka's Dick*: 61)

Bennett confesses to a 'sneaking sympathy' for Hermann Kafka, one of the most notorious parents in world literature and a character in the play. If we follow the argument Bennett has set up for an artist's creativity to be fuelled by a miserable childhood, fathers like Hermann Kafka and Sydney Larkin (see above) have to be thanked for supplying their sons with the 'necessary' deprivation and contributing to their literary success. Larkin's poem 'This be the Verse' illustrates the debate about the function of a writer's parents:

'They fuck you up your Mum and Dad' and if you're planning on writing that's probably a good thing. But if you are planning on writing and they haven't fucked you up, well, you've got nothing to go on, so then they've fucked you up good and proper. (Introduction, *Two Kafka Plays*: xiii)

Bennett's sympathies are normally with characters with a bad reputation, often without a voice of their own to defend themselves: characters range from George III to the Cambridge Spies and Kenneth Halliwell, Joe Orton's lover and murderer. While Hermann Kafka survives as the oppressive monster occupying a map of the world in a famous drawing by his son, it is not known how the real person relates to this image. Literary and public perception of Kafka's father shows he has stopped being a person, having become a literary monument, just as his son has. In the play, Bennett shows how volatile public views are. One minute, Hermann K. behaves like the monster from Kafka's works, the next minute he decides he wants to change his literary role to that of a loving parent and blackmails his reluctant son into hugging him ('Love me, you pillock!', *Kafka's Dick*: 47). This is commented on as 'a breakthrough in Kafka studies' (ibid.) by the bogus-biographer Sydney who refuses to acknowledge what he sees – a son being bullied by his father – but chooses to interpret the situation in a way that enables him to launch a sensational publication.

Kafka's Dick explores the part of the biographer, the reader and the literary critic (all having the unifying characteristic that all they want to do is to find connections between Kafka and themselves, thinly disguised as literary criticism.

> Kafka: He says he understands me: if he did understand me he'd understand that I don't want to be understood.
> Linda: Of course. I understand that.
>
> *(She doesn't)*
> (*Kafka's Dick*: 40)

Bennett is simultaneously intimidated and inspired by other writers, showing awareness of both literary tradition and the need of an author to 'make it new' (Ezra Pound). He acknowledges his audience's preference for autobiographical information, but rejects the assumptions about his private life that this brings. Bennett demonstrates ambivalence in the contradicting needs for recognition and for privacy, and in his apparent pleasure in gossiping, juxtaposed by the aim to be historically and biographically accurate. To be forgotten or to be misrepresented? There is no other choice. If Bennett is interested in elements of Kafka's biography he himself identifies with, what distinguishes him from the 'normal' biographer? Is it the intention? A biographer claims objectivity, Bennett stresses subjectivity and fictionality. In both plays, he has shaped the character Kafka to explore an idea he cannot find an answer to. The idea, of course, was shaped by Kafka's works, then transferred to Bennett as a writer, and then transferred back to the *construct* Kafka, or, to say it with Max Brod:

> He knows he's Kafka. He doesn't know he's *Kafka*. (*Kafka's Dick*: 25)

The deprivation olympics?

In *Kafka's Dick*, Kafka shows an artist's vanity: when he hears about Marcel Proust being 'one of the greatest writers of the twentieth century', despite being a 'lifelong invalid', Kafka retaliates:

> Kafka: Oh shut up, Max. My room was noisy. It was next door to my parents. When I was trying to write I had to listen to them having sexual intercourse. I'm the one who needed the cork-lined room. And he's the greatest writer of the twentieth century. Oh God.
>
> (*Kafka's Dick*: 27)

Kafka is protective of what he sees as his domain: a writer's illness and deprivation. Max Brod counters that it is not a special merit to be more ill than someone else: 'What is this anyway? The TB-Olympics?' (*Kafka's Dick*: 27). Bennett shows insight into the writer's psyche in this exchange, but nevertheless enters into competition with Philip Larkin himself about something normally considered undesirable: childhood deprivation and boring lives.

> Still, to anyone (I mean me) whose childhood was more sparsely accoutred with characters, Larkin's insistence on its dullness is galling, if only in the 'I should be so lucky' principle. (*WH*: 358)

Kafka, in Bennett's play, feels Proust's disease takes too much attention away from his own; and Bennett claims that Larkin should not have the right to complain about deprivation: he should be grateful for it, as Bennett sees it as prerequisite for a writer's success in the marketplace. Sales figures seem to support Bennett's point:

> Is there any way of avoiding the assumption that a miserable childhood is a prerequisite for a bestseller? It looks like the two are inextricably linked: the current bestseller list is comprised of a number of competitors in the 'my-childhood-was-more-miserable-than-yours' stakes.[25]

Frank McCourt (*Angela's Ashes*, 1997) and Dave Pelzer (in a series of books on his childhood full of abuse and neglect, including *A Child Called It*) are but two examples which suggest that Bennett is right to make a link between the deprivation and suffering these authors write about, and their popular success and recognition. In his view, a childhood lacking these extremes is a serious obstacle for a writer who depends so much on the material his life has generated. Bennett's lack of a miserable or spectacular childhood has been expressed many times since *Kafka's Dick*, in journalistic works and in diary entries and, most recently, in *Telling Tales* and *Hymn*.

> Art is pain. It must be. Otherwise it is not fair. (*WH*: 385)

Bennett's approach to portraying authors, or artists, on screen is not a documentary one. Felix (2000: 10) points out that accuracy is not necessarily the primary function of artists featured in films, but that the artists can be 'vehicles' for reflections on art in more general terms.[26]

> As a screen hero, the artist exists/ interests mainly as an exceptional existence, especially as an 'exemplary sufferer', suffering from a world that has to be transcended through. (Felix 2000: 10)[27]

Kafka seems an ideal object for a biographical film. Röwekamp (2000: 167) sees a reason for this: the mythologising of artists, and specifically writers, but primarily of the enigmatic persona Kafka which seems so suited for filmic use. His writing contains signs without referents, and he is seen as someone who mysteriously encodes his narratives, and is in his turn made mysterious.[28]

The Insurance Man

Bennett's 1985 play *The Insurance Man*, directed by Richard Eyre, shows Franz Kafka not as a writer, but as an employee of the Worker's Accident Insurance Institute in Prague: the insurance man in the play's title.

The *Insurance Man* is a multi-layered text. Firstly, it is a biographical text on Franz Kafka, albeit a speculative one on his 'other', his professional life, only sketchily documented in his diaries.

Secondly, the play is a commentary on Kafkaesque concepts and an opportunity to interpret visually/filmically/aurally what Bennett calls 'Kafka's fearful universe' (Introduction, *Two Kafka Plays*: xvii). It is full of defamiliarised and deconstructed shots that only gradually reveal their meaning, analogous to Kafka's literary 'enigmatic signs without referent' (Röwekamp 2000: 167).

Thirdly, *The Insurance Man* also functions as a commentary on the profession of writing as 'the devil's work' (Introduction, *Two Kafka Plays*: 78). Over the years, Bennett has developed a topos around this question in his work, exploring the varied questions about writing, ethics and biography in another of many guises.

Finally, *The Insurance Man* is a text inspired by and commenting on various Kafka texts, most notably *The Trial* and *The Judgement*. It also has a narrative frame that takes place twenty years later than the story itself. This frame links Kafka's works with events which they have often been said to prefigure: a totalitarian regime, secret police, or punishment without legislation or logic.

The first shot, accompanying the titles, shows the profile of a man, strangely positioned against the view of a street. Once the titles are over, the camera pans further away, and we realise that the man is dead, hanged from a lamppost outside a house in a Prague street, swinging slightly. Bennett explains:

> The doctor has heard the man running down the street the previous night, trying to find a refuge from his pursuers. He bangs on a door and it is opened – by his pursuers. His refuge turns out to be his doom. This kind of paradox is one associated with Kafka and it's also the paradox at the heart of the play. (Introduction, *Two Kafka Plays*: 74)

A man is walking towards the house in the dark. Cut to an X-ray of a pair of obviously diseased lungs, this fact also underlined by the doctor's expression as he is examining the X-ray. We see a caption 'Prague 1945'. In the next shot, two men, the doctor and old Franz are coming up a spiral staircase. They are shot from above, over the shoulder of a woman who is looking down on them. This could be a curious neighbour, the housekeeper who has not answered the doctor's call just before, or simply a watchful 'presence'. In the treatment room, old Franz says to the doctor 'So I'm not going to die?' This is followed by a distant bomb exploding. The doctor covers up the truth with euphemisms and starts questioning Franz about the jobs he has had, obviously looking for a connection between his work and his lung disease. Franz starts talking about a brief period working in a dyehouse: 'It's funny. I thought I was a goner then' (*Insurance Man*: 86). This introduces the actual story, and we move to the life of Franz in his twenties, when he developed a mysterious skin condition while working in dyeworks. The pun 'dying' and 'dyeing' is much employed by Bennett in this scene: 'Funny process, dyeing' and 'Dyeing won't do you any harm' (*Insurance Man*: 87). It is this skin condition and his employers' subsequent dismissal that leads Franz to the Worker's Accident Insurance Institute. Here, he is greeted by a calamitous procession of invalids and injured streaming towards the main entrance of the vast and forbidding building. It is in this scene that the visual style of *The Insurance Man* is introduced. It is shot as a blue and grey tinted modernist, surrealist nightmare, employing conventions of film noir.[29]

The soundtrack produces a brass-dominated, at times cacophonous and strict march for the procession of the damaged workers. The foyer of the Institute is a frightening place with herds of people rushing in different directions and clerks calling out orders harshly. A clap of thunder introduces the arrival of the 'tribunal' of assessing doctors and other experts, in top hats, and every bit as god-like as many of Kafka's figures of authority.

The Insurance Man and a subsequent 'biopic', Kafka (Stephen Soderbergh, 1992), show some interesting parallels. O'Mealy (2001) also points out similarities in visual style between Eyre and a 1962 adaptation of The Trial (Orson Welles). Bennett/Eyre's and Soderbergh's films do not approach Kafka as a literary monument, not even predominantly as a writer, but as a precise and critical observer of his surroundings, distant, friendly but determined. Röwekamp (2000: 170) also points out that 'the strategy of filmic mixing of facts and fictions corresponds to the fragmented narrative of the film, and also to the central principle of creation of Kafka's literature.'[30] He is commenting on Soderbergh's Kafka, but the point easily transfers to The Insurance Man with its Kafkaesque visual dramaturgy. Most of its narrative takes place in the labyrinthine world of the Insurance Institute. Shots often paraphrase Kafka's style of withholding a reaction, and do not reveal what they are or what they are signifying immediately. It is through changes in angle that these shots gradually reveal themselves. The camera manages to make another point that is prominent in Kafka's writing: that of deconstruction, unravelling, minute description. This style forces the viewer to look at something in the components shown, thus discarding the 'shortcut' of familiarity, resulting in an alienation effect from the familiar, the usual.

The young protagonist, Franz, whose life and social advancement are suddenly in doubt through his skin disease, starts out by thinking that there must be a straightforward solution to his problem. The notion of unwitting guilt is presented to him for the first time when, as a consequence of telling his employers about the problem, he is sacked. The sympathetic secretary prompts him to ask about compensation and insurance. This mirrors Dr Kafka's 'good turn' later in the play, as Franz' misery starts in earnest once he has experienced the fearful Worker's Accident Insurance Institute. Just as the building is not designed to be accessible, corridors and staircases leading nowhere, the system that governs it is rigid, but not transparent. Nobody knows the rules, and the only lesson to be learnt is that, without being at fault, one can still be guilty. Franz does not recognise this lesson at first, but when it sinks in, he reacts with aggression, just as the protagonists in Kafka's plots do. It is the battle of the individual against inflexible machinery, the individuals following the regulations bureaucracy and not knowing why. But there are other pressures in Franz' life as well. He is engaged to a girl from a well-to-do family, and the social pressure of the strained encounters in her home have possibly contributed to the skin eruption.

Dr Kafka (Daniel Day Lewis) stands out from the army of bureaucrats around him. He moves in a characteristic stooped and lanky way, he talks slowly and with great deliberation, and is friendly in an absent-minded way. He often does not look at the person he is talking to, and is shot in profile looking into distance while the other is talking. Day-Lewis is the only one of the numerous cast to speak with a trace of a foreign accent, his detailed, methodological approach to his work evident in the Kafka persona he created. Bennett comments that Day-Lewis kept his Kafka mannerism at all times on set (Introduction, *Insurance Man*: 74).

Despite all its Kafka mimicry, *The Insurance Man* is a Bennett text, and there is one character in particular who carries the characteristic speech and attitude. Lily, just one of the many hundreds waiting for their turn to explain their case, is one of Bennett's women desperately trying to prove her status in a world that is indifferent to her. We see these ladies' quests, be they in a surreal location like the Institute, or in an office in suburban Leeds:

> Lily: You'll go to the bottom of the pile. (*Pause*) The girl said last week my file was taken out by the Assistant Manager. Of course I know them all here, I'm like one of the family. (*Another girl passes*) Sheila ... (*to Franz*) Sheila. I'd liked to have worked in a place like this. A sedentary occupation but with some coming and going. Banter. Whip-rounds. Relations between the sexes. Sat at home, it's no game is it?
>
> (*Insurance Man*: 110)

The 'trial' itself takes place in two parts. To make Franz' fate even more fearful, he witnesses somebody else's trial in front of the tribunal before it is his own turn. As often, he is seen in silhouette, running through one of the countless corridors, then hasting down another spiral staircase, and finally entering the tribunal room on the gallery. It is a steeply raked lecture theatre, its seats covered in white material. We see the podium from above, Franz' point of view, the semi-circle of the table where the tribunal doctors are sitting, and a woman standing in the centre in front of them. She is naked, avoiding eye contact, her arms folded at the front. As Franz enters and watches, she is asked to raise her arm again. The ensuing conversation between the doctors talks about her in the third person, and turns into a scornful monologue:

> Angry Doctor: One could say that this accident has brought her to her senses rather than deprived her of her of them. She now takes a dim view of the world. So do I. She can't keep her mind on the matter in hand. Nor can I. She winces when she looks in the mirror. So do I.

Thin Doctor: She's crying.
Fat Doctor: So am I.

(*Insurance Man*: 112)

When it comes to Franz' own trial, we first see a figure, soon recognised as Dr Kafka in his characteristic bowed posture, running up some stairs and entering the lecture theatre, where he sits down to watch the proceedings. A large audience of students listens to their lecturer's explanations of the pathologies of the various human case studies. The lighting turns the podium into a stage. Franz, sitting with other candidates ready for examination, comes onto the stage, takes his gown off and stands naked, looking at the floor. As he turns round, following the instructions from the lecturer, and revealing the full extent of his skin condition, the camera turns to his father, also present in the lecture theatre. He is crying. Franz' father, a railway worker, had hoped his son might escape a life of hard toil. The scenes between him and Franz show tenderness and concern (one sequence shows him pressing healing leaves against his son's chest), and the tears he sheds in the lecture theatre while his son is being exposed also bemoan an uncertain future. Among the questions asked by the students is that of whether the disease might be venereal. Nobody acknowledges Franz beyond his function as a demonstration object. Humiliated and tortured by both his exposure on stage and his ongoing exposure to the senseless bureaucracy of the Institute, Franz has a desperate outburst. During this, his father, still crying, leaves the lecture theatre, and we leave with him, hearing only the voice of the lecturer. The scene then switches to the next case, Lily, who nods solemnly, at times with discreet triumph, as her history is outlined by the lecturer.

Franz' own humiliating exposure is mirrored in many of Kafka's works, but Bennett was possibly also using his own experience to construct this scene. While he was in the army, a consultant at Radcliffe Infirmary discussed Bennett's naked body 'without reference to me with his class of smirking medical students' (*US*: 27).

Bennett integrates an issue that was causing fear and public concern at the time when *The Insurance Man* was written (see also *WH*: 259). He introduces the work-related illness of tuberculosis or similar lung diseases through one of Dr Kafka's elaborate descriptions of a mill-worker exposed to cotton dust over a long time:

Kafka: And day by day this cotton dust has crept into his lungs, but so slowly, so gradually that it cannot be called an accident. But suppose out lungs were not internal organs. Suppose they were not locked away in the chest. Suppose we carried our lungs outside our bodies, bore them before us, could hold and handle them, cradle them in our arms. And suppose further they were not made of flesh but of glass, or something like glass, not yet invented, something pliable. And thus the effect of each breath could be seen, the deposit of each intake of air, calculated, weighed even. What would we say then, as we saw the dust accumulate, the passages clog, the galleries close down, as cell by cell these lungs hardened, withered, died.

(*Insurance Man*: 123)

This clearly relates to the contemporary asbestos scandal in the mid 1980s, but also shows the effect of working conditions in mills or dyeworks in the early twentieth century, the time in which the play is set. On a level specific to the plot, this statement by Kafka prefigures what he is going to do to Franz, thinking he is doing a good deed. The two protagonists have different stories within the plot of the play. It is possible to see them as two Kafkaesque representatives: the author, Dr Kafka, and the protagonist, Franz, both inhabit 'Kafka's fearful universe'. When, late in the play, the two protagonists meet, the issue that unites Bennett and Kafka is raised: the responsibility of a person of authority. The, well, Kafkaesque system that Franz has been exposed to in his pursuit for guidance over his work-inflicted skin condition is known to Dr Kafka, and he is powerless to change it.

'You say you understand,' says Franz in the film, 'but if you do and you do nothing about it then you're worse than the others. You're evil.' This is an echo of Kafka's own remarks that to write is to do the devil's work. And to say that it is the devil's work does not excuse it. One glibly despises the photographer who zooms in on the starving child or the dying soldier without offering help. Writing is no different. (Introduction, *Two Kafka Plays*: 78)

Dr Kafka does, however, offer help: his brother-in-law has just opened a factory for building materials, specialising in asbestos. He is looking for employees, and Dr Kafka offers Franz a recommendation to work there. The two men, in a shot walking down a corridor together, then shake hands over this. The next scene shows Dr Kafka visiting the factory, coughing from the dust, but possibly already showing symptoms of the tuberculosis that is going to kill him. Franz, whose skin has returned to normal, thanks him for saving his life. It is this statement that returns the viewer to the frame narrative, directly to the shot of the diseased lungs of old Franz. While Dr Kafka had saved his life in the short term, he has cut it short in the long term, long since dead himself. Is this the devil's work? Or is it nobody's fault, and just an irreversible consequence, the necessary evil of living in the world of the Kafkaesque?

Doctor: You weren't to know. He wasn't to know. You breathed, that's all
you did wrong.

(Insurance Man: 126)

102 Boulevard Haussmann

Bennett's biographical play about Marcel Proust explores the notions
of art as sacrifice and suffering as a creative force. While based on an
episode from Proust's life, the play is also a discourse on these concepts.
The selfishness that accompanies the artist confirms further that life
and art differ considerably:

> 102 Boulevard Haussmann (1990) came out of wanting to write about
> Proust, which in turn came out of having written about Kafka ... writers
> and their lives, and how life and art don't always measure up. Virtual
> contemporaries, Kafka and Proust both gave up their loves for their
> work, though the self-sacrifice didn't quite make them saints – how they
> lived sometimes falling short of what they wrote. (Introduction in Private
> Function: x)

Like all other of Bennett's biographical plays, the idea leads the way
in the construction of the play. Nevertheless, the film shows considerable attention to historical and biographical detail, to recreate 'the actual
topography of Prousts's airless and cork-lined apartment' (Private Function: xi). In other respects, too, it's a film that is faithful to the facts
of Prousts's life. The reason for this seems to lie in the eccentricity of
Marcel Proust's lifestyle, or 'regime', as it is referred to in the play. While
Bennett has often commented on the lack of dramatic potential of the
act of writing – hence, perhaps, the focus on Kafka's 'day job', or his
transposition to suburban Leeds. With Proust, he has a subject that is
more suitable to be at the centre of a play than simply showing 'someone
tearing an unsatisfactory sheet from the typewriter, screwing it up and
throwing it in the wastepaper basket (Proust didn't have a typewriter
anyway)' (Private Function: x). This is the only Bennett play that actually
includes the act of writing, filmed in a number of ways: hearing the
author's voice while seeing him write, following a close-up of a pen on
paper, trying to show the connection between material (in this case the
string quartet, and particularly its viola player) and its way into Proust's
writing. The author is also shown trying out ideas, preferably on his
servant, Céleste, whom he values for her lack of education, and for her
lack of interest in what he is writing about. Céleste is a more reserved
relation of Linda in Kafka's Dick. The attraction between the characters Kafka and Linda can be compared to Franz Kafka's last love, Dora
Dymant, who was not interested in his writing in the slightest. Bennett

allegedly identifies with the wish to seek partners without ambitions of being a 'writer's wife', and to associate with people without ambitions to 'understand' his work. This was something that attracted him to Anne Davies, with whom he had a long relationship:

> And one enormous virtue was that she was not in the least interested in my work. She didn't want to be the artist's wife. And I like that, because I don't want to be explaining how far I got with it every day. (Bennett quoted in Games 2001: 249)

Proust's prioritising of his art over anything else is shown on many occasions in this play. Removed from the world, he has his sound-proofed cocoon of a bedroom, which is the only room he inhabits in his vast apartment, where everything else is clad in dust covers. Here, the outside world has no relevance, Proust's nights are days, and the rhythm of his writing dictates his and servant Céleste's life. World War I, which dominates everyone else's life, is insignificant to Proust, unless it is of direct relevance to him personally:

> Still, the war is not without its blessings. I have had a letter to say Monsieur Rivière is reading my novel in his prison camp. (*Haussmann*, in *Private Function*: 198)

If the war threatens any of the 'necessities' of Proust's art, such as recalling his protégé, the viola player Massis, to the front, he uses his extensive connections to prevent this. Proust is unapologetic about his lack of patriotic or emotional involvement:

> One has lost so many friends, and that one feels, of course. But the deaths of tens of thousands happening every day is the most insignifi-cant of sensations, hardly as disagreeable as a draught. ... One death means more than a thousand. When men are dying like flies, that is what they are dying like. (*Haussmann*, in *Private Function*: 212)

The play, for all its subtlety, also presents the politics of relationships surrounding Proust. Céleste is devoted to his welfare and anachronisms, and discreetly but fiercely protective of him. This is shown through her disapproval of Proust bringing the string quartet to his flat to play him a piece by César Franck. She treats the young men as intruders, ordering them not to touch anything in the flat, and talking to them coldly and only when necessary. Her feelings seem of little importance to her employer, who is taking a special interest in the viola player, Massis. And while Proust shows affection towards Céleste, she ceases to exist as soon as his work takes over. Proust is also possessive of her: when Odilon, Céleste's husband, visits on a day's leave, he is immediately appointed as chauffeur. In a very poignant scene, Proust steps outside his bedroom, having heard the sound of Céleste and Odilon making love. He deliberately cuts this short by ringing the bell to summon her ('I can't seem to get comfortable', Haussmann, in *Private Function*: 211). She appears, seemingly unperturbed, to settle him back into bed, and as he takes her hand in his, we can see his satisfaction that he takes priority over her marriage. Proust's work overrides any other relationships. Proust indirectly makes this information available to Céleste, when he asks her to read a passage back to him.

> Céleste: (*With some hesitation*) 'Sometimes when we have made a rough sketch of a painful passage in our writing and can advance no further a new affection and a new suffering come our way which enable us to complete it, to give substance. And on the score of these great but useful unhappinesses we have little ground for complaint; they are plentiful and we seldom have to wait long for one.'
>
> (*Private Funtion*: 223)

She reads this without expression and with occasional hesitation, not realising that Proust is reflecting on his unhappiness of young Massis' disappearance from his life. Céleste thus demonstrates again what her employer values in her: lack of judgement and an unquestioning acceptance of his exceptional circumstances and lifestyle. Of course, it is Céleste's conspiracy with the doctor which has brought about the situation, so indirectly she has contributed to Prousts's unhappiness, thus furthering his productivity. This is also shown when Céleste notices Proust's ink-stained hands and wipes them, leading him to comment on writing as a 'dirty business'. It goes without saying that these ink stains are heavily metaphorical.

Two other familiar Bennett topoi also make an appearance in *102 Boulevard Haussmann*: one is the quality of great literature to permeate public consciousness without these works actually having been read. Proust triggers associations of a cork-lined room and of the famous moment the narrator, Marcel, is transported back to his childhood by eating a *madeleine*.[31]

> Bize: Maitre Proust is a sensitive man. He lives for his work.
> Massis: You call him maitre. Have you read his books?
> Bize: Not exactly. But he's a great man nonetheless.
>
> (*Haussmann*, in *Private Function*: 221)

The other theme is the transfer of life to art, and the indirectness which is rarely credited by a biography-obsessed readership:

> People think of a novel as a sort of cube, one side of which has been removed, so that the author can put in the people he meets. But it's more like a huge cemetery in which on the majority of tombs the names are

effaced and can no longer be read, even by the author. (*Haussmann*, in *Private Function*: 195)

Bennett also finds time for some self-reflection through the 'great precursor' Proust:

> When I hit thirty with still not much done I then took comfort from Proust, who had been an even later starter than Virginia Woolf: whatever else can be said about Proust, he did not hit the ground running. (*US*: 544)

As we move from Bennett's biographical works, they provide a link to the more directly autobiographical work, as the plays and essays on writers are reflections of his own 'condition':

> If I could write ... a play, a short story, anything ... I would, writing about writing (or not writing) is just vamping till ready. (*US*: 543)

Conclusion

> We love to categorize: Amis is the money-grabbing bloke who needed a big advance to fix his dodgy teeth; Stoppard is that clever fellow with a neat line in cod Shakespeare; Pinter is the chap who goes puce, tells journalists to fuck off, and is forever banging on about Iraq or the Kurds or the iniquities of US imperialism. We prefer idées fixes to ideas. (Stephen Moss in McAfee 2002: 162)

This chapter has aimed to illustrate the interfaces between writing and spying, between biography and persecution, between treachery and patriotism, between the fear of great precursors and the debates they spark off. It has shown writing as the devil's work for *The Insurance Man*, literary biography as persecution in *Kafka's Dick*, and art as sacrifice in *102 Boulevard Haussmann*.

According to Bennett, biography should be approached in a reflective way that stresses its subjective use for the investigator, confirming the common thesis that biographical writing is at least as much about its writer as it is about its object. The genre is driven by the reader's need to believe that deprivation can be overcome, talent is not determined by financial or educational circumstances and that true talent will prevail. Bennett half confirms, half satirises the readership's need for fairytales in Sydney's monologue at the end of *Kafka's Dick*:

> Sydney: And yet, in our heart of hearts, we know that like children we
> prefer the familiar stories, the tales we have been told before. And
> there is one story we never fail to like because it is always the same. The

myth of the artist's life. How one struggled for years against poverty and indifference only to die and find himself famous. Another is a prodigy finding his way straight to the public's heart to be loved and celebrated while still young, but paying the price by dying and being forgotten. ... He plunges from a bridge and she hits the bottle. Both of them paid. That is the myth. Art is not a gift, it is a transaction, and somewhere an account has to be settled. It may be in the gas oven, in front of a train or even at the altar ... We prefer artists to die poor and forgotten, like Rembrandt, Mozart or Beethoven, none of whom did, quite. One reason why Kafka is so celebrated is because his life conforms in every particular to what we have convinced ourselves an artist's life should be.

(*Kafka's Dick*: 64)

At the heart of Bennett's work about other writers is his urge to demonstrate the relevance authors like Kafka, Proust and Larkin have for him, and maybe for the reader or viewer as a consequence of his 'takes' on these writers. Bennett (through the mouth of Proust) acknowledges the power of literature when it makes the reader identify with an emotion or an idea:

Proust: You are reading a book, a novel say, and you come across something familiar. It is a thought or an emotion you yourself have had but thought secret, even shameful, but peculiar to you. And here it is, set down in the book. And it is as if a hand has come out and taken yours.

(*Haussmann*, in *Private Function*: 226)[32]

Does the approach through biography popularise the plays, or indeed the writers, or make them more accessible? The British readership is used to biographical approaches, and takes an acute interest in the connection between life and art. In acknowledging this through his biographical plays, Bennett manages to integrate the ideas that are of such importance to him – a 'Trojan Horse' approach? It would not be the only instance where Bennett smuggles intellectually rigorous concepts into a broad audience's consciousness through the use of familiar formats.

Notes

1 *The Old Country* was revived for English Touring Theatre in 2006 (director: Stephen Unwin). Critics remarked that Bennett's play was 'easy on the traitor', the protagonist Hilary ('a Kim Philby-esque turncoat stuck in a Soviet summer shack, bemoaning the decline of Lyons Corner Houses and the bowdlerising of the Eucharist back home'), *Evening Standard*, 21 March 2006, www.thisislondon.

co.uk/theatre/articles/22046316?source=Evening%20Standard.

2 Alexander Walker, 'Running the tap over a traitor', *Standard*, 17 November 1983.

3 In the published script (in *Objects of Affection*), this line reads 'He popped by my dressing room last night and threw up in the basin. It was our first meeting.' During production, this was obviously changed to '... It was love at first sight'.

4 This discussion is based on the television text, whereas the published version is the play as it was performed in stage. As quotes are transcribed, there is no pagination.

5 'I have to confess that I've never had a sensation of rapture, or any physical sensation in fact, standing in front of a painting, except maybe aching legs' (Bennett in 'Going to the Pictures', in *Untold Stories*: 455).

6 A compromise was reached, documented in Eyre's diaries, in an exchange between himself, Victor Mishcon and Max Raynor (both Labour peers): 'don't tell the Board, face the consequences when the play's on, put a note in the programme' (Eyre, *National Service: Diaries*, London: Bloomsbury, 2003: 49).

7 See, for example, Pamela Church Gibson's chapter 'From dancing queen to plaster virgin – Elizabeth and the end of English heritage?' in *Journal of Popular British Cinema*, vol. 5, 2002; and my chapter 'Taking liberties with the monarch – the royal biopic' in Monk and Sargeant (*British Historical Cinema*, London: Routledge, 2002), in *British Historical Cinema*, London: Routledge.

8 'One consideration that had kept me away from the book [*The Wind in the Willows*] for so long, gave it a protective coating every bit as off-putting as those black and maroon bindings of my childhood, was that it had *fans*. It's often a children's book – *Winnie the Pooh*, *Alice* and *The Hobbit* are examples – or it is a grown-up children's book such as those of Wodehouse, E.F. Benson and Conan Doyle. But Jane Austen and Anthony Trollope are nothing if not adult and they have fans too ...' (*Willows*: x).

9 'Asked to read *The Good Companions* for a possible production, I find I can only get as far as the end of Act I. It's interesting, though, in that it's Priestley on one of his favourite themes, that of escape and escape from the North particularly.

> Act I, Scene I ends like this:
>
> Leonard: Where yer going?
> Oakroyd: [at door] Down south.
> *Exit to triumphant music from the gramophone.*
>
> And earlier:
>
> Oakroyd: I'd like to go down south again. I'd like to have a look at ... oh well ... Bristol. I'd like to see ... yer know ... some of them places ... Bedfordshire.
> Oglethorpe: I nivver hear tell much o'that place; is there owt special I' Bedfordshire?
> Oakroyd: I don't know but it's summat to see.

Which was my attitude exactly when I was 16. And my father's in 1944 when the family upped sticks and migrated disastrously from Leeds to Guildford for a year. In the end Oakroyd goes off to Canada, between Bedfordshire and Canada there not being much to choose' (Bennett in 'Diaries 1998', *LRB*, 21 January 1999).

10 'The Treachery of Books' was first published in *The Independent on Sunday* in 1990, and was published in *Writing Home* in 1994.

11 Six revisionary movements in the strong poet's life-cycle present Bloom's model for 'the way one poet deviates from another' (*The Anxiety of Influence*, Oxford: Oxford University Press, 1975: 10-11). Influence, or 'poetic misprision' (ibid.: 7) is about the desire to 'wrestle with strong precursors' (ibid.: 5) and to emerge as a strong poet oneself. However, 'self-appropriation involves the immense anxieties of indebtedness' (ibid.).

12 'My concern is only with strong poets, major figures with the persistence to wrestle with their strong precursors, even to the death. Weaker talents idealize; figures of capable imagination appropriate for themselves' (Bloom, *The Anxiety of Influence*, 1975: 5).

13 See Humphrey Carpenter's (*That Was Satire That Was*, London: Victor Gollancz, 2000) comprehensive study of satire in the 1960s and *Beyond the Fringe*'s part in its development and transformation.

14 'Satire: A writing in which the language or sentiment of an author is mimicked; especially, a kind of literary pleasantry, in which what is written on one subject is altered, and applied to another by way of burlesque; travesty', www.hyperdictionary.com/dictionary/parody, accessed 2 April 2003.

15 Director Jonathan Stedall in the series *Betjeman and I*, BBC TV, August 2006.

16 'With Shakespeare, whatever you do, you know that he has been there first', Bennett, speaking in the programme *The Genius of Shakespeare*, BBC2, 6 November 2002.

17 The reading of *Poetry in Motion* is mainly textual, as the Channel 4 series is only available as an illustrated script, and no recordings could be obtained.

18 'Instead of a Present' (*WH*: 498), 'Alas! Deceived' (*WH*: 548), 'Philip Larkin' in *Poetry in Motion* (1990: 87), 'England Gone: Philip Larkin' (*US*: 358).

19 Later published in the collections *The Writer in Disguise* and *Me, I'm Afraid of Virginia Woolf* respectively; see also Chapter 2; the play was directed and produced by Stephen Frears as part of the *Six Plays* season for LWT in 1979.

20 'I tell folks you're at the Polytechnic and they think you teach woodwork', as Hopkins' mother puts it (*Me:* 100). It might be seen as an unusual statement, considering that Hopkins, like Bennett, is probably the first in his family to obtain a degree, and to work in Higher Education.

21 *Me, I'm Afraid of Virginia Woolf* is widely accepted as a gay text, and has been screened at the NFT's Gay and Lesbian Film Festival. Bennett himself has referred to it as a play that suddenly turns into a love story.

22 Other examples: Mole in *The Wind in the Willows*, Dennis Midgley in *Intensive Care*.

23 The separation of the text from the author after production was announced, meaning that the author's intentions were declared no more significant than a reader's interpretation, and that the text acquired autonomy after being made public. Post-structuralist ideas surrounding the independence of the text heighten the awareness of the instability of a text's meaning, and, therefore, the instability and potential artificiality of the authorial persona *within* that text.

24 See also Tomasevskij in Burke (*Authorship*, Edinburgh: Edinburgh University Press, 1995: 84).

25 Radio 4, *Front Row*, 27 February 2002.

26 *Nicht immer muß der dargestellte Künstler einem historischen Vorbild entsprechen; auch die Fiktion macht Exemplarisches sichtbar: über den Mythos des Künstlers und die Signatur seiner Epoche als literarische und kunsthistorische Gattung ist die Darstellung eines Künstlerlebens, einer historischen oder fiktiven Künstlerexistenz, in Wort oder Bild, immer auch Selbstreflexion der Kunst* (Felix, *Genie und Leidenschaft – Künstlerleben im Film*, St Augustin: Gardez Verlag, 2000: 10).

27 My translation from German: *Als Leinwandheld existiert/ interessiert der Künstler vorrangig als Ausnahmeexistenz, insbesondere als ‚exemplarisch Leidender'. Leiden an einer Welt, die es durch die Kunst zu transzendieren gilt.*

28 'Es ist die Form der Mythologisierung von Literatur und die Person des Schriftstellers Franz Kafka, die Verrätselung eines Verrätselers, die auch heutzutage vollkommen kinotauglich erscheint. Rätselhafte Zeichen ohne Referenten, Geheimnisse und tragische Anti-Helden, Auflösung und Dekadenz, Delirium und Wahn. Diese Zutaten*

eignen sich nach wie vor zur Entfesselung wildester Spekulationen, und immer noch scheint kaum ein Ort geeigneter, solchen Spekulationen Raum und Zeit zur Verfügung zu stellen und sie in audiovisuelle Muster zu übersetzen – als das Kino resp. das bewegte Bild' (Röwekamp, 'Kafkaeske Visionen. Das Beobachtungsmuster "Schriftsteller" im zeitgenössischen Film', in Felix, *Genie und Leidenschaft – Künstlerleben im Film*, St Augustin: Gardez Verlag, 2000: 167).

29 Film noir is seen less as a genre than a visual style or mood. Most films associated with 'noir' were produced after World War II and had elements such as a cynical and hardened anti-hero, a femme fatale, and often a sense of purposelessness and a sense of injustice. *The Insurance Man* references this style of film mainly visually. See also Copjec (*Shades of Noir: A Reader*, New York: Verso, 1993).

30 *'Die Strategie der filmischen Vermischung von Fakten und Fiktionen korrespondiert die fragmentarische Erzählweise des Films und damit zugleich einem zentralen Gestaltungsprinzip von Kafkas Literatur'* (Röwekamp, 'Kafkaeske Visionen', 2000: 170).

31 In Marcel Proust, *A la recherche du temps perdu*, Part 1: *Du coté de chez Swann*.

32 This statement resonates in many of Bennett's works: he uses it in his essays, and, after putting it into the mouth of Proust in *Boulevard Haussmann*, the character Hector says it in Bennett's latest play and subsequent film adaptation, *The History Boys* (Nicholas Hytner, 2004 and 2006).

'If I start off undressed, I have nowhere to go': documentaries and autobiography

4

Dinner at Noon (1988)
Portrait or Bust (1994)
The Abbey (1995)

Only what is seen sideways sinks deep. (*US*: 458)

Alan Bennett has stated that he writes plays when he is in two minds about something (see also Wu 2000: 79). The issue of Englishness, and Bennett's ambivalence towards it, features in most of his works from the late 1960s onwards. As seen in Chapter 3, ideas are explored through biography, which Bennett frequently employs in the 1980s and early 1990s. Through the 'writer in disguise' protagonists, discussed in Chapter 2, he uses autobiographical material indirectly and transfers it to his characters. In the 1990s, Bennett starts to develop a strand of auto-biographical work. Since 1981, Bennett's diaries have been published in annual instalments,[1] but they deal mainly with social and political commentary, and offer findings and observations. The first time Alan Bennett spoke in a television piece as himself, without the protective layers of fictionality or disguise, was in the documentary *Dinner at Noon* (Jonathan Stedall, BBC TV, 1988). It is an exploration of behaviour in public places. The documentary serial *Poetry in Motion* (Channel 4 TV, 1990) is an introduction to the lives and works of British poets of the twentieth century, selected, contextualised and read by Bennett. *Portrait or Bust* (Jonathan Stedall, BBC TV, 1994) is an exploration of the Leeds Art Gallery and, starting with Bennett's childhood, his relationship with fine art. *The Abbey* (Jonathan Stedall, BBC TV, 1995) is a three-part documentary on the history of Westminster Abbey. All these programmes offer insight into Bennett's love-hate relationship with Englishness. The documentary series *Poetry in Motion* (Channel 4, 1990), although touching on biography and Englishness through examining lives and works of writers, is different in its style and remit to the three documentaries discussed in this chapter, and is therefore part of the previous chapter, together with other works on writers and writing.

The documentary in its many variations (docusoap, mockumentary, docudrama) is among the most rapidly expanding programming choices in British television. The national preoccupation with biography and 'factuality' has resulted in an expansion of 'reality television', a trend that has its roots in documentaries centring on the depiction of 'true stories' and 'real people'. Documentaries often rely on celebrity presentation: names such as David Attenborough and Simon Schama stand for a certain predictable style, and a certain level of quality. The regular suppliers of voice-overs for documentaries, normally well-established actors or presenters, are similar signifiers of reliability and quality, thus ideal for the communication of 'factuality'. There is normally a trustworthy, serious, but still benign quality to either the (visible) presenters or the voice-overs, making it easy for the viewer willingly to suspend disbelief and to buy into the 'promise of fact' (see also Paget 1990: 3). Documentaries are presented as 'factual' and are equipped with the appropriate conventions to convey authenticity.

Bennett's most famous predecessor on issues of Englishness was John Betjeman, who wrote and presented numerous documentaries (*Metroland*, 1973) and various documentary series. Although it is problematic to draw direct comparisons between Betjeman and Bennett, there are some poignant parallels. Given their carefully crafted scripts, their topics centred on English identity and public institutions and monuments, Betjeman's and Bennett's documentaries can be seen in the 'it's-good-for-you' tradition of the BBC, 'the long and distinguished tradition of public service broadcasting' (Creeber 2001: 125). Both authors are popular, and to a certain extent populist, but do not compromise their values and are unafraid to communicate them. Betjeman's campaigns for the preservation of Victorian architecture at a time when it was unfashionable are proof of this. Bennett mirrors Betjeman's values in that he has always condemned 1960s brutalism and its damage to British cityscapes. He is the Chairman of the Settle Conservation Society, and has been known to issue warnings about mock-period details on houses in its newsletter. His other targets are wide-ranging and cannot be aligned with party politics: he has urged the public to support independent bookshops, and has spoken out for the pardoning of soldiers in World War I, shot for defection and cowardice. Betjeman and Bennett were and are both skilful, personable and humorous presenters who have the ear of the public. Their documentaries, often very personal narratives, are authored by them and constructed around them as authors. They also worked with the same director and producer, Jonathan Stedall. He was the director of

Summoned by Bells (1976), Betjeman's autobiographical documentary, seen as a televisual testament towards the end of his life. Stedall is the director and producer of all Bennett's documentaries, except for *Poetry in Motion*. All documentaries fronted by a presenter are to some extent auteurist, but Betjeman and Bennett's are particularly personalised and dependent on their 'figurehead'. Bennett's public persona means he is ideally suited for this convincing transmission of 'fact'. Although he is seen as an authority, he is not perceived as patronising. He is able to maintain a 'one of us' appeal. In theatrical terms, this could be described as deliberately playing low status to maintain the favour of the audience. Bennett is aware of the target audience and thus approaches his topics in an accessible and inclusive way, similar to Betjeman. Bennett is wary of the intimidation created by the elitist constructs of 'Art' and 'Literature' and seems to prefer to position himself on a par with the viewer.

All Bennett's documentaries, *Dinner at Noon* and *Portrait or Bust* in particular, are 'hybrids': although well-researched and informative about their topics, they are about Bennett's life *in relation* to these topics. The documentaries often accommodate Bennett's autobiographical material and his historical and sociological interests. As these works are not easy to categorise; one has to give them new names, sometimes fairly long-winded ones. Daphne Turner (1997: 133) calls what I have called 'the Bennett-documentaries' 'semi-autobiographical television documentary'.

Goode (2003: 312) remarks on the different locations of the three documentaries, covering the provincial (Harrogate), the municipal (Leeds) and the national (Westminster Abbey). Director Jonathan Stedall mentioned in a 1998 interview that the next documentary he and Bennett had planned was on the public library service, a project that has not come to fruition thus far. The choice of topic, however, shows that Bennett seems to want to remind the viewer of the significance of the public sphere, funding for arts and education and issues of public accountability. Tradition, acknowledgement of the past, and local specificities are also dominant themes in Bennett's plays, but they have a more educational, 'caring' and accessible character in the documentaries. Bennett's insistence on parochialism, which has made him invisible to critics of television drama, is ironically the key to his success in the documentaries, where he can be seen to be educating the public, in the 'worthwhile' tradition of the BBC. The documentaries show distinctive ways of combining and managing autobiography and approaches to topics, as the following aims to demonstrate.

Bennett as Observer: *Dinner at Noon*

> I have had unfortunate experiences in hotels. I was once invited to Claridge's by the late John Huston in order to discuss a script he had sent me. The screenplay was bulky (that was what he wanted to discuss) and looked like a small parcel. Seeing it and (I suppose) me, the commissionaire insisted I use the tradesman's entrance. (*Dinner*, in *WH*: 39)

A documentary about a typical day in a hotel, *Dinner at Noon* is a study in observation. It explores the social front, pretence, and the importance of environment. From a sociological angle, following Goffman's theories about behaviour as performance, this would be observation without involvement (see also *WH*: 40). Bourdieu (quoted in Robbins 2006: 18) claims that the reflexivity that follows observation exempts the sociologist from participating or demonstrating his or her own cultural capital. This can be related to Bennett's working method in his earlier works for television, and he claims it is a general precondition to being a writer – being on the outside, looking in. Although Bennett and Jonathan Stedall originally set out to work along these lines, it quickly became clear that their scheduled shoot at the Crown Hotel in Harrogate would not generate enough material for this. Bennett therefore, somewhat spontaneously, wrote the linking script, which is a very personal exploration of his family and their demeanour in public places. Bennett takes on the role of a character among other hotel guests, an on-screen narrator of his past, an eavesdropper, commenting on other people's behaviour. So, we eavesdrop on hotel guests and marvel at the way they present themselves through Bennett's eyes. His accounts of eating in public are illustrated with close-ups of other people eating, potentially embarrassing themselves, but largely at ease and unselfconscious. Bennett contrasts this with seeing 'hotels and restaurants as theatres of humiliation' for years. His family could not afford much, so some tea would be ordered, and food brought in had to be shared under the table, and Bennett and his brother would have to drink sips of tea from his parents' cups. The fear of discovery, exposure and expulsion stayed with him for a very long time. The pleasure of observing has made Bennett like hotels, as they are ideal for seeing people when they are on their best behaviour (but not necessarily at their best, as Bennett remarks, *Dinner*, in *WH*: 42). Bennett's parents enjoyed watching people in public places, making up stories about them, and drawing social distinctions. In *Dinner at Noon*, Bennett introduces the intricate social scale his mother developed: 'She'd talk about people being "better-class", "well-off", "nicely spoken", "refined", "genuine", "ordinary" and – the ultimate condemnation – "common"' (*Dinner*, in *WH*: 43–4). According to someone who grew up in similar circumstances to Bennett, 'common' is still a worse insult than a four-letter word, is mainly used with reference to a woman, and is a judgement that will not depend on money, origin or class background.[2] It implies a lack of appropriate behaviour or dress sense and a lack of restraint for one's 'station'. By contrast, the sense of 'knowing one's place' cancels out aspirations, but often Bennett's elderly characters will blame their social restrictions on their lack of education, just as Bennett's parents might have done. Bennett's conclusion is that feelings of social ease are more shaped by temperament than by social status. After he had overcome his own embarrassment in public places, he no longer wished for his parents to have more social sophistication, instead delighting in their idiosyncrasies:

> I think it was the Ritz of which my mother said, 'It's a grand place. You can have anything you want – at least you can have egg and chips, which is what *we* want.' (Kingsley 1988: 83)

The social distinctions Bennett's parents made, as well as the way they saw themselves, were obviously heavily influenced by perceptions of class. Bennett, however, maintains that *Dinner at Noon* is not an observation to verify class-determined behaviour:

> ... a good social mix. I hope that's what the film's about. Not class, which I don't like, but classes, types, which I do; and a hotel like this is a good place to see them. (*Dinner*, in *WH*: 42)

In a review based on a short interview with Bennett, Madeleine Kingsley (1988: 83) points out that Bennett is not interested in class in the 'bold, three-tier divisive sense', but as an expression of individuality: 'as a magnifying glass of myriad human types'. Human behaviour that involves recipients is, according to the dramaturgical-behaviourist approach, impression management (Brissett and Edgley 1990: 17). The self is not seen as an entity, but as the meaning created from the process of self-expression (1990: 16), and is established only in interaction with the recipient. 'It is in the doings, not the minds and hearts, that selves emerge' (1990: 18). Apart from managing their behaviour in a public place, some of the hotel guests are also trying to act as if the camera was not there – so there are two layers of observation they have to take into account while 'just being themselves'. Some manage this better than others, prompting Bennett to satirise them from the sidelines, such as in the case of the Mayor's wife at a reception, who does not speak French and does not want to admit it. The annual disco held by the Boston Spa Tennis Club makes Bennett muse about 'the joys of the Zimmer Frame' (*Dinner* in *WH*: 49). There is one type of guest who will always have Bennett's full attention and respect: middle aged to elderly ladies, 'women in sensible shoes':

> I like ladies like Mrs Baker and Miss Wood – and don't think of them as old people. Just as Paris is geared to thirty-five-year-old career women, so is the North to women like these. In London they'd be displaced and fearful; here, accomplished pianists and stylish ballroom dancers, they still help rule the roost. (*Dinner*, in *WH*: 50)

The relevance of Goffman within *Dinner at Noon* would have been more obvious to audiences in 1988, as Bennett's autobiographical discourse was not in the public domain as much as it is now, nearly twenty years later. Both audiences and critics can become blinded by the familiar feature of Bennett talking about his childhood and about being embarrassed. The impression management that is undertaken to establish the self and the impression management undertaken to establish an authorial persona have obvious parallels, as both take place in the knowledge that meaning will be read into behaviour, ideally the meaning that the constructor intends. Audience perception means that work like this will be received in terms of what it reveals about *Bennett*, not how it transfers to others. Bennett plans but then withdraws the transparency between being and seeming for his self in this documentary, using 'real' settings and commentary. The audience is made aware of the performative behaviour of the people observed in the hotel, but will probably not realise that Bennett is part of this performance. It is he who puts on the performance, but the audience, preoccupied by the question of 'what he is really like', does not seem to realise that Bennett is performing Bennett. Wherever possible, behaviour will be categorised as familiar.

> In a sense, Goffman reaffirms ... that 'the imaginations which people have of one another are the solid facts of society' (Cooley 1902, quoted in Brissett and Edgley 1990: 87). So Goffman was about guises, semblances, veneers, surfaces, illusion, images, shells, and acts. He was not, as most scholars pompously try to bill themselves, about substances, things, facts, truths, and depths. (Brissett and Edgley 1990: 37)

The most interesting moments within observing behaviour as performance occur when there is a flaw in a performance, and suddenly the social front shows a crack (see Brissett and Edgley 1990: 38–9). Bennett frequently offers insight into the process of a failed performance by referring to his own persona. As with his characters, it is always apparent what the author is trying to achieve with his performance, but the failure of Bennett's impression management is then dissected with a self-awareness that is sometimes almost painful to watch. It also provides comic effects through its strong sense of self-mockery. Bennett describes the following scene at the British Film Week in Los Angeles, where *A Private Function* premiered in 1985. The British Ambassador introduced the director, the producer and Bennett, who were all sitting in different parts of the cinema:

> Mark [Shivas] is introduced first, the spotlight locates him, and there is scattered applause, then Malcolm [Mowbray] similarly. When my turn comes I stand up, but since I am sitting further back than the others the spotlight doesn't locate me. 'What's this guy playing at?' says someone behind. 'Sit down, you jerk.' So I do. The film begins. (*WH*: 193)

Such stories make the process of performing the self more transparent. An unsuccessful performance is easier to analyse, because a successful one will not be identified as a performance. Its performer's intention is for it to seem real, and if it does so, its success is in its deception for reality. For the discourse on being and seeming, an imperfect performance is also more useful. Furthermore, it shows different ways of perception. Where an insecure character's failure to perform convincingly may seem monstrously big to himself or herself, it is either not properly noticed by the surrounding 'audience' or interpreted as a different kind of performance. Bennett often manages to show both the way in which characters see themselves and how this differs in others' perception. Goffman's reader shares the sociologist's privilege of being able to see through performances given to particular means and becomes an 'insider'. This position of the privileged observer is very similar to the position of Bennett's audience. Bennett is a writer who empowers his reader through laying open his line of inquiry, just as Goffman makes his fieldwork findings available to the reader.

Bennett, at the end of *Dinner at Noon*, concludes that his field trip to research people's embarrassment in public places revealed that his own discomfort is not mirrored by the modern hotel guest: 'Class isn't what it was; or nowadays perhaps people's embarrassments are differently located' (*Dinner*, in *WH*: 60). At the end of the production, there was a cruel reminder for Bennett that nothing much had changed for him since he was sent to the tradesman's entrance decades earlier. Having bought a first class supplement, he was asked to leave his seat, as it was for 'proper First Class people' (*Dinner*, in *WH*: 61). In a parallel to the 1979 play *One Fine Day*, *Dinner at Noon* ends with a 'coda' of voices from its different characters:

> Environmental Health Officer: Today I feel very proud to stand before you.
> Old Man: It's a funny thing, this puberty business when you think of it, isn't it?

Lecturer: ... just keep taking pound notes from people and keep them smiling as you do it.

Old Lady: I used to come in my youth to Harrogate.

Receptionist: Crown Hotel, good morning. Can I help you?

(Dinner, in *WH*: 62)

The Bennett Persona: *Portrait or Bust*[3]

What makes Alan Bennett's stylish and witty diaries so remarkable is that this ostentatiously diffident and private playwright has turned himself into a public act. Alan Bennett is having a fantastic success playing Alan Bennett. (Buruma 1995: 15–18)

'I'd rather the public had an image, and not quite fit it. That way, you're free.'(Bennett in Adams 2000: 3)

This quotation implies that Alan Bennett sees his public and his private selves as separate. Moreover, he encourages the fact that there is a public image of himself, which he feels his 'real self' does not match. From an early stage, the concept of self plays a part in Bennett's work, as he comments on the contradiction of acquiring a voice through education in order to 'speak properly', but still being urged to 'be himself' by his family (*WH*: xii–xiii).

Somehow, we do manage to become our own persons over the course of time; we find that we become able to 'just be ourselves' rather than the imitative, other-driven beings we used to be. This is largely what is meant by the idea of identity. But isn't it also clear that the self ... is an idealization, an imaginary vision of completion? Can we ever really become the authors of our own actions, our own selves? (Freeman 1993: 66–7)

Freeman suggests that an identity is defined through being distinctive of others and relatively independent of former influences, but also concedes that identity cannot be finite, nor can it be separated from the influences that have shaped it.[4] Is it more convenient to claim to have two selves – one private and one public – rather than conceding that there is no such fixture as a self? Does this mean that there only has to be one fixture – the public self – and the other can be the true, liberated self? Bennett, always interested in concepts of self-representation, has made a contribution to this discussion with his 1999 play *The Lady in the Van,* where there is an Alan Bennett and an Alan Bennett 2.

An observation of Bennett as an Oxford Undergraduate shows that the author might have been aware from early on in his career that there were different versions of his self he could adopt:

Alan Bennett was not, in short, some student Garbo; he was, from the word go, a performer who – onstage and off – played versions of himself. The shrinking, querulous diffidence which made his vicar from *Beyond the Fringe* an instant classic was just a part of his act. (Preston 2001: 15)

In analogy with Bennett's pronounced interest in behaviourism (sometimes referred to as dramaturgy, here understood in the sociological rather than the theatrical sense), it should not be in the interest of the critic whether Bennett is being 'true to himself'. The focus of the analysis is his performance of himself. Bennett's persona passes as him, but is compared to a mask, made to look like his own face.

Portrait or Bust is a documentary just as personal as *Dinner at Noon*, and there is a sense of repeating a winning formula about it, with Bennett and Jonathan Stedall teaming up again. The two documentaries have in common that their focus is northern (Harrogate in *Dinner at Noon*, Leeds in *Portrait or Bust*) and site-specific (a hotel, an art gallery, and later a library).

Portrait or Bust accompanied an exhibition at Leeds City Art Gallery, *Mr Bennett's Pictures*, which Bennett curated in 1993. In the volume *Untold Stories*, the three pieces on Bennett's art outreach work, 'Going to the Pictures', 'Spoiled for Choice' (written for the scheme for art dissemination in schools) and 'Portrait or Bust',[5] based on the documentary, complement each other well. Although accessible, and designed to dispel notions of art as elitist, the documentary film *Portrait* is a text bristling with multiple layers. As in *Dinner*, Bennett's early life provides the narrative for the pictures Bennett has chosen to highlight. Landmarks in his art appreciation from an early age are told as stories, and are then taken as an opportunity to expand on his choice of pictures. Without exception, all the works of art chosen in the documentary (and thus in the exhibition) are wrapped up in Bennett's autobiographical narrative, and his sense of place for his home city, Leeds. The notion of bathos is very prominent, just as it is in Bennett's lecture at the National Gallery, where he, for example, brings saints and martyrs down to earth by transposing them into contemporary life, or equipping them with a contemporary voice: St Peter Martyr, Bennett claims, is only recognisable with an axe in his head, and he imagines him entering saying 'Hello everybody [pointing to the axe in his head] Remember me?' (*US*: 461). Just as Bennett cheerfully dismantles writers' monuments of eminence through musing on whether Proust would have been Proust had he been called Trevor, he creates disarming comedy through looking at art from unexpected angles. And so we hear about the common convention of painting Jesus without any bodily hair, and Bennett's association of his own torments in puberty, as a late developer. Bennett also shares the reason he dislikes Dutch landscape and marine paintings: 'it was because as a child I'd been given far too many pictures like them to do as jigsaws. So much sky and so many browns: they may be masterpieces, but as jigsaws they are a bugger' (*US*: 462).

The documentary *Portrait or Bust* starts with a simple version of the song 'Mona Lisa' on a piano. A canvas is being painted, and we then see the sitter for the emerging portrait: Alan Bennett, sitting for Tom Wood, who is painting his portrait, commissioned by the National Portrait Gallery. Bennett is seen to briefly acknowledge the camera, then speaks with pursed lips, not wanting to upset his pose during the sitting. He mutters his analysis of sitting for portraits, which he feels as uncomfortable about as his father did when posing for photographs: 'they tell you to be yourself – what they really mean is "imitate yourself"' (*Portrait or Bust*, television script, see note 3). And as if to show us a typical Bennett attribute, which will also appear in his portrait, there is a close-up of his hands holding a tea cup. And so Bennett performs himself for the rest of the programme, and the viewer settles into being instructed in his unhurried tones, always with a slight inflection and a drop of the voice at the end of the sentence.

When Leeds City Art Gallery is introduced, we approach it in a shot from above, and then see the figure of Bennett running up the stairs in long shot, just as he might have done in the 1940s, when he came to the gallery for a break from homework in next doors' Reference Library. Inside the Gallery, we are treated to a cleverly edited pastiche of visitors of all ages, with emphasis on old people and children. Bennett comments that 'old ladies are unfazed by the avant-garde, just as children are. Outrage is for middle age' (*Portrait*). Their way of approaching art from their own perspective and comparing it to things familiar to them suits Bennett, ever suspicious of pretence and jargon, and always eager to seize on connections with his own life.

A group of old ladies, shown through the gallery by a much younger outreach worker, obviously delighted Bennett and Stedall, as these ladies are given more footage and attention than any expert commentator. Unfazed though they are, they are convinced that their opinions are relevant, and are unapologetic for saying what they think. One old lady feels she is not being given due attention by the guide, and when the much younger woman tries to rectify her mistake by addressing a question about a picture directly to her, the old lady snaps 'I won't say now, I'll just keep it to myself'.

Although responding spontaneously to pictures, invariably the old ladies make their judgement on pictures based on whether they would like them in their homes. This resonates with Bennett, who claims never to have been able to separate 'appreciation from possession, so I know I like a picture only when I'm tempted to walk out with it under my raincoat' (*Portrait*, in *US*: 495). Bennett mistrusts monumental, emotional responses to art, but remarks that the trajectory of art history from appreciation to iconographic interpretation suited him well:

> To find, though, that paintings could be decided, that they were intellectual as well as aesthetic experiences, was something of a relief because it straightaway put them in a familiar and much more English context if only because a lot of iconography, saying who's who and what's what in a painting, could be taken as a higher form of that very English preoccupation, gossip. (*Portrait*, in *US*: 458)

The notion of performing the self is also given emphasis by one of the old ladies, who has obviously been told to pretend the camera is not there, but who cannot quite avoid acknowledging it, or including the person behind the camera in her remarks. Pleased with herself for liking a modern and very colourful picture, she confirms 'It's good, very nice', smiling and nodding delightedly at the camera. Together with Bennett and his personal way of talking to his viewers, this old ladies' direct address heightens the inclusiveness of *Portrait*.

The other noticeable 'performer' is an elderly man who has a very loud voice and a restless, manic demeanour. He is taking his brief of being a gallery visitor very seriously (and has probably been told to 'just be himself'), and does not cross the camera threshold as such. However, his behaviour is entirely performative, shouting, so as to make sure his voice can be heard. Interestingly, the old man's remarks are all about biography: an artist called 'Jack Yeats' makes him tell his companion that this is the brother of W.B. Yeats, makes the same connection between Stanley and Gilbert Spencer, and tells confused and biographical anecdotes about the painters whose names he thinks he recognises. Going into a room with contemporary sculpture and painting, the man exclaims cheerfully 'Ah, modern art – I shan't understand anything at all!', and then, after looking at a painting for a few seconds, triumphantly confirms: 'This, I don't understand!' His excited ramblings are at one point intercut with a man sleeping peacefully on a sofa in one of the gallery's rooms.

As Bennett slowly walks through the gallery, he appears in the background of shots, out of focus, an unobtrusive but nonetheless alert eavesdropper. Again, this is similar to *Dinner*, where we are given the opportunity to overhear people's conversations, but it is made clear that this is the material from which Bennett distils his work.

We see the exhibition rooms over Bennett's shoulder, and the camera moves to a frontal shot when he starts telling the story of his first visit to the Gallery during World War II at the age of eight. Class Standard 3 from Upper Armley National School was meant to listen to a rendition of 'Pedro the Fisherman' with their teacher, Miss Timpson, but were soon distracted. At this point, Bennett softly whistles the same song, accompanying a contemporary class of primary school children who are just entering one of the gallery's spaces. On Bennett's 1940s visit, some boys noticed a vast canvas of a scene depicting the aftermath of a battle. One wounded warrior was being tended to by 'a striking figure (what my mother would have called 'a big woman') – bold, scornful ... with whom she is on familiar terms, because she has torn aside her bodice and, standing back from the prostrate figure, displays an ample breast' (*Portrait*, in *US*: 496) Some classmates were already sniggering at the picture and the uncommon sight of a breast, but their 'mirth turned to awe' when they saw that the woman, possibly Boudicea, was expressing the contents of her breast into the mouth of the wounded warrior from a considerable distance. It is this, of course, not heroic art, that impresses eight-year-olds. Bennett, with usual forensic detail, describes his own reaction. Intrigued and excited, he was nevertheless mindful of his reputation and did not want to risk it – therefore 'I hedge my bets, keeping one eye on Miss Timpson while stealing looks at this extraordinary canvas' (*Portrait*, in *US*: 497). Also, the accuracy of the squirted milk reminds him of his own inadequacy, in this case his inability to spit over large distances, as some of his bolder classmates can. Bennett re-enacts his dialogue with Miss Timpson as a precocious child in a minimalist but animated way:

> 'Miss,' I asked innocently, 'is this what they mean by succouring the wounded?'

> 'No, Alan,' said Miss Timpson crisply, 'it is what they mean by smut. But very good. Do any of you others know the word "succour"? And what are you smirking about, Roland Ellis, perhaps you can spell it?'

> 'S-U-C-K-E-R,' says Roland Ellis proudly, and is mystified to get a clip over the ear.

> (*Portrait*, in *US*: 498)

Bennett's childhood narrative is complemented by pictures that enforce a sense of place, for example, Atkinson Grimshaw's painting of Park Row in Leeds. Bennett introduces this picture while his face is mirrored in the glass covering the picture. This then cross-fades to a view of Leeds townscape, and continues in a series of shots that juxtapose classic nineteenth-century civic architecture with 1960s concrete high-rise buildings, and glass-fronted, anonymous blocks.

Specialising in 'ready made suits and rhubarb' from his early childhood onwards, Leeds had an air of the 'safe, innocent and dull', Bennett comments (*Portrait*). To illustrate this, he tells the tale of the City Art Gallery's evacuation of its pictures to Temple Newsam. In contrast to the furtive and adventurous campaign of the National Gallery, transporting their pictures to a disused mine in Wales, the unassuming journey with the pictures on the tram seems to symbolise the provincial status of Leeds. The story is illustrated by interchanging shots of old and new trams and buses making their way through two very different versions of Leeds. Bennett's excursion to Temple Newsam, the site of the gallery's evacuation, ends with his pensive, solitary figure walking down a long corridor in silhouette, shot from behind.

The footage of Leeds City Art Gallery is then contrasted with the National Gallery in London, brimming with metropolitan importance and grandeur and accompanied by festive music by Handel. The unveiling of Bennett's portrait by Tom Wood is shown. Bennett's pose is frontal, but looking sideways, up to his left, head propped up on his left arm. The props are familiar and enigmatic. The tea cup will provide a welcome association for Bennett lovers, the brown paper bag and the plug pointing towards Bennett are less clear in their attribution. When it comes to the actual unveiling, the camera switches between Bennett's portrait and more classic ones, George III in particular showing a very similar pose to that of the playwright who staged his madness only a few years previously. Bennett's portrait has provided a frame to the documentary's narrative. Characteristically, the footage of the celebration for its unveiling ends with the picture being wheeled out, possibly to the stores, for later exhibition ('if one is lucky', remarks Bennett, not really expecting this).

Although it is not the last shot in the documentary, it is appropriate here to end with a little boy in Leeds City Art Gallery, as Bennett also places him at the end of his essay based on the film. The boy is seen deciphering the label on a small Barbara Hepworth sculpture, then looking up at it, smiling, and remarking confidently 'It's good, is that!'. This is a joyful image, underlining what impact the free use of galleries and libraries might have in the boy's future. Yet, Bennett muses that the government is actively dismantling the spirit of free education that is at the core of his own success and development:

> I see myself fifty years ago and I know that through no fault of his own he [the boy] is going to have a harder time of it than I had. And I think that is wrong. (*Portrait*, in *US*: 514)

And to the whistling and singing of 'Pedro the Fisherman' by the Little London Primary School, Leeds, this poignant exploration of art, public and personal history concludes.

The Abbey: Englishness and subversion

> Alan Bennett has done three films for television about Westminster Abbey. He's brilliant and they're wholly compelling, but he's in danger of self-parody, of his modesty becoming a form of pride, backing diffidently into the limelight to castigate those who hungered for 'fame', 'wealth' and 'power'. (Eyre 2003: 320)

Although it has the same 'winning team' to the previous two documentaries, *The Abbey* differs considerably from *Dinner* and *Portrait*. It shows a few parallels with John Betjeman's documentary *A Passion for Churches* (1974). To use an analogy, in his essay accompanying *Portrait or Bust*, Bennett comments on a dog in a drawing by Rembrandt:

> He's one of Rembrandt's frisky and utterly non-symbolic dogs. Maybe that's why he's frisky, because he knows he doesn't have to represent fidelity or trust or anything at all from Hall's Dictionary of Subjects and Symbols. He's just happy to be All Dog. (*Portrait,* in *US:* 501)

In comparison with *Dinner* and *Portrait, The Abbey* is happy to be 'All Documentary'. Its first part was broadcast at Christmas 1995 – a treat for the nation from one of its national treasures? Bennett is a significant presence in the three parts, and history is presented to us through his eyes. The Bennett persona in *The Abbey* is a balance between his two professions: the original one of historian, and that of the performing writer. He makes far fewer connections with his life than he does in the preceding documentaries, and the narrative is not shaped as much by personal experience and comparison as are the previous two documentaries. This said, in the way the script is presented, illustrated with footage from the Abbey and juxtaposed with Bennett's idiosyncratic comparisons, *The Abbey* is every bit as recognisably 'Bennett' as are the other documentaries he has produced. Atmospheric shots of the building's splendour are blended with choral singing from the Abbey Choir, and show respect and admiration. Bennett's script is not 'cosy' history, however, and mixes the sublime with the ridiculous, as we have come to expect. Although all these programmes are about the past, contemporary politics are made more meaningful when scrutinised alongside a historical comparison. Bennett compares the dissolution of the monasteries to privatisation, saying with slight cynicism that its barbarity must be more understandable from a late twentieth-century perspective, as redundancies (of monks and of employees) are seen as a short-term 'fix' for the government. Equally, Bennett brings the Abbey in line with the English psyche, featuring those well-known signifiers of biography, gossip, non-conformity, embarrassment and liking of clubs.

In *The Abbey*, Bennett does what a good historian might do within a popular context: he evokes a sense of the building, its monuments and its meaning to the nation, but in its own period. His description of the 'tremendous surprise' of the Lady Chapel, commissioned by Henry VII, communicates the 'last great flowering of mediaeval Christianity', every inch of it originally painted in bright colours. Detailed shots of the now grey interior accompany this, as Bennett explains that its glory was cut short by the start of the Reformation. In the next shot, a duster is seen moving over the tombs in the Lady Chapel, then cutting to a milkman delivering to the living quarters. The chapel's history was cut short; it is now preserved and rendered historical, while outside, contemporary life goes on.

Bennett refers to himself as 'just an eavesdropper', and he assumes this pose, just as he did in the other documentaries. When approaching the Abbey School, for example, Bennett is seen sitting in the cloisters outside, and we can hear the sound of a lesson being held inside. As it turns out, Bennett can also hear, as he answers the teacher's question with 'I don't know' from outside the classroom. Bennett and Stedall's approach is never sanctimonious, and sometimes quite mischievous, as in a sequence where visitors are listening to a guided tour. The camera furtively moves in on one visitor whose hairstyle and moustache make him seem as if he is trying to imitate the look of Adolf Hitler. At that moment, the viewer realises that the English guide's speech is counterpointed by another guide's voice, who is talking in staccato-like (because amplified) German. This non-sequitur snapshot is not commented on further, remaining an odd little *trouvaille*.

Bennett demonstrates the variety of Westminster Abbey, ranging from bureaucracy to theatricality (the guides in many different languages, all of them coming across as skilled performers). Naturally, Bennett focuses on features that separate the Abbey from other churches, and confirms it in its status as 'A Royal Peculiar' (also the title of the first part of the series). Central to this is, of course, Poet's Corner. Bennett's evaluation of this particular peculiarity exudes scepticism: he is wary of the 'Christopher Robin, Peter Pan, tourist board notion of Englishness' and the 'safe and cosy' version of English Literature with which it might align some of the dead writers – Auden, for example, who left Britain for its oppressive cosiness, but who is buried here, Bennett remarks, in the cosiest corner. Wordsworth, buried in such a confined and crowded space, is 'less lonely than a cloud' Bennett remarks, also noting in a burst of alliteration that the marble poet's pen has been taken by 'prying prizing fingers'. This section, commenting on the familiar territory of writers and assumptions about their lives, as well as posthumous modifications to reputations, is based on the ideas inherent in all his works about life, art, and writing in particular (see Chapter 3).

Bennett values the Abbey above all for its enduring independence and non-conformity, something his viewers have probably come to value in Bennett's presentations of history and the past by the mid 1990s:

> Were the Abbey run as the country's run, they (the non-conformists or 'the awkward squad' such as Milton, Shelley and Charles James Fox) would not get a mention. But this thank god is an independent place, conformity won't get you in, nor money, nor bullying. It is indeed a peculiar.

Bennett and Englishness

Bennett's artistic persona seems to mirror both the qualities and the insecurities that are seen as central to the English character. Yet he has been described, for example, as an 'anomaly' (Bull 1994: 10) amongst contemporary playwrights, serving to enforce a safe concern with the past and writing to reinforce the political status quo (the 'whimper of continuing decline', Bull 1994: 11). The shy, cycle-clipped neurotic with an accent that gravitates between Oxford and Leeds is the foundation on which Bennett develops contradictions. It gives him the freedom to accommodate his being in two minds. Bennett's political 'colour', for example, is difficult to pin down. In the 1970s he described himself as 'politically left-wing but socially right wing' (Carpenter 2001: 22).[6] This self-assessment is one of the keys to understanding Bennett, who wrote against Thatcherism, refused to condemn the Cambridge Spies as traitors, turned down an honorary doctorate from Oxford because of the creation of the Rupert Murdoch Chair, but has made a passionate protest against the replacement of The Book of Common Prayer in *Writing Home*. Nicholas de Jongh (1990) remarks that Bennett may lack party political punch, but 'there's no missing his political and social courage'. *Getting On* (1971), for example, is a play about the scheming duality of a Labour MP, and effectively a critique of Harold Wilson's government. Seeking an alternative in the SDP in the 1980s, Bennett's hatred of the Thatcher government drove him to disowning his Englishness at the invasion of Port Stanley: 'this is just where I happen to have been put down. No country. No party. No Church. No voice' (*WH*: 168). Margaret Thatcher's re-election in 1983 made him 'spit blood'. This anger has found its way into his works, especially the season of television plays, *Objects of Affection* (1982) and the play *The Madness of George III* (1991), where William Pitt the Younger is presented as an early propagator of

Thatcherism. Bennett expresses strong opinions, but often approaches a problem or a conflict from several angles. His characteristic of being in two minds has been interpreted as timidity, when it should be seen as investigation, prompted by thorough thinking. Bennett remarks on the way his popularity and his ambiguity seem to produce a political void: 'An article on playwrights in the *Daily Mail*, listed according to Hard Left, Soft Left, Hard Right, Soft Right and Centre. I am not listed. I should probably come under Soft Centre. (*WH*: 117). Bennett seems to be a Labour traditionalist, displaying beliefs in social welfare and in 'fair shares for all', but at the same time showing respect for Queen and Church, associated more with reformist socialism.

Bennett's autobiographical discourses can be seen to enforce owner-ship of a life that almost works as a shield to ward off intruders threat-ening to usurp his 'real' life. Thus, the autobiographical trajectory of Bennett's career moves towards finding creative solutions that allow his life as source, but avoid being judged on it.

Hiding and stripping: strategies of autobiography

> Sometimes, particularly in summers in New York, I have tried to write in shorts or with no shirt on and found myself unable to do so, the reason being, I take it, that writing, even of the most impersonal sort, is for me a kind of divestment, a striptease even, so that if I start off undressed I have nowhere to go. (*US*: 547)

Bennett has often spoken about autobiographical writing in terms of exhibitionism or voyeurism: exposure, unmasking, and, as above, as a striptease. For a long time, confessions were guarded, exposure was coded. Bennett's prefaces, however, pre-empted the personal and confes-sional material of later autobiographical works such as *The Lady in the Van*, sometimes by many years. It must be assumed that, for Bennett, the prefaces must be a 'safe' place, if he chooses to undergo rigorous self-scrutiny in full view of the reader. In doing so, he strengthens his position when facing critics of his work: he will normally have pointed out mistakes before any critic can do so, or will have collated critical views that were formulated when the work was first shown without its protective framework. The in-between status of the prefaces contributes to the thesis of their relative safety: Bennett smuggles in personal reve-lations, but they can always be claimed as not being part of the *actual* work, giving the author space for ambiguity.

It is difficult to find a work of Bennett's that does not come with an explanation of the reasons for its shortcomings. The inherent apology can be compared to the classical rhetorical figure of *captatio benevolen-tiae*. It translates as 'the capturing of [the audience's] benevolence'. The speaker or author points out the shortcomings of his work, seemingly appealing to the audience to be generous and understanding. One of the most well-known examples is the beginning of *Henry V*, where the Chorus introduces the scene by apologising for its sparseness.[7] Apart from the introductory function of the Chorus's words, there is a clear sense of lowering expectations, and gaining sympathy in return. Often, *captatio benevolentiae* has an air of 'tongue in cheek' about it. This is evident from the prologue of *Henry V*: an audience will not come to the theatre expecting 'the vast fields of France', so there will be no disappointment in receiving the address by the Chorus, but more a sense of flattery ('benevolence') at being spoken to with such reverence, and being asked kindly to accept what has been produced for their entertainment.

As Stephen Frears points out,[8] the understanding of the importance of modesty to Bennett's generation is paramount to the understanding of the self-deprecating tone of Bennett talking about himself: 'That generation was brought up to be self-effacing, modest and not to take themselves too seriously.' Talking about oneself is seen as 'showing off', so if one *does* talk about oneself, one must dismiss it as unimportant. Coming back to Bennett, this does not, however, mean that one wants others to take that line, too. Frears remembers Bennett talking to a journalist about *A Day Out*, his first television play. Bennett described it as 'not very much', which was replicated by the journalist in his article, causing frustration with writer and director. The rationale is that, because of modest delivery, the personal vanity of the artist clears the way for admiration of the actual *work*. It can be argued that Bennett occasionally employs the device of *captatio benevolentiae*, particularly when talking about his work, or in a preface or introduction. An example: at a platform presentation of *George III* at the National Theatre, Bennett said how he had always felt pleasure and excitement when, at the very beginning of the play, the King and Queen and their Court came down the enormous staircase centre stage. After he had finished, there was a brief pause, after which he said in a cheerful tone 'Not that that had anything to do with me, of course.'[9] It was this cheerfulness and the routine delivery of the phrase that hinted at the possibility that this was a well-practised way in which Bennett ruled out any kind of conceptions of him as 'aloof' or a 'show-off'. He made sure the audience's sympathy was captured. In interview, both Peter Hall and Stephen Frears immediately dismissed suggestions of Bennett declaring his inferiority through these frequent put-downs of himself.

Bennett could be seen as a moderator between his work and his audience, sometimes deliberately positioning himself (or his persona) in between the play text and its introduction, guiding the reader's perception of his work. He therefore volunteers his technique, his motivation for writing the piece that is to follow, and, above all, his opinions and evaluations of his own work. That this initially takes place outside the actual piece, or is at least formally separate from it, could be seen as a safety measure – at least this information is not inside the actual work he is preparing the reader for. Thus exposed, Bennett awaits judgement by his reader, whom he has equipped with as the knowledge, rationale and gossip he considers necessary.

Bennett has made clear that he resents biographers, journalists or academics 'doing' him (Bennett used this expression talking to a journalist from the *Independent*, who was writing his profile: 'you're doing me'). It might be seen as hypocritical that Bennett, 'protesting too much', claims not to want any revelation, but provides revelations himself throughout the 1990s. However, it is here not seen as paradoxical that a decision was obviously made that henceforth the only personal information would come from Bennett, in his own terms, at a time set by himself and in his own form and wording. This leads to the conclusion that it is of great importance to Bennett to retain ownership of his life and of his self within his texts. Autobiography is sold as something the public demands, and which the author (seemingly grudgingly) provides, preferring to do it himself, before the invaders (the biographers, the journalists, the academics) get it wrong. Bennett the biographer knows the impulse of biographical investigation and the literary (that is, unreliable) editing of information the construction of somebody else's life involves. Bennett's resentment of biographical writing on him is in line with what Jürgen Schläger (in Batchelor 1995: 57) describes as follows:

> Biography ... is a discourse of usurpation. The truth-criterion does not consist in the authenticity of an inside view but in the consistency of the narrative and the explanatory power of the arguments.

In 2001, Alexander Games produced an unauthorised biography of Alan Bennett. When *Backing into the Limelight* was published, critics commented on the fact that the biography did not provide any new revelations on Bennett's life beyond those already in circulation:

> [H]e [Bennett] was, from the word go, a performer who – on stage and off – played versions of himself. ... And any biography worth its salt has to grapple with that amorphous duality. (Preston 2001: 15)

It was 'the real Bennett' everyone was interested in, and consequently, the conclusion was drawn that a more ruthless investigator should have been given the commission to write the book. The lack of ground-breaking new facts is partly due to Bennett's refusal to co-operate with Games, a refusal that seemed to extend to most of his friends and colleagues. There is no lack of material available on Bennett, and, for want of the author's participation, Games declared his work that of a chronicler and of an eavesdropper (Games 2001: 4). He freely admits he cannot present a straightforward answer to the central question of what Bennett 'is really like', but can only show patterns and investigate parallels between life and art. After a chance encounter with Bennett in the street in Camden Town, which saw the playwright running away, Games decided that one of his aims was to conduct 'an investigation into why Alan Bennett is running away' (Games 2001: 6) from journalists, admirers, biographers and academics.[10] Games mainly reads Bennett's personal life through his works, doing in effect what many readers do: reading the work to know more about the life, Games' archival research suggests that there is a pattern that takes shape earlier than assumed, and that Bennett had a public self before he became a well-known public figure. If one is convinced by Games' findings, Bennett has retrospectively created the wistful, inarticulate persona, when in reality he was a performer at an early stage.[11] Games points out that the accumulated picture points to Bennett as 'opinionated, articulate, self-possessed, and nowhere near as hunched or crab-like as he has made himself out to be' (Games 2001: 24). When describing these contradictions between the supposed Bennett person and the constructed persona, Games is doing what is expected of him as a biographer: uncovering, comparing and searching for early determining factors for later patterns.

For Alan Bennett, Games' biography increased the urgency of claiming his life back by writing it down himself:

> Knowing there is not much to be done to prevent such an enterprise, I had given the author no help but not made much of a fuss about it. When the book came out it was thought to be kind but dull, not unlike its subject, with the author complaining rather forlornly about how little help he'd received in his self-imposed task. Still, it was the publication of this book that made me press on with my own autobiographical efforts and start thinking of them as pre-posthumous. (*US*: xii)

Bennett's other trigger to write more 'explicit' autobiographical material was the diagnosis of cancer of the bowel in 1997, making it more urgent to tidy up his 'Nachlass'. Bennett's decision to bring his life out of its former protective disguise seems like a charging forward out of the realisation that a controlled *autobiographical* output might keep biographical usurpation at bay. This explains Bennett's seemingly illogical reaction to the increasing demand for revelation: detailed introductions are like pre-emptive strikes, Bennett acting on his fear of being exposed by others through exposing himself on his own terms.

> Ultimately, autobiography is a discourse of anxiety. Autobiographers have to be true to themselves and true to the image they would like to present to the public or to posterity. Very often these two obligations are extremely difficult to reconcile. (Schläger in Batchelor 1995: 57)

Bennett is therefore fighting off the biographical usurpation, and trading it in for exposing his life in a discourse of anxiety. This exposure does not seem to come out of a spirit of confidence, but out of the necessity Bennett feels to tell his own story, according to how he wishes his life to be presented. Bennett has experienced exposure of people close to him (the press's 'hounding' of Russell Harty before his death, for example), and has been the victim of tabloid exposure himself (the uproar the *Daily Mail* caused by revealing Bennett's and Anne Davies' *heterosexual* affair, for example). It is important to understand that the trauma of 'uncontrolled' exposure is transferred to his works from encounters in Bennett's life. In *Writing Home* and in the title piece of *Untold Stories*,[12] Bennett's parents are also shown to suffer from fear of exposure and discovery: his mother could not cope with the notion of being 'the centre-piece'. On occasions where this was inevitably the case, such as the time before her wedding, or after a move to a small Dales village, she experienced serious episodes of depression and delusion. Bennett's father enforced the idea that exposure equalled 'showing-off' by showing dislike for Bennett demonstrating intelligence and inquisitiveness as a child, and doubting he was telling the truth on a number of occasions. When Bennett was molested by a man in a cinema and ran home 'in mild distress', his mother became 'satisfyingly hysterical':

> [B]ut Dad, a shy and fastidious man who I knew regarded me as a liar and a show-off, was just made angry, refusing even to believe anything had happened and, if it had, 'It was all nowt.' Certainly I hadn't been damaged, and if damage was done at all it was only in Dad's refusal to acknowledge the situation. (*US*: 162)

Bennett has stated that he has felt frustrated by overly simple connections made about the way he presents his life in his works. It is therefore believed that Bennett has attempted a solution of 'controlled exposure' in order to regain artistic control over his life. Through providing this information, Bennett has chosen to be a 'stripper' rather than a 'hider' (see Schläger in Batchelor 1995: 58). Recalling the title of this chapter, Bennett metaphorically strips out of his own accord, at a pace and in a style that suit him, rather than having his clothes taken off by force. The amount of 'life' Bennett exposes in his works seems to be increasing ('stripping'), while his collaboration with investigators of his life and the part it plays in his art is decreasing ('hiding'). Closely interdependent, the two tendencies move in opposite directions. We can visualise this by applying the *chiasmus* model of connected opposite movement (Greek: 'a placing crosswise', from the name of the Gr. letter 'chi'), which expresses the tension between Bennett's urge for self-revelation and secrecy:

It is suggested in summary that Bennett's life writing does not prioritise the narration of events as they really happened, but the fact that he wants to tell his story in his own, unmediated way.

Notes

1 Bennett's diaries have been published in the *London Review of Books* annually each January since 1981, apart from 2001. Entries for the years 1980–95 appear in the volume *Writing Home*; entries from 1996–2004 in *Untold Stories*.

2 I am grateful to my neighbour, Simon Child, for clarifying the use of this expression.

3 There are two pieces of the same title, the television documentary and the accompanying essay, published in *Untold Stories* in 2005.The quotations are taken from the documentary and, as the script itself has not been published, are not paginated.

4 David Hume (*A Treatise on Human Nature*, 1739–40) states that the idea of a self 'beyond the evidence of a demonstration, both of its perfect identity and simplicity' is fictitious, due to the absence of constant impression, and the fluctuation of influence (quoted in Freeman, *Rewriting the Self: History, Memory, Narrative*, London: Routledge, 1993: 69).

5 *Portrait* refers to the documentar, *Portrait*, in *US* to the essay of the same name.

6 Games (*Backing into the Limelight: The Biography of Alan Bennett*, London: Headline, 2001: 2) describes Bennett as 'politically liberal, architecturally conservative'.

7   But pardon, gentles all,
    The flat unraised spirits that hath dar'd
    On this unworthy scaffold to bring forth
    So great an object. Can this cockpit hold

The vast fields of France? Or may we cram
Within this wooden O the very casques
That did affright the air at Agincourt?
O, pardon! since a crooked figure may
Attest in little place a million;
...
Admit me Chorus to this history;
Who, prologue-like, your humble patience pray,
Gently to hear, kindly to judge, our play.
(*Henry V*, Prologue)

8 Interview with Stephen Frears, London, 31 December 2002.

9 Platform *George III*, National Theatre, London, 16 November 1999.

10 Bennett declared in the *Guardian* (25 May 1992; see Games, *Backing into the Limelight*, 2001: 245) that 'not to be interviewed is the only answer', although several profiles have appeared since 1992.

11 For example, Games points out that Bennett won the Declamation Prize and the Leeds Institute Sixth Form Prize in 1950/51, became honorary secretary of the Literary and Historical Society and was made senior prefect. This contradicts the shy, ill at ease and inarticulate presence Bennett 'sells' as his earlier persona.

12 This piece was later integrated into a long essay of the same title, and published in Bennett's 2005 autobiographical volume, also called *Untold Stories*.

5

'They want to be seen as they see themselves': reinventing the monologue

Talking Heads 1 and *2*

Despite shying away from rejection and wanting to please, Bennett is always trying to fight 'niceness'. 'It can't just be being nice. Nice is so dull', as one of the two Alan Bennetts remarks in *The Lady in the Van* (28). Audiences will not register the use of swearwords, graphic language, or think of murderers or paedophiles in connection with Bennett. Yet most of his plays approach dangerous subjects, both thematically and linguistically, as this chapter aims to show.

Meet Graham. He lives with his elderly mother, who refers to him as her 'boyfriend'. This is not how he would like us to see him, but gradually, he unmasks himself as a mentally instable closet homosexual who is jealous of his mother's late flowering.

Meet Lesley. She is an actress, 'professional to my fingertips'. Her conversations with directors, however, do not centre around Stanislavski, but on whether she suits their demands for the latest porn flick.

Meet Muriel. Her husband has died, having possibly abused their daughter in the past. Meanwhile her son speculates away her inheritance and leaves her isolated and penniless. To admit this, however, would add to her shame.

These are all characters from the first series of *Talking Heads 1*. The monologues follow other Bennett plays in showing us the fissure between 'seeming' and 'being' and in addressing the concept of 'behaviour as performance'. What is often overlooked, however, is their formal and generic innovation. Todorov (in Chandler 2000: 4) remarks that 'a new genre is always the transformation of one or several old genres,' and this is certainly true for *Talking Heads*. The form of the monologue is, as Bennett remarks, the oldest form in theatre: a person telling a story. In theatre, the convention at first mainly existed as part of larger dramatic structures, ranging from a brief aside to a lengthy soliloquy. During the twentieth century, the monologue has emerged as a theatrical form of its own. The television monologue is a recent expansion of this development.

The *Talking Heads* monologues are Bennett's most widely known work for television. After the success of the first series in 1988, he wrote and co-produced a second series in 1998. The plays are cast with well-known actors (most of them with careers both on stage and screen) such as Maggie Smith, Penelope Wilton or Eileen Atkins. Patricia Routledge, Thora Hird and Julie Walters appear both in the first and second series, Routledge's and Hird's pieces written specially for them. Both series generated a large amount of merchandise with continuing successful sales figures: videos, audiotapes and scripts. The scripts for the first series were published at the time of their first transmission, and the volume *The Complete Talking Heads* (*CTH*) was published at the time of the transmission of the second series, in late 1998. The simultaneous availability of the monologues on screen and in print demonstrates confidence in their success. *Talking Heads* have continued to be highly successful in different adaptations, such as audio recordings and stage versions. The monologues transferred to the stage soon after they were broadcast.[1] No textual changes were made, and it is up to directors, actors and scenographers to adapt the monologues for the stage.

The first series of *Talking Heads* was put on the A-level syllabus in the early 1990s, ensuring young and diverse readers' familiarity with an author who is more often associated with middle-aged, middle-class audiences. As a consequence of *Talking Heads'* success, Bennett now dominates the market for the genre of monologue, and all monologue plays, be they for stage or screen, are compared to his work. A steady stream of monologues in the *Talking Heads* style are sent to television production companies and producing theatres, and are mostly rejected because they are too similar to Bennett's monologues. The Literary Manager of the West Yorkshire Playhouse,[2] for example, remarks that the market for monologues by authors other than Bennett is saturated. If monologues by other authors *do* go into production, critics normally complain either that the authors are imitating Bennett's voice, or that Bennett himself has better contributions to make to the genre. *Talking Heads* has proved to be a benchmark for the television monologue.

Talking Heads and monologue conventions

The monologues, although *formally* providing a shift from Bennett's other work, employ well-established thematic and linguistic patterns.[3]

> He [Bennett] allows us to overhear them saying what remains unspoken in their [the *Talking Heads* protagonists'] fictional world, a world whose

> presence and pressures on the characters are convincingly included. Monologues by definition cannot use several defining features of drama: the interaction of characters, dialogue, the meeting and clashing of voices and points of view, the population of the world of the play by other characters. However, Bennett manages to create a detailed network of relationships for each *Talking Head* by means of reported conversations with others. (Turner 1997: 59)

The monologues are formally simple, but generically complex. 'Talking heads' is a phrase used to describe a talk-dominated, visually static programme or programme section on television, typically a news programme, or other formats associated with factuality broadcasting rather than drama. The choice of title, and the fact that Bennett originally intended to call the monologues 'Dull Lives', comes across as ironic insistence that the pieces are unspectacular and visually unexciting.

> Though none of these characters are bores I'm not sure I'd want to get saddled with them on a long railway journey. I wouldn't mind eavesdropping, though, overhearing them talking to someone else which is, I suppose, what I've ended up doing in these programmes. (Bennett in *Radio Times* 1988)

Bennett's remark about 'eavesdropping' mirrors the real-life attitude most of us would have towards the *Talking Heads* protagonists. We would be intrigued, and happy to observe, but would not want to get involved. Bennett challenges this instinctive avoidance through the televisual framing. He also lowers expectations, leaving the viewer to realise that instead of dullness and simplicity, the monologues demonstrate the complexity, subtlety and formal innovation of his work.

The monologue as an independent form has mainly been a feature of twentieth-century literature, and often takes place by one actor impersonating or representing several characters. Alan Bennett calls the *Talking Heads* 'monologues' or 'monologue plays'. Delia Dick (1999) points out that the correct term would probably be 'monopolylogues', as the character re-enacts many others. On a basic level, a monologue is defined as 'a literary device used to convey innermost thoughts and feelings of a character'.[4] This definition leaves open whether the monologue is self-contained or part of a play, although the latter is more commonly referred to as a 'soliloquy'. Here, a character, alone on stage, may voice thoughts too personal or too dangerous to convey to others, or consults with himself or herself on a dilemma, expressing thoughts aloud. Dramaturgically, a soliloquy is often needed in order to equip the audience with information necessary to their understanding of the plot, but cannot be heard by any other characters participating in a play. For the purpose of this study, a 'monologue' is defined as a self-contained piece of theatre, and a 'soliloquy' as part of a larger framework.

The character types, the settings and the iconography in *Talking Heads* are often modelled on ordinary people and places, without adapting any particular life, although Bennett's family is a strong influence. Often, an overheard phrase or an image might have sparked off the creation of one of Bennett's characters. A pushy boy at an audition proved the earliest ancestor for Lesley in *Her Big Chance*; the phrase 'Get lost Jesus' written in 'tiny, timid letters in a prayer book' proved the starting point for the vicar's wife Susan in *Bed Among the Lentils*, who 'hasn't got much time for God' (Bennett in *Radio Times* 1988). The monologues have a certain documentary, mimetic quality. They deal with the lives of unspectacular people, but signal that these lives are worthy of being presented in minute detail and that attention must be paid while these characters are placed centre-stage. Some of the characters are as trapped in their lives as many an Ibsen character, and there is a sense that the future will not see them breaking free from their confines, imposed by habit, class, circumstance and fear of change. Some of the monologues reveal glimpses of what might be if restrictions disappeared.

Talking Heads' kind of realism is considered to be different from the 'realisms' generally employed in Bennett's other work for television:

> These [*Talking Heads*] are not naturalistic pieces but even plays that claim to be faithful accounts of ordinary life can seldom accommodate this garrulous intruder [a television set]. The world of everything that is the case is not the world of drama. (*CTH*: 124)

Here, Bennett shows understanding of the genre's ambivalent relationship with realism, also due to its convention of a character speaking alone, but 'everything that is the case is not the world of drama' is something that has become important for Bennett, particularly in his writing for the stage. According to Williams (1968), the monologue is particularly clear in showing the paradox of realism in the theatre: wanting to represent life as accurately as possibly, but being in an inescapably artificial situation for the purpose of doing so.[5] Clemen (1972: 148) points out, that 'the convention of the monologue with its lack of psychological probability and its artificiality has often been a stumbling block to critics'. Gottsched (quoted in Clemen 1972), for example, remarks that 'clever people do not speak aloud when they are alone'.[6] The setting of a soliloquy contradicts conventions of naturalism, but is often part of a play that has naturalistic characteristics. This is particularly evident in soliloquies in Shakespeare's plays, where they can have a range of different functions. The opening monologue in *Richard III*, for example, provides essential information for the audience, both within the exposition of the plot and Richard's own introduction of his character. This introduction also contains an element of self-exploration, but then moves towards the revelation of the protagonist's plans. Clemen (1972: 153) states that 'the plan laid open before us is a ready-made one, we are not present – as in later soliloquies – while it is hatched.' While Richard is expressing thoughts and character traits too private or dangerous for any other characters' ears, the protagonist still seems to be speaking and 'editing' for an extradiegetic audience. The performer seems to be conscious of this audience without making any reference to this consciousness. It is possible to see this convention in *Talking Heads*, where 'thoughts and feelings of a character are conveyed' (*Colliers Encyclopaedia*). It is difficult to add 'innermost', however, as there is always the impression that the character is holding back some information, and 'editing' his or her narrative. As in the opening monologue of *Richard III*, the nature of the *Talking Heads* monologues will often be tailored towards self-presentation or self-justification rather than self-revelation.

> Given the monologue convention, then, the potentially dramatic material described above is distanced by the single narrating voice, who has already experienced it, worked it through, and frequently treats it with irony and humour. (Rose 1993: 539)

Patricia Routledge in *Miss Fozzard Finds Her Feet* offers a useful example for self-editing through her balancing and resulting contradiction of verbal and non-verbal information. Routledge as Miss Fozzard gives her account of her ongoing appointments with the chiropodist, Mr Dunderdale. She does this to camera, firstly through verbal narrative, which includes plenty of evaluative detail on clothing and appearance, thus on class, and, crucially, gives us information on Miss Fozzard's perception and pretence. The real information, especially as the encounters become more surprising, is in the non-verbal narrative: slightly raised eyebrows, amused, slightly concerned about where this is going to lead, and a little bit flattered. A glance directly at the camera, and then she looks to the side, as though suddenly found out, and worried that the duality of her narrative is starting to become apparent. Her face also tells us when she is pragmatically convincing herself (or us?) of something she does not really believe. The words say one thing, the face tells us that she knows she is editing the truth.

The *Talking Heads* protagonists look straight at the camera, and thus at the viewer, but the characters do not refer to this, nor do they use any form of personal address.[7] The hypothesis of the characters speaking to an invisible viewer suggests a link with the poetic form of dramatic monologue, such as Robert Browning's 'My Last Duchess' (Woolford and Karlin 1991). Here, the speaker addresses a silent listener, whose presence is referred to, and to whom the monologue is often addressed, but who otherwise does not take part in the narrative:

> ... a first-person speaker not the poet, a tie and place, and auditor – revelation of character, colloquial language and some dramatic interaction between speaker and auditor. It may then seem that dramatic monologue is a truncated play. If the principal elements of drama are, as Aristotle said, plot and character, then dramatic monologue has very little plot and only one real character. (Sinfield 1977: 3)

In comparison, some of the *Talking Heads* protagonists address someone, although this silent presence is normally not specified any further, for example in *Soldiering On* (*TH I*): 'I wouldn't want you to think this was a tragic story' (*CTH*: 105). Who is meant by 'you'? The viewer? A stranger? But how can a stranger be present at various stages of this character's decline, at different times, and in different locations?

Apart from the possibility of the character performing for a viewer, talking to an undefined presence could also be a symptom of the characters' deep-rooted self-deception. This is certainly how Bennett sees his own work:

> They don't quite know what they are saying and are telling a story to the meaning of which they are not entirely privy. (Introduction, *CTH*: 32)

Some of the information revealed to an invisible viewer would actually be dangerous or damaging to the character if it left the confines of the monologue, in keeping with the above definition of 'too private or dangerous for any other characters' ears'. Examples are Rosemary in *Nights in the Gardens of Spain* and Marjory in *The Outside Dog* (both *TH 2*). Both women suspect their husbands as instigators of or participators in a criminal act, and keep that information to themselves – but tell the story to an invisible viewer nonetheless. The audience is addressed (mainly through eye contact), and although the performer is 'protected' from direct contact, the implied judgement of the onlooker governs the performer's behaviour to a certain extent.

The invisible listener

Most self-contained monologue plays seem to involve an invisible or visible, but largely passive, third party. The following examples examine the position and the address of the narrator of a monologue or monologue play.

Harold Pinter's *Monologue*, for example, starts with the stage direction 'Man alone in a chair. He refers to another chair, which is empty' (Pinter 1973). Throughout, the monologue is addressed to an absent friend from the speaker's past, giving every indication that this addressee is firmly believed to be present. Unlike stage soliloquies, self-contained monologue plays often seem to incorporate the invisible presence of one or more other people. This is something they have in common with the dramatic monologue in poetry.

Similar to Pinter's *Monologue*, Arnold Wesker's *One Woman Plays* (*Four Portraits – of Mothers, Yardsdale* (2001), for example) are often addressed to someone who is not present or visible, but clearly identified. Monologues such as *Whatever Happened to Betty Lemon* are written in the style of a stream of consciousness. This gives the impression that the protagonist's thoughts are simply made audible, as she talks to herself, addressing a variety of absent people in doing so.

In Willy Russell's monologue play, *Shirley Valentine* (1988), the protagonist, Shirley Bradshaw, tells her story not to absent characters, but to inanimate objects: first, this is a wall in her kitchen; later, it is a rock by the sea in Greece, the site of Shirley's escape and transformation back to Shirley Valentine, her maiden name. Despite the fact that she talks to objects, the character seems to be performing to an audience. At times, she seems to do this in order to enlarge her statements, which gives her more courage to face the changes she is undertaking. The uncertainty over who exactly she is talking to links *Shirley Valentine* to *Talking Heads* (see also Rose 1993: 537).

In Samuel Beckett's short monologue *Not I* (1972; version for television), a mouth is the only visible part of the speaker, 'Mouth', the person it belongs to remaining invisible throughout. Mouth's story is not told out of free will, however, and her life is described with aggressive defensiveness. The piece is a structured stream of consciousness: sections finish with the denial of self ('what? ... who? ... no! ... she!', Beckett 1984). In the stage version, there is another presence on stage, a silent and passive 'other': the Auditor. The sex of this person is indistinguishable, and it is covered in a black djellabah and hood. Its only function is to listen to the ruptured speech of Mouth and to occasionally lift its arm in a gesture of 'helpless empathy'. In the television version, Mouth is 'facing' the viewer, but not acknowledging any presence. Are we supposed to assume the role of 'Auditor', or are we the merciless presence who makes Mouth tell its torturous tale? Out of the examples discussed, the television version of *Not I* is similar to *Talking Heads* in its unresolved question of who is being addressed. Both seem to transcend the diegesis of the character's world, but neither do they acknowledge the viewer's presence, nor do they act on it.

Talking Heads does not have a definite or defined addressee, and offers ambivalent conclusions as to whether there is a fourth wall. The addressees of many monologue plays are silent but identifiable participators in the action. The undefined and uncertain presence of an observer in the *Talking Heads* monologues makes for a 'safer' choice for the disclosure of deeply private, embarrassing or dangerous information. Given that many of the *Talking Heads* characters fail to see that they are concealing a central truth from themselves, it is suggested that they use an imagined listener like a mirror, allowing them to check their story and their performance. As spectators behind this mirror, we are witnesses to the developing duality of each *Talking Heads* character, which is clearly detectable to us, but evidently not to them.

The unreliable narrator: *A Chip in the Sugar*

Alan Bennett, playing Graham in *A Chip in the Sugar*, shows the performative aspect of a typical *Talking Heads* character. When he is just airing his own thoughts, Bennett demonstrates Graham's slightly patronising (and as we shall see, misleading) attitude towards his elderly mother ('she will look at my *Guardian* and she actually thinks for herself', *CTH*: 42). When Graham talks about thus 'educating' his mother, his pose and voice change to a heightened version of himself, and one feels that Bennett is overacting to a good purpose, namely to show that this might not be the whole truth. This is a delicate balance, but Bennett manages his imitations of people he talks about, and more importantly the impact they are supposed to make, wisely. When other characters start talking through Graham's quoted conversations, the method Bennett applies could be termed 'biased imitation'. The voices Graham acts out in his story are his own, his mother's, and Mr Turnbull's, his mother's admirer. There are subtle (or sometimes not so subtle) signifiers as to which of these three differing voices to believe. The following is a reported three-way conversation between Graham, Mam and Mr Turnbull. It also includes Graham's thoughts and 'stage directions' such as 'she said'. He delivers it in retrospect, but it is transcribed like dialogue here, to show the different voices and implied commentaries Graham's character (and, of course, the actor 'behind' him) has to establish:

> Graham: Mr Turnbull said 'Do you like these Pakistanis?'
> 'Well in moderation,' Mother said. 'We have a nice newsagent. Graham thinks we're all the same.'
> I said, 'I thought you did.'

> She said, 'Well, I do when you explain it all to me, Graham, but then I forget the explanation and I'm back to square one.'
> 'There is no explanation,' Mr Turnbull said. 'They sell mangoes in our post office, what explanation is there for that?'
> 'I know,' Mother said, 'I smelled curry on my *Woman's Own*. You have to be educated to understand.'
> I didn't say anything.
>
> *(CTH*: 45–6)

Although there are only two interjections by Graham himself in this reported conversation, its delivery is obviously 'managed' by him, and meant to have a certain effect. It is useful to look at Graham's performance as 'impression management', Erving Goffman's concept of influencing the impression others have of us through behaviour (Goffman 1990: 14). For the actor, this is a complex task. He has to communicate who is saying what, how it is being said, and how the character Graham wants it to come across. On top of this complexity in imitation and demonstration, there is yet another level of biased imitation, which is the actor's: this is to show the general unreliability of Graham's narrative. While Graham is telling the story from his perspective, he is also gradually unmasking himself, turning from the well-read, liberal and tolerant carer to a frightened, unstable, sexually repressed man as the narrative progresses. As in all of the *Talking Heads* monologues, clues are given: at first, a reference to a day centre, then a damning deconstruction of Graham's clothes by Mr Turnbull, then euphemisms by his mother as to Graham being 'between jobs' in his day centre, having made soft toys and paper flowers in the past. References to a previous spell of what could be persecution mania, and to Graham's conviction that the house is being watched, confirm the real picture. But, of course, this real picture is delivered to us by the character Graham, who would not be so careless to mention it, would he *really* want to keep up the appearance he strives to give earlier in the piece. For all its dramaturgical effectiveness and narrative elegance, this question as to why *Talking Heads* characters unmask themselves is another enigma alongside the question of to whom exactly they are talking.

The story as it is told and the story as it is decoded by the recipient is determined by textual and visual clues in the story. The interactions and contradictions of speech and behaviour give away much more about a character than the text on its own could. The tale is told in a selective way, its protagonist deliberately or subconsciously withholding information from the recipient. The subtextual information enables Bennett to write a character as withholding this information, while he, the author, still presents 'the real picture'. In the monologues, the silent voice and steering presence of the implied author have more authority than the audible voice of the protagonist. How can an implied text or a subtext thus have more reliability than the main text and its on-stage or on-screen narrator? The concept of the 'unreliable narrator' offers a solution in that it is defined as:

> A narrator whose trustworthiness is undermined by events as deduced from the narrative.

> More technically, a narrator whose actions are not in accordance with the implied author's norms and values. (McQuillan 2000: 329)[8]

Through the unreliability of the protagonists' narrative Bennett demonstrates that the subtext of their stories is generally more reliable than their words.

Structure and technique

> One thing at the time is my motto and keep children out of it. (Bennett in *CTH*: 123)

At first glance, it is difficult to imagine a simpler form of television drama than the *Talking Heads* monologues: two cameras, a performer, and a few breaks with unintrusive music to indicate the passing of time. Several critics have addressed these structural and stylistic characteristics (see Hunt in Brandt 1993: Rose 1993, 1995). The formula first created with *A Woman of No Importance* (Giles Foster, 1982) has remained almost unchanged through the two series of *TH*. Bennett has embraced simplicity as a principle: although events are told in the past tense, there are no flashbacks; although a lot of the action happens in between takes, this is only dealt with within the narrative; although there is a complex subtext to the text, this is not made visible, but left to the viewer's imagination. Each monologue is divided into four or five sections of a few minutes' each; a section often ending with a seemingly throwaway remark, which is a clue that will increase the viewer's knowledge of the plot. The short interludes are marked by a fade to black with intermediate music composed by George Fenton, one of Bennett's long-term collaborators. These breaks indicate the passing of time; anything from a few hours to a few years. They also help to give the viewer a sense of immediacy, as the protagonist tells of the recent past in each new section (see also Rose 1993: 541). Peter Davison points out that the suggestion of the passing of time can also be seen as a technical convenience, as the audience will not feel that a break has simply been inserted for the performer's sake.[9] The monologues' stories themselves take place in between sections – what has happened is recalled by the speaker rather than narrated as it occurs. Important clues for the progression of the plot and the character are given through costume, props and (very sparse) settings. Proxemics can also deliver information – the way a character is positioned, comparing the beginning and the end of a monologue, for example. The narrative's 'breakthrough' moments often happen during pauses, where the significance of what has been said previously is processed by character and listener.

The monologues are built on the dramaturgical principle of two distinctive levels of narrative, representing two versions of the same material: linguistic and visual, where the face does all the telling on television. The weighting of the two narrative levels, verbal and non-verbal, is almost equal on screen, whereas this balance greatly shifts in favour of the verbal on stage, as the performer's face is normally too far away from the audience to produce the minimalist non-verbal story that is so clearly communicated on screen. The narrative device of the face in close-up is obviously missing on stage. The emphasis on words and especially silences has to 'fill in' for the closeness of performer and viewer which is provided in the television version. The 'liveness' of the event in the theatre might offer compensation; the presence of the audience contributes to the monologue and creates an ephemeral quality to each performance, the experience of which is obviously not possible in the television version. On stage, the tale has to be supported by 'larger' gestures and hints in the way the performer structures the text. It can be argued that silences still remain an integral part of the expressive total of the monologues, but even these have a different function on stage to that on screen. In the television plays, silences are invitations to scrutinise the face, the gestures and the posture of the protagonist. On stage, silences emphasise the words spoken previously, giving the audience time for their meaning to 'sink in'.

> There is a tension built up between the stage dialogue and the thoughts of each individual member of the audience and, implicitly between each member of the audience. It is this implicit tension which gives the play its strange theatrical power. (Davison 1982: 64)

This quotation is made with reference to Harold Pinter's 'early sketch' *Last to Go* (1991), but it can be applied to Bennett's technique in *Talking Heads*. The following diagram, suggested by the critic Peter Davison, clarifies the potential function of a silence:

| A: speaker's statement | B: silence | C: speaker's follow-up statement (may not logically follow on) |

| B1: silence in which speaker processes statement |

There are two outcomes for this sequence. In the first case, the pause (B1) follows up the statement just made and processes it, C then moving on from this different level of information.

Silences: *Nights in the Gardens of Spain*

The monologue *Nights in the Gardens of Spain* from the second series of *Talking Heads* has been praised for the understated clarity of Penelope Wilton's performance and the trust of director Tristram Powell in the audience's ability to pick up nuances. It serves as a powerful example for Bennett's orchestration and dramaturgical use of silences.

At first sight, Rosemary (aptly named, for her passion is gardening) is just another *Talking Heads* character. She has all the attributes of the 'typical' monologue protagonists (essentially all the same character, as remarked in an unfavourable review).[10] Rosemary is shy, easy to influence, as her confidence is low, and has given up on what all Bennett-characters call 'Life': 'I didn't have another remark up my sleeve ready, so that was the end of that. I do that all he time, start a conversation but can't keep it going' (*CTH*: 184). Rosemary does not have a proper voice, only internalised thoughts, somehow brought to the surface in the *Talking Heads* situation. But there *is* a voice waiting to be discovered.

In this suburban, muted and middle-class environment, a murder has occurred, and, paradoxically, Rosemary's witnessing its aftermath is the start of her flowering. She develops a friendship with the wife, Fran, who has shot her husband after years of ritual sexual abuse. Their shared passion for gardening develops into a passion for each other. The prison garden Fran cultivates can be seen as a metaphor for things growing within confines – something that also applies to Rosemary's life with her husband. Henry, who whistles under his breath when tense, calls Rosemary 'young lady' and is planning to sell the house and move to Marbella to play golf. Rosemary is fenced in by her husband, but her friendship and blossoming love for Fran grow inside these confines. She compares the idea of Marbella to being jerked around by a dog collar, as Fran was by her sadistic husband, but Henry does not hear her objections: we do. Henry is what Rosemary calls 'the face of suburbia', jovially patronising and '"very ..." and I said such a silly word "very considerate"' (*CTH*: 188). This statement to a neighbour is punctuated by pauses, and the hesitation before 'considerate' and Rosemary's subsequent expression are such that it becomes clear that 'considerate' is a euphemism for not having sex. When Rosemary does briefly stand up to Henry, she recounts it, then pauses and looks at the camera, almost seeking affirmation. We have had clues very early, but it is quite a while before Rosemary understands that Henry has taken part in the sexual abuse of Fran. The realisation is accompanied by the camera moving closer, and by soft music.

> One of them had a funny habit ... and I knew what she was going to say the second before she said it ... a funny habit of whistling under his breath.
>
> *Pause*
>
> Of course, a lot of people do that.
>
> *Fade*

(*CTH*: 190)

The realisation seems to hit Rosemary after the statement, and in the pause she is searching for explanations, and for ways of protecting herself from this dangerous truth. But it is clear from Penelope Wilton's delivery that Rosemary knows that it is her husband: after saying 'whistling under his breath', one eyebrow goes up, she then looks away, blinks in an attempt to collect herself and says 'of course, a lot of people do that' slowly and without much conviction. This signals that this is what she is going to have to *pretend* to think in order not to have to confront her husband.

The final section of *Nights* finds Rosemary in an austere Spanish garden with a window with iron grids. This casts a shadow onto the terrace and gives the scene a feel of prison, in line with Rosemary referring to the garden as 'an exercise yard'. The scene is also in grim contrast to the connotations of the monologue's title, *Nights in the Gardens of Spain*. After these remarks, there is a silence, in which the camera almost seems to ask a question, not audible to us. Rosemary responds with 'She died, did Fran' (*CTH*: 192). The conversations with Fran are nearly almost reported in indirect speech, which suggests that direct quoting in *Talking Heads* is reserved for characters the protagonists want to show up.

For the very final part of the monologue, the camera is almost relentlessly close, at times almost coaxing Rosemary to keep talking. She is like the plants she so lovingly cultivates: she doesn't make a noise, she just stops growing when deprived of love and interest. When she receives it, she blossoms, when she doesn't, she does not die, she just continues to exist on the bare necessities. Not flourishing any more, but a life in the shade in Marbella.

> The gardening books talk about the plants that are supposed to like shade. They say they prefer it.
>
> I don't believe it. I don't believe anything likes shade. They do perfectly well in the shade, it's true. But give them even ...(*and there's quite a long pause*) give them a bit of sun and suddenly they come into their own. (*CTH*: 193)

The long pause is emotional, Rosemary fighting tears, but she then delivers the next statement with quiet and intense passion. Afterwards, her glance wanders around, as she talks about listening to the frogs and crickets, and there's a long pause, full of loathing, before she says 'and Henry, whistling under his breath'. The shot fades with Rosemary staring at the ground, not wanting to answer any more questions by the invisible presence behind the camera. Rosemary's story relates to many of the *Talking Heads* characters. They are trapped in their lives, but sometimes they briefly flourish. These small victories are often sexual, but invariably the protagonists fall back into helpless and frustrated silence.

The influence of other forms and media

Television drama often has a hybridized nature and displays a host of influences (see also Creeber 2001: 4). It is on these influences that I wish to begin discussion on the generic nature of *Talking Heads*. Although written for television, the monologues' simplicity has been interpreted as pointing both towards stage conventions of the monologue and the short story (for example, by Albert Hunt in Brandt 1993: 21). The *Talking Heads* characters are recognisably 'Bennettian': the pieces are about ordinary people in their everyday environment, telling their story. *How* this story is told marks a significant formal departure from Bennett's previous television plays, and constitutes a complex case of 'generic crossing', an example of 'novelists and dramatists sallying into each others' territories' (Dorrit Cohn in Rose 1995: 17).

Drama at its most literary

> Here television shows its affinity not only with the stage – the monologue
> is after all a well-established minor theatrical form – but with the short
> story as well. This is TV drama at its most literary. (Brandt 1993: 6)

Brandt demonstrates how theatre, television and short story are all part
of what makes the form of *Talking Heads* 'as full as a novel, ripe as an
apple, a miniature masterpiece' (Reynolds 1998: 21). The monologues
thus combine many generic elements to create a new form.

Apart from being produced for television and for the stage, both
series of *Talking Heads* have been extremely successful as 'talking
books'. Both volumes were best -selling audio books when they came
out, and continue to add to Bennett's success in this medium. The
reason why they transferred to another medium so effortlessly, it might
be argued, is that the monologues have certain features of the radio play:
storytelling, the tradition of the narrator, the single speaker in personal
narrative. Also, the economy of production is not restricted to *Talking
Heads*' visual style: there are no sound effects, and music is used only
over the titles, and between sections, to indicate the passing of time.
Losing the visual part of the narrative simply lends greater weight to
the spoken word: the listener concentrates on the meanings of silence
and the nuances in the voice, which carry the text and its subtext. The
performer either talks to an invisible third party or pretends to be part
of a group of people while suggesting all the characters the audience
cannot see. In radio drama, the voice and accompanying sounds are all
the listener has got to build a character. This means that the visualisa-
tion provided in the television version of *Talking Heads* is taken on by
the audience themselves, who will imagine a character according to the
suggestions the actor's voice provides.

The television monologues are not very demanding technically. The
viewer sees the protagonist's face in close-up or medium close-up virtually the whole time. Although the shot size changes, within sections, the
angle generally does not. Bennett states that, for reasons of technical
simplicity, he conceived the individual sections of the monologues as
uninterrupted shots, with two cameras. Some are over ten minutes long,
and all the actors agreed that they could not work with an autocue (*CTH*:
10). To achieve an uninterrupted build-up within each of the sections,
director and performer had to fall back on takes of almost a theatrical
length. The concentration on the sole performer and his or her closeness to the camera made it virtually impossible to interrupt a take, as
cuts would have been too noticeable. This made the shooting of any
one section similar to giving a performance, as uninterrupted build-up

and the memorising of a large amount of text became necessary. Albert Hunt (in Brandt 1993: 21) calls this filmed live performance a 'reassertion of theatricality', claiming that 'demands made on the performers' bring back 'a theatrical quality of immediacy, which created its own tension on screen'. It is also part of theatrical tradition to put the actor at the centre of a play, and to create a performance environment where nothing distracts from the achievement of this actor. Bennett planned to direct his first monologue in the style of *Talking Heads, A Woman of No Importance*. In the following, he attributes the format's simplicity partly to his inexperience as a director:

> Thinking I would be able to manage at the most two cameras, I planned the play as a series of midshots with the camera tracking in very slowly to a close-up, holding the close-up for a while, then just as slowly, coming out again. I didn't figure on there being any cuts within scenes, though this would place a heavy burden on the performer, some sections being pretty lengthy: the first speech, for instance lasts twelve minutes. To shoot in such a way makes cutting virtually impossible: one fluff, and it's back to the top of the scene again. (Introduction, *CTH*: 10)

Bennett's simple conception of *Talking Heads* put considerable demands on the performer. The acting style required is more televisual than theatrical. *Talking Heads* on television offers the viewer a closeness to the protagonist which cannot be achieved by an adaptation of the monologue on stage.

Short story or snapshot?

> His endings are not merely a surprise or contrary to expectation, they appear in a sort of lateral way, as if popping out from around the corner; and it is only then that the reader realizes that certain details here and there had hinted at the possibility of such an ending. (Eixenbaum 2002)[11]

The above describes the short stories of O. Henry, but it could easily be applied to a *Talking Heads* monologue. As with many short stories, *Talking Heads* are structured in a way that brings gradual revelation through 'clues'. Sometimes the endings are also quite surprising: in *Playing Sandwiches*, for example, the last section is set in prison. Between the penultimate and the last episode, the protagonist has been arrested, has stood trial and has been imprisoned. All these events are then narrated, but the surprise is in the 'jump', and in the eventfulness of the gap between episodes:

> Creating a social and physical world by reporting in the past tense what
> has been done, seen and said is a strategy primarily of narrative fiction.
> (Turner 1997: 59)

The sparseness of the performance environment and the heavy reliance
on words to evoke situations also point to links with the form of short
story. Artlessness is a feature of the *Talking Heads* concept, stressing
the 'realness' of the character and the language used. Some authors
have described the short story as having its origins in a single image, a
snapshot that developed into a story:

> The special appeal of the snapshot is its seeming casualness, its subject
> caught perhaps in a moment of total unselfconsciousness, creating
> the illusion that the photographer ... is included in the artlessness he
> captures. (Shaw 1983: 14–15)

Talking Heads characters are often the evolution of 'snapshots' Bennett
has observed and remembered. In 1986, Bennett discovered a book
of photographs, *Interior America* by Chauncy Hare, which became an
influence for *Talking Heads 1*:

> As the title suggests the photographs are of people in their rooms and
> in my series of TV monologues, *Talking Heads*, I tried to capture some
> of the bleak atmosphere of Hare's photographs and to animate the kind
> of characters who in England might have been his sitters. (Bennett in
> Segal 1993: 1)

He also compares the approach of *Talking Heads* to the work of the English
photographer Magda Segal, who has taken widely known photographs
of Alan Bennett. The key lies in the decision not to catch the sitters
(Segal or Hare) or the deliverers of the monologues (Bennett) unawares;
all of them present themselves for the camera. Bennett comments: 'they
want to be seen as they see themselves .... And without condescending
to her subjects Magda Segal shows that the way they present themselves
is part of their personality and their appeal. Letting us see them as they
see themselves she confers dignity on them' (Bennett in Segal 1993: 1).
Segal and Bennett also both realise that, in leaving the way of presentation to the characters, they reveal more about themselves than author or
photographer could have done:

> People in rooms
> Sitters in settings
> Subjects with objects
>> These are the threshold of drama
>> Something is about to happen

> (Bennett in Segal 1993: 1)

The comic monologue

> But how do you explain what a monologue is to someone who does want to know and has no Greek. I would say: 'I'm not talking to myself, I'm pretending there is someone else on stage with me and I talk to him. If I pretend clearly enough I should be able to make you, the audience, accept the invisible character I'm imagining. (Grenfell 1977: 251)

In *Contemporary Drama and the Popular Dramatic Tradition in England*, Peter Davison (1982) demonstrates the significant influence of music hall conventions on contemporary drama. One of the most popular forms of music hall entertainment was the comic monologue. It is evident that the format of *Talking Heads* has some of its roots in the conventions of the comic monologue: the setting is simple (not *just* due to economic limitations), the performer relies on powers of characterisation, mime and mimicry to signify environment, circumstance and to recall or re-enact conversations, and the comic effect will often arise from the audience's familiarity with characters similar to those on stage/screen. Obviously, there are also differences between the monologues performed in music halls and *Talking Heads*, some of them determined by the medium of television. *Talking Heads* is more economical with other characters in the narrative, for example. In comic monologues, there will often be an imaginary second person, or even more, such as in Grenfell's legendary 'Nursery School' series of sketches. Although she performs these pieces entirely on her own, through her interaction and her addressing of other characters, the viewer is invited to believe there are other characters there with her.[12] In *Talking Heads* there is no interaction with invisible characters at the time of the story being told, although there are re-enactments in retrospect for the purpose of demonstration, sometimes in reported speech, sometimes in a direct quotation of what was said by another character. The monologues do not go as far as classic comic monologues, where the performer imitates other characters. *Talking Heads* protagonists re-enact people they have talked to, but remain firmly themselves.

Famous performers of this century include Stanley Holloway (1890–1982), Mabel Constanduros (d. 1957), Ruth Draper (1884–1956) and Joyce Grenfell (1910–79).

Draper's way of sourcing material for her monologues shows similarities with Bennett's method: both use people they have known or encountered to create realistic characters. In this process, linguistic, facial and gestural observation make the character 'come alive'. Some of Joyce Grenfell's characters seem to be direct ancestors of Bennett's *Talking Heads* protagonists. Grenfell's monologues, deliberately artless in form and language, are based on a similar dramaturgy to that of

Talking Heads: quite early on, the audience will understand more than the protagonists, who are telling 'a story to the meaning of which they are not entirely privy' (*CTH*, Introduction: 32).

Norman Evans' Yorkshire housewife in 'Over the Garden Wall' (1950) (less a 'drag act', than performed in the tradition of the Pantomime Dame or the Ugly Sisters) could also be counted among *Talking Heads*-predecessors, as Bennett remarks in the documentary *Looks Like a Chair, Actually it's a Lavatory* (BBC TV, 5 July 1992). There are similarities in language, dialect, register and linguistic and physical mannerism, and both Bennett's and Evans' monologues are based on an amalgamation of northern 'types' the creators have observed. This 'real' quality ensures an involvement on the part of the audience. Indeed, a frequent response to Bennett's monologues is that viewers state they know somebody very similar to a protagonist. Within the field of comic monologue, the character will always have a heightened quality to it, but laughter is still sparked by recognition, not detachment. This provides a feeling of inclusiveness, a reassuring familiarity, important in times of crisis or deprivation.

Talking Heads can be compared to the comic monologue in that the two share certain aspects in the creation of a comic effect – repetition, innuendo, delivered with a certain 'deadpan' quality:

> I saw this feller's what-do-you-call-it today. Except I'm not supposed to say 'what-do-you-call-it'. Verity says, 'Violet. What-do-you-call-it is banned. When we cannot find the word we want we describe, we do not say what-do-you-call it'. Well, you won't catch me describing that. Besides, 'what-do-you-call-it' *is* what I call it. Somebody's what-do-you-call-it. Anyway I saw it. (*CTH*: 196)

This is not from a music-hall routine; it is the opening of the last of *Talking Heads 2*, *Waiting for the Telegram*, spoken by a woman in her mid-nineties.

Talking Heads and comic monologues also employ the convention of characters incongruously juxtaposing ideas:

> I wasn't at home in that sort of hotel I can tell you. I said to the man I'd been put next to, who I took to be my husband, I said, 'Curtains in orange nylon and no place mats, there's not even the veneer of civilisation.' He said, 'Don't talk to me about orange nylon. I was on a jury once that sentenced Richard Attenborough to death.' (Lesley in *Her Big Chance*, *CTH*: 82)

The notions of 'funny' and 'sad' are often sharply juxtaposed:

> Just then there's a little toot on the horn and she runs to the lav again. I said, 'Don't go. Don't leave me, Mam.' She said, 'I'm not giving in to

you, you're a grown man. Is my underskirt showing?' He toots again.
She says, 'Look at your magazines, make yourself a poached egg.' I said,
'Mam.' She said, 'There's a bit of chicken in the fridge. You could iron
those two vests. Take a tablet. Give us a kiss. Toodle pip.' (Graham in *A
Chip in the Sugar*, CTH: 51)

Although aware of the inherent sadness of this scene, we laugh at the
juxtaposition of important and trivial statements – Graham is expressing
existential fear of abandonment, and his mother, although she is aware
of this, is deflecting her acknowledgement by a stream of unimportant
banter:

> It is this technique that Pinter develops even further, first allowing us to
> laugh, and then surprising us by making us realise what we are laughing
> at. (Davison 1982: 56)

This occasionally gives the monologues a dimension of tragedy, even
if they are never concerned with the heroic, but with flawed and self-
deceiving characters.

Talking Heads and comic monologues also have in common that
there is often a focus on the unmasking of a characters' pretence; in the
case below, an upper-class character's unease about talking casually to
the servant is shown:

> Oh, Mrs Finley, is there a favourable chance of your finding yourself in
> close proximity to a kettle? I think Mr Wimble and I are both very well
> disposed towards the idea of some tea. And something crunchy? Lovely.
> (Joyce Grenfell, *Stately as a Galleon*, quoted in Rose 1995: 71)

Miss Fozzard (*TH 2*) shows her pretentious side through describing
somebody she considers to be 'refined':

> Refined-looking feller, seventy-odd but with a lovely head of hair, one of
> the double-fronted houses that look over the cricket field. Rests my foot
> on a large silk handkerchief which I thought was a civilised touch; Mr
> Suddaby just used to use yesterday's *Evening Post*. (*Miss Fozzard Finds
> Her Feet*, CTH: 148)

Skirting around it: *Miss Fozzard Finds her Feet*

When showing characters for whom outward respectability and sophistication are the most important things in their lives, Bennett often turns
their carefully constructed performances on their head. Miss Fozzard is
the personification of a middle-class, middle-aged and vaguely conservative Englishwoman. Throughout the monologue, she is filmed in an
environment that does not suggest anything other than this image; she

is perceived as one of the pretentious middle-class women that Bennett is so famous for, talking about 'spearhead[ing] the provision of pot-pourri in the ladies' toilets' (*CTH*: 153). Like Peggy Schofield (*A Woman of No Importance*) and Miss Ruddock (*A Lady of Letters*) and, of course, Bennett's aunties, Miss Fozzard's life is dominated by the urge to increase her importance in a world that is largely indifferent to her. While her appearance and speech do not change throughout the monologue, the subtext gradually makes us realise that she is offering sexual services to her chiropodist, who is a shoe fetishist. The encounters between him and Miss Fozzard are described in minute detail, yet we are unsure until the very end whether Miss Fozzard realises (or wants to realise) what she is actually doing. Miss Fozzard's method of not facing uncomfort-able truths is to not verbalise them. As long as they stay suggestions, she can pretend that nothing untoward is happening. Miss Fozzard is, however, more aware of what she is doing than the other *Talking Heads* characters, and the monologue ends with her admitting that she also skirts around giving a name to what she does with Mr Dunderdale, just like her disabled brother Bernard is advised to skirt around words when he can't remember them. As long as there are no words for her actions, she can continue to convince herself of her respectability:

> Little envelope on the hall table as I go out, never mentioned, and if there's been anything beyond the call of duty there'll be that little bit extra. Buys me no end of footwear generally. I keep thinking where's it all going to end but we'll walk that plank when we come to it .... I suppose there's a word for what I'm doing but ... I skirt round it. [*Fade*] (*CTH*: 157)

Looking at Bennett's television characters, we have come across this prototype, inspired by his own aunties, time and time again: be it Miss Fozzard, the office workers Doris and Doreen, various mother and auntie figures, or even a deluded woman in a Prague insurance institute. Pretence comes out of the urge to matter, to be acknowledged and to be treated with respect. Although this is employed to great comic effect, Joyce Grenfell and Bennett also grasp the real need that prompts state-ments like the following: 'Those are the biggest gas works in Britain, Alan. (Pause) And I know the owner' (*The South Bank Show*, October 2005).

Talking Heads differ from monologues by authors contemporary to Bennett in the way in which the characters directly address the camera (or the audience, in the stage version). It is suggested here that this is a stylistic device Bennett has transferred to his work from conven-tions associated with the comic monologue. He does not, however, use it in the same fashion as the comedians described above. The *Talking*

Heads protagonists never 'leave' their character, and they do not talk to the viewers, they merely address them. Do they do this for greater empathy? Who are the characters actually talking to, and in some cases performing for? Finally, the answers to these questions will be the decision of the director and the actor working on the monologues.

Having examined the above range of formal influences, it is evident that, although first conceived for television, *Talking Heads* can be described as drawing on conventions of the comic monologue, television play, short story or radio play. This 'pick and mix' approach, the fact that the monologues straddle conventions of different media makes them suitable for transfer to these very media. The ease with which Bennett's work is adapted suggests a non-specific approach to both form and medium. It also reveals Bennett's craftsmanship in realising what medium-specific conventions an adapted work needs to make the transition. We can therefore diagnose a certain generic anarchy, also caused by Bennett's increasing auteurist identity and the artistic control that comes with it. Bennett has reached a status where he can disregard generic boundaries:

> There are no distractions. Every word counts. Every moment matters. 'Sui generis,' as Shivas [producer and director] says of Bennett, 'sui generis'. (Reynold 1998)

Reception

All *Talking Heads* monologues are preceded by an animation of Alan Bennett with music by George Fenton. It shows Bennett talking, looking pensive, laughing and then taking pen to paper to write the words 'Talking Heads, by Alan Bennett' with his fountain pen (the words appear on screen in Bennett's own handwriting), followed by the title of the individual monologue, and the name of the actor playing the protagonist. This animation was, of course, contemporary with the Alan Bennett puppet in the satirical series *Spitting Image*, where he always appeared as a double act with Thora Hird, invariably ending on 'a nice cup of tea'. Both the *Talking Heads* animation and the *Spitting Image* caricature make use of Bennett's public persona. These images confirm the image of a befuddled, but funny Bennett, shy, but sincere, dressed in tweed jacket with elbow patches and corduroy trousers. The way Bennett is presented is connected to the audience's expectations of his works: non-experimental, safe, mildly eccentric, but ultimately reactionary. This is also confirmed by the still chosen to accompany the 'Alan Bennett Season' in 1988: we see an old-fashioned television set, its age connecting the 1980s viewer with the 'Golden Age' of television. There is a comfy chair in the corner, but, as everything else in the room apart from the television, it is covered in white material. This communicates the preservation of the past in a strangely museum-like picture, accompanied by string pizzicato. The implication is that Bennett's work harks back to the earlier days of television, and keeps the values associated with that age alive: slower pace, recognisable characters, long, unchanging sequences.

Talking Heads 1 turned Bennett into a brand and can be seen as a non-standard contribution to the preferred format of late 1980s television drama: the mini-series. It is, however, not suggested that Bennett deliberately offered to conform to commissioners' preferred form of production. However, he seems to have found the perfect intermedial form of telling the stories of unspectacular people from their own perspective, and this happened to suit the favourable climate for such mini-series. *Talking Heads 1* fitted into developments in television drama in the 1980s, a decade called 'oppressively reactionary' (Bignell et al. 2000: 1) in its approach to innovative television drama. Although *formally* innovative, *Talking Heads* fits into an age concerned with the creation of brands and the recreation of familiar formats, and has lent itself to marketing outside the broadcast medium. The monologues are cheap to produce and keep the risk of failure to a minimum. They are straightforward, if slightly restrictive, to direct. Bennett's recognisable style and language ensure familiarity, even though the form is at first new. It is accessible, though, and every one of the six monologues is constructed in exactly the same way. The character types, taken from life, are similar to those that have populated Bennett's television work for a long time. *Talking Heads* is 'pure' Bennett, without the frills of location or relationships between different characters. The pieces are direct, to the point, unornamented, and seem to have been made for the market that the author has already established. Both series are marketed around Bennett's appeal, in a classic 'auteurist' fashion, comparable to Potter and the mini-series *The Singing Detective* (BBC1, 1986), or Stephen Poliakoff's *Shooting the Past* (BBC1 1999). Through its success with audiences and readers, *Talking Heads 1* presented a breakthrough for Bennett, and the effect on commissioning agencies was that Bennett was given free reign to develop any work he wanted, although audiences and agencies alike always expressed the wish for more variation on the same format. Bennett confirms the pressure to repeat a winning formula in the preface to *Talking Heads 2*: 'The success of the first series made this lot harder to write' (*CTH*: 121). The television critics' and the audience's reception generally focused more on the individual performances than on formal matters, and this has meant that the monologues have not been sufficiently recognised as the innovative works they undoubtedly are.

The whole truth? *Telling Tales* (2000)

In his last project for television so far,[13] *Telling Tales* (2000), Bennett presents yet another hybrid form, tailored to match his thematic and narrative concerns. The monologue, thanks to *Talking Heads*, has become Bennett's 'televisual signature', as the critic Victor Lewis-Smith (2000) remarks. The series comprises ten monologues, told by Bennett himself. The visual conventions are very close to those of *Talking Heads* 1 and 2: a single 'talking head' – Bennett himself, addressing the camera with a small number of varieties in angle and shot size.

The expression 'telling tales' can mean 'lying', but Bennett's detailed delivery points to a meaning more akin to the Yorkshire expression of 'Telling t'tale from start to finish' (*TT*: 8). Unlike *Talking Heads*, the narrative is not fictional, but autobiographical. It is not plot-based, but a series of reflections on themes, sometimes sparked off by a childhood memory, such as the 'strip of blue' under the arm rest of his parents' sofa, its colour and freshness a reminder of the muted colours of wartime. *Telling Tales* are densely detailed autobiographical narratives, at times confessions and reminiscences, grouped thematically rather than chronologically. The monologues display similar formal influences to those discussed in the *Talking Heads* above, although they are applied in different measures. The form is just as protagonist-centred as the *Talking Heads* monologues. The generic classification could again be called intermedial: conventions employed in *Telling Tales* can be assigned to different genres such as the monologue (albeit conventions defined by Bennett himself through *Talking Heads*), the documentary and storytelling, something that has all but disappeared from the television screen. Due to their documentary content, if not their form, the autobiographical monologues can be seen as transitional between Bennett's modes of playwriting and documentary. The narrative could also be associated with the medium of short story. The blurb on the front cover of the published scripts calls them 'Ten childhood snapshots from the master of the monologue'. Each of the ten monologues is accompanied by an actual photo from Bennett's childhood and youth: holiday snaps on the beach, childhood photos of his parents, days out with his mother, aunties and grandmother, Bennett at school or in the army. At the beginning of each instalment, we see what looks like a page in an old photo album. The camera moves close to snapshots of Bennett and his family, while the title of the monologue is introduced by a simple tune, played on the piano and the violin, the instrument Bennett's father played.

Bennett presents the monologues sitting on a chair in a studio that is styled to look like a room. The walls are painted in an uneven charcoal colour, giving the semblance of fading and patchiness in a designed way. It bears resemblance to the colours Bennett describes in the article 'My favourite things'.[14] He starts telling his memories in torso shot, which occasionally moves closer (although there is generally no emotional reason for doing so), and sometimes changes sides. He gesticulates, demonstrating or wringing his hands. Patrick Garland and Tristram Powell, both long-term collaborators of Bennett, both directed five monologues each. Their 'sparse direction' was generally praised, although the video editing was criticised as 'occasionally crude' (Lewis-Smith 2000: 39).[15] Bennett shows his characteristic trait of 'mining' contents, and one cannot but notice familiar sections in *Telling Tales*, adapted from material aired in, for example, the documentary *Dinner at Noon* and various other works for television. Bennett is not letting any of his childhood memories go to waste either, describing streets, houses, rooms, furniture and bric-a-brac on mantelpieces and dressing tables. There are acute childhood distinctions (which are adopted from adult social distinctions) in judging the status of houses and streets, his grandmother's house being slightly superior to the one next to it for being an end house on its terrace, and closer to the outside toilet. There is the bed in which he and his brother were born, and which still, according to family legend, bears the toenail scratches of his mother when she was enduring a long and painful labour at the birth of Bennett's brother, Gordon.

The Bennett household above his father's butcher's shop is described as permanently divided by, on the one hand, his father's insistence on rendering the dripping in the cellar and the resulting stench, and on the other, his mother's 'battered emblems of gentility' in the flat above the shop. The detailed listing of these items sometimes makes for an almost Brechtian strangeness in these monologues about northern provincial life: 'a parrot perched on the shoulder of an androgynous highlander in a kilt' (*TT*: 35), 'an embarrassment of cake knives and even cake forks' (*TT*: 36), 'the fish slice, still pristine in its original box' (*TT*: 36) and the curious child Bennett, furtively 'squeez[ing] the scrotum of the scent spray' on his mother's dressing table (*TT*: 38) or secretly cleaning his parents' dentures.

As a child, Bennett suffered from a painful certainty that his family failed to function as a proper family should. One can imagine the child or adolescent Alan Bennett suffering in silence because the cake stand was never put to use, or because his family never sat down to a cooked breakfast, as every other family in the British Isles undoubtedly did. It said so in the books he read. This is the most poignant impression left by *Telling Tales*, the chronic feeling of inadequacy, of not measuring up to some unrelenting standard, of being left behind by 'Life', which was happening anywhere but Leeds. Bennett claims that, at an age as early as seven or eight, he was already 'halfway to believing that we have had the best of it' (*TT*: 19). There is, however, a sense of regret for feeling embarrassed and ashamed of his surroundings and of his parents and their homemaking, as well as eventual delight in the idiosyncrasies which had haunted Bennett during his childhood and adolescent years. *Telling Tales* also displays notes of civic pride, which have been rewarded by Bennett being given the Freedom of the City of Leeds on 12 March 2006. The 2005 autobiographical volume *Untold Stories* gives the impression of a happier author, more at ease and comfortable with his life. The writer's guilt seems to haunt him less, which he demonstrates through a quotation from Flannery O'Connor:

'I once had the feeling I would dig my mother's grave with my writing but I later discovered this was vanity on my part. They are hardier than we think.' (*TT*: 15)

The late voice of Alan Bennett is still heavily influenced by his history, and especially his parents. He has, however, learned to turn the negatives into positives through their example:

Now we stroll back up to the village where she [Bennett's mother] had come in such despair and anguish of mind twenty-five years before. I still live here with my partner, as the phrase is, who is fonder of the house and the village even than I am. He is thirty years younger than me and what the village makes of this I do not know and now at last do not care. That, at least, my parents' lives have taught me. (*US*: 123)

Notes

1 West End production of *Talking Heads*, 1992, revived in 1994: *A Chip in the Sugar* (Alan Bennett), *Bed Among the Lentils* (Maggie Smith), *Soldiering On* (Stephanie Cole), *A Lady of Letters* (Patricia Routledge).
2 Conversation with Alex Chisholm, West Yorkshire Playhouse, March 2002.
3 It is on these, rather than on questions of form and genre, that critics have focused. Academic works on Bennett (Turner, *In a Manner of Speaking*, London: Faber & Faber, 1997, Chapter 5; Wolfe, *Understanding Alan Bennett*, Columbia: University of South Carolina Press, 1999, Chapter 6; Hunt in Brandt, *British Television*

Drama in the 1980s, Cambridge: Cambridge University Press, 1993, Chapter 2) provide detailed readings of the *Talking Heads 1* monologues. Hunt considers one of the monologues in the context of television genre. O'Mealy (*Alan Bennett: A Critical Introduction*, London: Routledge, 2001) continues the trend of discussing aspects of theme and plot only for the second series.

4 'Monologue' – *Colliers Encyclopaedia*.

5 'Not long ago, and perhaps still in some places, it was, however, thought very strange if a character spoke in soliloquy, whether this was thought of as "thinking aloud" or "directly addressing the audience". The complaints would be that this was "artificial", or "not true to life", or even "undramatic"; yet it is surely as natural and as "true to life", when one is on a stage before a thousand people, to address them, as to pretend to carry on as if they were not there. As for the soliloquy being "undramatic", this is the kind of conditional statement, elevated into a "law", which continually confuses dramatic criticism, since it is well known that the soliloquy, in many periods, has been a normally accepted part of dramatic method' (Williams, 'Realism and non-naturalism 1', in the official *Programme of the Edinburgh International Television Festival*, 1977: 14).

6 '*Kluge Leute aber pflegen nicht laut zu reden, wenn sie allein sind*', quoted in Clemen (*Shakespeare's Dramatic Art*, London: Methuen, 1972: 148).

7 It can be noted that the convention is used occasionally in television drama, notably in *House of Cards* (Andrew Davis, BBC TV, 1990), where the protagonist comments to the camera and cannot be overheard by others while doing so, even though he stays in the same environment. Andrew Davies also often uses direct address in his adaptations, most memorably in *Moll Flanders* (1997).

8 McQuillan (*The Narrative Reader*, London: Routledge, 2000: 326) describes a reliable narrator as 'a narrator who provides an accurate account of narrated events. More technically, a narrator who behaves in accordance with the implied author's norms.'

9 Informal conversation with Professor Peter Davison, 4 October 2002.

10 'But we knew Miss Fozzard not just by her tone of voice and her wallpaper. As a *Talking Heads* person, she had the *Talking Heads* personality. And there is only one. They are people – well, all but one of them, so far – who have no idea of what is going on' (Ian Parker, 'Her master's voice', *Observer*, 11 October 1998, p.11).

11 Excerpt from B.M Eixenbaum, 'The Literary Structure of an O. Henry Short Story', *The O. Henry Page*, accessed 4 April 2002, http://ppl.nhmccd.edu/~dcox/ohenry/crit9.html.

12 'Building up a complete and complex mental picture ... One of the possibilities of an act that depends upon mental images is that it can go beyond the limitations of actuality. The late Joyce Grenfell's brilliant monologues could conjure up real, almost palpable nursery schools' (Davison, *Contemporary Drama and the Popular British Tradition in England*, London: Macmillan, 1982: 42).

13 There is no indication of any forthcoming work for television by Bennett at the time of writing in 2006.

14 'My favourite things', *Guardian Weekend*, 11 December 1999, p.35.

15 Also, it was remarked that the BBC's scheduling was unhelpful, not giving the ten instalments a regular slot. Mark Lawson (*Guardian*, 13 November 2000, p. 17) speculated whether 'the BBC is punishing the series for under-achievement by transmitting it like this. Calling *Telling Tales* 'Bennett's least satisfying pieces for TV'. Lawson explained the paradox of Bennett's reclusiveness and relentless literary self-exposure. He stated that Bennett delivered the scripts 'hesitantly and even sometimes archly, as if tripped in the delivery by the paradox of being a recluse who delivers autobiographical monologues on TV'.

Conclusion: on the margin

In her 2005 book on Andrew Davies, Sarah Cardwell explains her approach to interpreting the writer's works: although she asked Davies questions and received answers which she considered, she did not prior- itise the representation of the author's views. Her approach is based on the 'embodied intention' (Cardwell 2005: 192) of Davies' work. Due to the biographical and autobiographical characteristics of Alan Bennett's television oeuvre, my approach could be described as auteurist, but also one of embodied intention. My book is not a biographical study, but is concerned with Bennett's 'authorship and artistry' (Cardwell 2005: 192). Where Bennett's life or persona spills over into his authorship and artistry, it is included. But it is the life which Bennett presents to his audience, not one based on speculation by biographers, journalists or academics seeking 'patterns'.

My study suggests that Bennett uses his talents in negotiating genre and pitch to underline his permanent state of being in two minds. He expresses, for example, two very different positions on the role of child- hood memories in an author's work:

> Anyone of any distinction at all should, on reaching a certain age, be taken away for a weekend at the state's expense, formally interviewed and stripped of all their recollections. (Alan Bennett, Diaries, *LRB* 2001: 6)

Despite this statement, Bennett has carefully been mining his childhood and earlier life, making his recollections the most important source in his works by far in the last ten years:

> The Boyhood of Alan Bennett must by now be one of the most closely described subjects in all literature, outdoing the life of Napoleon and the battlefields of the First World War. He has, surely, spent longer telling us about it now than he did living it. If only he had known at the time how the entire nation would come to share its every minute! Yet he has still not exhausted its riches of deprivation, incongruity and provinciality. (Sexton 2001:)

Liminal spaces

> I think in terms of the edge of tragedy and the edge of comedy, because I always think that's the best place to be, in everything really – in my television stuff as well, just to tread that line. People mistake extremes for edges ... I know that extremes aren't edges and extremes aren't for me, really. ... I like something that can just tip over from comedy to tragedy or comedy to sadness. (Bennett, in Wu 2000: 90)

Alan Bennett is not an author of extremes, and this also characterises his television work: he is at the edge of genres, at the edge of trends in television drama, and he occupies the territory between 'funny' and 'sad' more than any other contemporary writer in Britain. The marginality Bennett propagates is extended to his characters, of course. Often overlooked, and generally inarticulate, they don't move the action, but are moved along by it. Yet they need us to listen to them, and it is Bennett's recognition of this need that makes for the extraordinary television drama he has produced.

> 'It's also much better if things are happening on the edge of frame – ideally the best film would be where everything was on the edge of frame and just very ordinary things happening in the foreground.' (Badder 1978: 73)

Bennett's work reflects this statement. Until the late 1990s, his writing magnifies characters and occurrences in the background or on the margins of a picture.[1] With this technique, Bennett makes significant what might be passed over as unimportant, making sure that attention is paid to it. His literary preference for outsiders and marginalised characters creates seemingly banal lives, which then reveal unexpectedly complex worlds. The respectable middle-aged lady is a part-time prostitute, a vicar's wife enjoys sexual liberation with her Asian grocer, and a nonagenarian, fragile woman discusses sex. In exposing the territory between the mundane and the unexpected, the 'margins' of characters (but also characters on the margin), Bennett has formulated what can be deemed a preference for liminal spaces. He explains this using visual art as a metaphor. In a piece in the *Guardian Weekend* (1999: 35), he states that colour means more to him than line ('... so I've never much cared for drawings'), and that he prefers contiguity to contrast, liking 'the edge of colours'.

> I see this as a general principle going way beyond art or decoration. On television, for instance, it seems to me that people of widely differing views, contrasting colours, if you like, are less interesting to listen to than people whose views are different but quite close together. So when I came to start writing, I found I preferred to deal with the edges of

emotion rather than their extremes, irritation rather than anger, melancholy rather than grief. I avoid clash, my instinct always for adjacence, ambiguity and being in two minds.

Liminality,[2] a term that conceptualises the transition between two states, while belonging to neither, has become Bennett's permanent place. Occupying a liminal space has many advantages for Bennett: he can relate back to the more definitive areas on either side, without fully committing to their rules and restrictions. Bennett thus travels with ease between genres, occupying their liminal spaces, between northern and southern literary landscapes, and between being politically left and socially conservative. This thesis locates Bennett not as an author who breaks the rules of conventions, but one who excludes himself from being subject to these rules. He can either be a conformist who enjoys playing the non-conformist, or conform where he is not expected to conform.

Other aspects of liminality have been discussed in this study, with particular emphasis on the principle of autobiographical exposure made safe through a number of measures, notably disguise and narrative unreliability. Bennett has developed measures that allow him to occupy a permanent transitional stage, and has protected himself from exposure, while simultaneously disclosing detailed and intimate accounts of what might be his private or his real self. Bennett performs a 'double bluff' – he tells the biographically interested audience the story of his 'life', but edits it through multiple versions to avoid committing himself to any single account. He remains resistant to the biographical usurpation by others.

> The spy exists with equal authenticity in two opposing worlds, while feeling authentic in neither. He moves back and forth, observing, recording, seeing without being seen. He can even (as Burgess was constantly doing) reveal his secret from time to time, knowing that no one will take it entirely seriously. (Eyre 2000: 330)

Bennett can be said to have escaped the initial engrossment with other writers, although they are still a constant presence in his works, and often an inhibiting one. He has, however, developed a voice that is entirely his own, and instantly recognisable:

> Patricia Routledge is only a couple of minutes into the monologue and you know it is by Alan Bennett. The style and tone are unmistakable. The acute ear for the banalities of everyday speech, the unerring social detail, the wry humour and the underlying sadness all evoke the singular Bennett world.[3]

This book has sought to establish Bennett's place in the canon of the 1970s, 1980s and 1990s. Dave Rolinson (2005: 153) points out that the initially unquestioned status of the writer as the auteur has changed: 'directors gained more influence than writers as drama shifted to a more visual form of storytelling.' Bennett's work is 'writer-centric' in that his voice is so recognisable, but particularly his early plays certainly have a 'visual way of storytelling' that is shaped by his directors and filmographers.

An auteurist interpretation of Bennett's works is possible mainly from a literary and thematic perspective. Aesthetically, the style of the directors Bennett has worked with is at least as important as his own input. This is clearly visible when comparing the work Bennett has done with different directors and producers. He seems happy to merge his literary style with their visual styles. The Frears–Bennett–Lloyd collaborations in the 1970s have a distinctive look, and a style that is heavily dependent on the interaction of character and a northern landscape or environment. Narrative and argument are secondary, and the issue the plays are pursuing will be communicated subtextually. In his study on Alan Clarke, Rolinson (2005: 156) talks about 'the articulacy of inarticulacy – but then, who made inarticulacy such a long word?' Bennett's tongue-tied protagonists can also be seen as having the 'not quite' quality of Alan Clarke's creations, whereas other typical characters in Bennett's television plays are certainly not tongue-tied. The middle-aged, respectable ladies offer a constant flow of talk, often not even conversation, where even the smallest event is described in relentless detail. It could be said that these plays use language atmospherically rather than informatively.

This is not true of the Bennett–Schlesinger collaborations, the spy plays. The plays are frames for the articulation and discussion of questions Bennett is in two minds about. In a different way, this is also the case for the two televisual 'biopics', collaborations with Richard Eyre and Udayan Prasad. *The Insurance Man* juxtaposes Bennettian characters with the question of writing as 'the devil's work' in a film noir setting. *102 Boulevard Haussmann* recreates Proust's world visually, and offers a matching blend of biography, fiction and criticism. In a way, Bennett's documentaries are also vehicles for ideas and concepts. The investigative and accessible character of the films, combined with Bennett's authorial persona, naturally prompt comparisons with documentaries featuring John Betjeman, enforced by the fact that Bennett and Betjeman both worked with the same director, Jonathan Stedall.

The Talking Heads monologues are probably the television pieces most determined visually by the way they are written. The structure and style of the plays demand a minimalist directorial approach. Bennett's involvement was also considerable, as writer, actor, director (*Bed Among the Lentils, TH 1*) and latterly as executive producer (*TH 2*). He would have therefore had more input into the production process, and the directors' individual styles can only be defined through small features. The same is true for the autobiographical monologues *Telling Tales*. Bennett remarks that episodes directed by either Tristram Powell or Gavin Millar could be distinguished through whether he was wringing his hands when delivering them, as Garland did not mind, but Powell preferred a 'less anguished mode' and kept the hand-wringing out of shot (*TT*: 15).

One of the most fruitful collaborative relationships in Bennett's later career has been with Nicholas Hytner, resulting in four stage plays and two feature films, the latter adapted from the stage. Bennett and Hytner have not worked for television together. The reason for this might well be that Hytner does not generally work for television, but mainly as a stage director (and as the Director of the National Theatre since 2003). But it seems to be Bennett's decision as well to move away from television. In 1984, he stated that on his 'subjective scale' of writing, theatre was at the top, followed by film and television.[4] When I asked him in 2006 whether this hierarchy had changed, he responded:

> No. I'd still rather write for the theatre – and it is only place where you're free of all sorts of constraints, e.g. in *The History Boys* on stage characters just turn to the audience and talk. In the film this only happens once or twice because it doesn't work in the same way – you have to lead up to it and repeat the procedure – whereas on the stage you just go ahead and do it.[5]

With the exception of *Writing Home*, and especially *Untold Stories*, a confessional autobiographical work, television has been the medium in which Bennett has produced his most personal writing. Yet he has moved away from television, judging theatrical conventions as more suitable to breaking up the naturalist and realist conventions he sees himself prone to. The fact that, in Hytner, he has found a collaborator who can help him to overcome these restraints has obviously fuelled his interest in writing for the stage.

Typically English?

Alan Bennett manages to mirror both the qualities and the insecurities that are seen as essentially English: the embarrassment, the understatement, the self-deprecation. He seems to represent both national and regionally specific English characteristics. Bennett's preface to a publication on the local history of Headingley reinforces his pride in the parochial:

> I'm glad that so much of the area has survived and that it's more valued for its character and interest now than then it ever was then. Leeds is full of such submerged villages. Armley, Bramley and Kirkstall are others, with buildings often of remarkable antiquity and it's right that their history should be told as David Hall tells Far Headingley's here. It will enhance the pleasure of living in such a definite community and foster its sense of identity. I'm just a little disturbed, though, that I've passed so soon into history. (Hall 2000: xxi)

Bennett engages with notions of Englishness in literature, history and art, relating mainly to the past. He does so in a voice that is accessible to a wide audience and through a public persona that manages to combine the sharpness of an Oxford wit and the familiarity of a favourite teacher. 'I always think the reason why I'm popular is that I'm no threat.'[6]

> Bennett has become 'a universally recognised turn' who knows what is expected of him. Readers and audience 'want more of the same, please, with just enough variation to show it's not actually a repeat. It can't be easy.' (Sexton 2001: 20)

Public adoration obviously brings with it an obligation. Consequently, Bennett often censors his own work when he feels it does not correspond to his image. He has spoken about not wanting to inflict the dark side of his writing on his readership, calling some developments in his writing 'too bleak to visit on the public' (Hill 2001). His 2001 short story, 'The Laying on of Hands' is 'as dark as I could let myself be publicly without being rejected altogether' (ibid.). However, Bennett was enthusiastic about the chance to take experimental approaches in projects such as *Enjoy* (1980) and *The Old Crowd* (1979). About the latter, he stated that 'the play's greatest virtue is that it does not seem like mine' (*Writer*: 15). Also, recent stage plays and autobiographical writings have challenged public perceptions of Bennett considerably, through controversial topics and openness to a sometimes forensic degree. Bennett has been successful in negotiating his various identities through quiet and persistent subversion, trying to make sure he is not usurped by others' attempts to categorise, analyse and simplify his work and persona:

> Audience question: You said once you'd rather the public had an image of you you'd not quite fit – that way, you're free. So, in a sense, you're playing a game which you've managed to win.
>
> Alan Bennett: Up to a point, yes. But there's always ... they get you in the end![7]

However, despite the growing critical interest in his work and the inaccuracies this might present for the author in the way he would like to be seen, Bennett has the option of politely ignoring interventions from what he has called the 'academic undergrowth' (*Poetry*: 2):

> I think when I've finished trying to write I'll then start reading what's been written about me.[8]

Notes

1 Stephen Frears: 'I think I sometimes tend to concentrate on the peripheral events in my films rather than what's happening at the centre. It seems to happen every time and I'm sure it comes from the three writers, Alan Bennett, Peter Price and Neville Smith, whom I've mainly worked with. If you think of those three writers, the bits they write at the edges are wonderful. You can't pretend that Neville has a strong sense of plot, and Alan writes a very simple short story, and with Peter the convolutions are more interesting than the simplicities' (Badder, 'Frears and company: conversations with Stephen Frears, Alan Bennett, Brian Tufano, Chris Menges', *Sight and Sound*, vol. 47, no. 2: pp. 70–5, 1978: 73).

2 The term 'liminality' (from Latin *limen* – threshold) is often used in reference to the transitional state within a rite of passage. It refers to the condition in which one state of being is left and another is entered. While in liminal transition, the subject is 'in between' and is therefore a kind of non-person until he or she emerges on the other side. See also www.wordreference.com.

3 *The Times*, London, 6 October 1998 (also quoted in O'Mealy, *Alan Bennett: A Critical Introduction*, London: Routledge, 2001: xiv–xv).

4 For the full quotation, see Chapter 1, p. 12.

5 Alan Bennett, Letter to K. McKechnie, September 2006.

6 Alan Bennett in *Book of the Month*, 5 January 2003, BBC Radio 4.

7 Alan Bennett in *Book of the Month*, 5 January 2003, BBC Radio 4.

8 Postcard to K. McKechnie, acknowledging receipt of MA thesis *The Theatre of Alan Bennett*, 27 August 1997.

Appendix: list of television programmes, films, stage plays and other works

Single plays

A Day Out, Director Stephen Frears (LWT, 24 December 1972)
Sunset Across the Bay, Director Stephen Frears (LWT, 20 February 1975)
A Little Outing, Director Brian Tufano (BBC TV, 20 October 1977)
A Visit from Miss Prothero, Director Stephen Frears (BBC TV, 11 January 1978)
Intensive Care, Director Gavin Millar (BBC TV, *Play for Today*, 9 November 1982)
An Englishman Abroad, Director John Schlesinger (BBC TV, 29 November 1983)
The Insurance Man, Director Richard Eyre (BBC TV, 23 February 1986)
102 Boulevard Haussmann, Director Udayan Prasad (BBC TV, 17 February 1991)
A Question of Attribution, Director John Schlesinger (BBC TV, 20 October 1991)

Seasons of plays

Six Plays

Me, I'm Afraid of Virginia Woolf, Director Stephen Frears (LWT, 2 December 1978)
Doris and Doreen (later published as *Green Forms*), Director Stephen Frears (LWT, 16 December 1978)
The Old Crowd, Director Lindsay Anderson (LWT, 27 January 1979)
Afternoon Off, Director Stephen Frears (LWT, 3 February 1979)
One Fine Day, Director Stephen Frears (LWT, 17 February 1979)
All Day on the Sands, Director Giles Foster (LWT, 24 February 1979)

Playhouse (later *Objects of Affection*)

Our Winnie, Director Malcolm Mowbray (BBC TV, 12 November 1982)
A Woman of No Importance, Director Giles Foster (BBC TV, 19 November 1982)
Rolling Home, Director Piers Haggard (BBC TV, 3 December 1982)
Marks, Director Piers Haggard (BBC TV, 10 December 1982)
Say Something Happened, Director Giles Foster (BBC TV, 17 December 1982)

Series

On the Margin (November/December 1966)

Talking Heads 1 (six monologues for television, BBC TV, 19 April–24 May 1988)

A Chip in the Sugar, Graham: Alan Bennett, Director Stuart Burge
A Lady of Letters, Irene Ruddock: Patricia Routledge, Director Giles Foster
Bed Among the Lentils, Susan: Maggie Smith, Director Alan Bennett
Soldiering On, Muriel: Stephanie Cole, Director Tristram Powell
Her Big Chance, Lesley: Julie Walters, Director Giles Foster
A Cream Cracker Under the Settee, Doris: Thora Hird, Director Stuart Burge

Talking Heads 2 (six monologues for television, Slow Motion Ltd/BBC TV, 6 October–11 November 1998)

Miss Fozzard Finds Her Feet, Miss Fozzard: Patricia Routledge, Director Patrick Garland
The Hand of God, Celia: Eileen Atkins, Director Stuart Burge
Playing Sandwiches, Wilfred: David Haig, Director Udayan Prasad
Nights in the Gardens of Spain, Rosemary: Penelope Wilton, Director Tristram Powell
The Outside Dog, Marjory: Julie Walters, Director Gavin Millar
Waiting for the Telegram, Violet: Thora Hird, Director Stuart Burge

Telling Tales (ten autobiographical monologues performed by Alan Bennett, Slow Motion Ltd/BBC TV, 4 November–6 December 2000)

A Strip of Blue, Director Tristram Powell
Our War, Director Patrick Garland
An Ideal Home, Director Tristram Powell
A Shy Butcher, Director Tristram Powell

Days Out, Director Patrick Garland
Proper Names, Director Tristram Powell
Eating Out, Director Patrick Garland
Aunt Eveline, Director Tristram Powell
Unsaid Prayers, Director Patrick Garland
No Mean City, Director Patrick Garland

Documentaries

Poetry in Motion 1 (Channel 4, Six parts, 6 June – 11 July 1988)
Dinner at Noon, Director Jonathan Stedall (BBC TV, 9 August 1988)
'Childhood', in *Poetry in Motion* 2 (Channel 4, 29 November 1990)
Looks Like a Chair, Actually it's a Lavatory (Presenter, BBC TV, 5 July 1992)
Portrait or Bust, Director Jonathan Stedall (BBC TV, 4 April 1994)
The Abbey, Director Jonathan Stedall (BBC TV, three parts, 25–27 December
   1995)

Produced feature films

A Private Function, Director Malcolm Mowbraw (Handmade Films, 1984)
Prick Up Your Ears, Director Stephen Frears (Civilland/Zenith, 1987)
The Madness of King George, Director Nicholas Hytner (Samuel Goldwyn/
   Channel 4 Films, 1994)
The History Boys, Director Nicholas Hytner (Channel 4 Films, 2006)

First productions of stage plays

Forty Years On, London, Apollo Theatre, 31 October 1968
Getting On, London, Queen's Theatre, 14 October 1971
Habeas Corpus, Lyric Theatre, London, 10 May 1973
The Old Country, Queen's Theatre, London, 7 September 1977
Enjoy, Vaudeville Theatre, London, 15 October 1980
Kafka's Dick, Royal Court Theatre, London, 23 September 1986
An Englishman Abroad and *A Question of Attribution*, National Theatre,
   London, 1 December 1988
The Wind in the Willows (adaptation of Kenneth Grahame's children's book),
   National Theatre, London 14 December 1990
The Madness of George III, National Theatre, London, 28 November 1991
Talking Heads (adaptation of Bennett's television monologues), Comedy
   Theatre, London, 6 February 1992
The Lady in the Van, Queen's Theatre, London, 1 December 1999
The History Boys, National Theatre, London, 18 May 2004

Bibliography

Works by Alan Bennett

Television plays: scripts

(1981) *Office Suite*, London: Faber & Faber.

(1985) *The Writer in Disguise*, London: Faber & Faber (Contents: Me, I'm Afraid of Virginia Woolf, All Day on the Sands, One Fine Day, The Old Crowd, An Introduction by Lindsay Anderson, Afternoon Off).

(1996) *Objects of Affection*, 2nd edn, London: BBC Books (Contents: Our Winnie, A Woman of No Importance, Rolling Home, Marks, Say Something Happened, A Day Out, Intensive Care, An Englishman Abroad).

(1998) *The Complete Talking Heads*, London: BBC Books.

(2003) *Rolling Home*, London: Faber & Faber (Contents: One Fine Day, All Day on the Sands, Our Winnie, Rolling Home, Marks, Say Something Happened, Intensive Care).

(2003) *Me, I'm Afraid of Virginia Woolf*, London: Faber & Faber (Contents: A Day Out, Sunset Across the Bay, A Visit from Miss Prothero, Me, I'm Afraid of Virginia Woolf, Green Forms, The Old Crowd, An Introduction by Lindsay Anderson, Afternoon Off).

(2003) 'Two in Torquay', in *London Review of Books*, vol. 25, no. 13.

Documentaries (scripts)

(1988) *Dinner at Noon*, in A. Bennett (1997) *Writing Home*, London: Faber & Faber, p. 39.

(1990) *Poetry in Motion*, London: Channel 4 Television.

Anon (1992) *Poetry in Motion 2*, London: Channel 4 Television.

Bennett, Alan and Leeds City Art Galleries (1994) *Mr Bennett's Pictures*, Leeds: City Art Galleries.

(2000) *Telling Tales*, London: BBC Worldwide.

Films (scripts)

(1987) *Prick Up Your Ears*, London: Faber & Faber.
(1994) *A Private Function*, London: Faber & Faber.
(1995) *The Madness of King George*, London: Faber & Faber.

Plays for the stage (published)

(1991) *The Wind in the Willows*, London: Faber & Faber.
(1995; reissue) *The Madness of George III*, London: Faber & Faber.
(1996; reissue) *Plays 1*, London: Faber & Faber (Contents: Forty Years On, Getting On, Habeas Corpus, Enjoy).
(1998) *Plays 2*, London: Faber & Faber (Contents: Kafka's Dick, The Insurance Man, The Old Country, An Englishman Abroad, A Question of Attribution).
(1991) *Two Kafka Plays*, 2nd edn, London: Faber & Faber.
(2000) *The Lady in the Van*, London: Faber & Faber.
(2004) *The History Boys*, London: Faber & Faber.

Short stories

(2003) *Three Short Stories*, London: Profile Books (Contents: 'The Clothes They Stood Up in', 1998; 'Father! Father! Burning Bright!', 1998; 'The Laying on of Hands', 2001).

Diaries, journalism, prefaces and introductions

(1985) 'Preface' in C, Smith (ed.), (1985) *The Let's Join In Storybook*, London: BBC.
(1988) 'Preface' in W.R. Mitchell (ed), (1988) *The Changing Dales:. A Half-Century of 'Progress'*, Clapham/Lancaster: Dalesman Books.
(1991) 'Every picture tells a story', in *Radio Times*, 19–25 October, p. 20–1.
(1993) 'Foreword', in M. Segal (1993) *London at Home*, Manchester: Cornerhouse.
(1997) *Writing Home*, 2nd edn, London: Faber & Faber.
(1997) 'What I did in 1996', in *London Review of Books*, vol. 19, no. 1.
(1998) 'Notes on 1997', in *London Review of Books*, vol.20, no. 1.
(1998) 'Alan Bennett chooses four paintings for schools' in *London Review of Books*, vol. 20, no. 7.
(1999) '*Untold Stories*', in *London Review of Books*, vol. 21, no. 19 p. 11.
(1999) 'What I did in 1998', in *London Review of Books*, vol. 21, no. 2.
(1999) 'My favourite things', *Guardian Weekend*, 11 December, p.35.
(2000) 'What I did in 1999', in *London Review of Books*, vol. 22, no. 2.
(2000) 'A cure for arthritis and other tales' in *London Review of Books*, vol. 22, no. 21.

(2000) 'Foreword', in M. Mayne (2000) *Pray, Love, Remember*, London: Darton Longman Todd.

(2001) 'Alan Bennett's 2000 Diary', in *London Review of Books*, vol. 21, no. 2, p. 3.

(2002) 'Seeing Stars', in *London Review of Books*, vol. 22, no. 1, p. 12.

(2002) 'Memories of Lindsay Anderson', in *London Review of Books*, vol. 22, no. 14. p. 17.

(2003) 'Secrets are best kept by those who have no sense of humour', in *London Review of Books*, vol. 25, no. 1.

(2004) 'A Shameful Year', in *London Review of Books*, vol. 15, no. 2.

(2004) 'Postscript', in *London Review of Books*, vol. 26, no. 4.

(2005) *Untold Stories*, London: Profile Books.

(2006) 'Diary', *London Review of Books*, vol. 28, no. 1, p. 36.

Transcripts

(2001) *Hymn*, transcript from audio recording, BBC Radio 4, November 2001.

(1999) Platform: *The Madness of George III*, notes of discussion, National Theatre (Lyttelton), London, 6 November.

(2003) *The Book Club*, transcript of interview with Alan Bennett, BBC Radio 4, 5 January 2003.

The South Bank Show (ITV: The Old Crowd 1979, A Private Function 1984, Untold Stories 2005)

The Late Review, BBC2, November 1998.

Platform, *The Madness of George III*, National Theatre, London, November 2000.

Fame, Set and Match, Beyond the Fringe, BBC 2, 23 November 2002.

An Audience with Alan Bennett, South Bank, London, June 2004.

Front Row Special, BBC Radio 3, October 2005.

Interview material

Anty, Martin (1984) 'A Yorkshireman abroad', in *Time Out*, London, 13 September, p. 13.)

Bennett, Alan (1984) Interview at the National Film Theatre, www.screenonline.org.uk/audio/id/1115595/index.html

Works on Alan Bennett

Monographs

Dick, Delia (1999) *Talking Heads*: York Notes, London: Pearson Education.
Games, Alexander (2001) *Backing into the Limelight: The Biography of Alan Bennett*, London: Headline.
O'Mealy, Joseph (2001) *Alan Bennett: A Critical Introduction*, London: Routledge.
Turner, Daphne (1997) *In a Manner of Speaking*, London: Faber & Faber.
Wolfe, Peter (1999) *Understanding Alan Bennett*, Columbia: University of South Carolina Press.

Journal articles and chapters

Badder, D. (1978) 'Frears and company: conversations with Stephen Frears, Alan Bennett, Brian Tufano, Chris Menges', *Sight and Sound*, vol. 47, no. 2, pp. 70–5.
Bennett, Alan (1982) 'Observation', *Radio Times*, 6–12 November, p. 8.
—— (1984) 'British cinema: life before death on television', *Sight and Sound*, vol. 53, no. 2, pp. 115–21.
—— (1988) 'Talking Heads', *Radio Times*, 16–22 April.
—— (1999) 'My favourite things', *Guardian Weekend*, 11 December, p. 35.
Bull, John (1994) 'Introduction' and 'Alan Bennett: The Leftovers', in *Stage Right: Crisis and Recovery in British Contemporary Mainstream Theatre*, London: St Martin's Press.
Dawson, J. (1972) 'Day out', *Sight and Sound*, vol. 41, no. 4, pp. 189–190.
Goode, Ian (2003) 'A pattern of inheritances: Alan Bennett, heritage and the British film and television', in *SCREEN*, 44, 3.
Hood, Thomas (1826) 'I remember, I remember', Representative Poetry Online, http://rpo.library.utoronto.ca/poem/1035.html, accessed 29 March 2007.
McKechnie, Kara (2001) 'Mrs Brown's mourning and Mr King's madness', in D. Cartmell, I.Q. Hunter and I. Whelehan (eds) (2001) *Retrovisions: Reinventing the Past*, London: Pluto Press.
—— (2002) 'Taking liberties with the monarch: the royal biopic in the 1990s', in C. Monk and A. Sargeant (eds) (2002) *British Historical Cinema*, British Popular Cinema Series, London: Routledge.
—— (2003) 'Northern women in sensible shoes – Alan Bennett and the pleasures of provincialism', in M. Middecke, B. Daewes, I. Bergmann (eds) (2003) *Global Challenges and Regional Responses*, Society for Contemporary Drama in English, Trier: WVT.
—— (2005) 'Alan Bennett', in John Bull (ed.) (2005) *Dictionary of Literary Biography*, fourth series, British and Irish Dramatists Since World War II, New York/London: Thomson Gale.
Macnab, G. (1995) 'The Madness of King George', *Sight and Sound*, vol. 5, no. 4.
O'Mealy, Joseph (1999) 'Royal family values: the Americanization of Alan

Bennett's *The Madness of George III'*, in *Literature/Film Quarterly*, vol. 27, no. 2, 90–6.

Pym, J. (1988) 'Older Women – *Talking Heads'*, *Sight and Sound*, vol. 57, no. 3.

Raab, Michael (1998) 'Ein Königsdrama – very british', in *Die Deutsche Bühne*, no. 11, p. 27.

—— (1999) 'Der Preis der Selbstkontrolle: Alan Bennett', in *Erfahrungsräume: Das englische Drama der neunziger Jahre*, Trier: WVT.

Rose, Margaret (1993) 'The repression of the melodramatic in Alan Bennett's *Talking Heads* monologue plays', in R. Rutelli and A. Johnson (eds) (1993) *I linguaggi della passione*, Udine: Campanotto Editore.

Röwekamp, Burkhard (2000) 'Kafkaeske Visionen. Das Beobachtungsmuster "Schriftsteller" im zeitgenössischen Film', in Felix, J (ed.) *Genie und Leidenschaft – Künstlerleben im Film*, St Augustin: Gardez Verlag, pp. 167–82.

—— (2003) 'Film Noir. Vom "film noir" zur "methode noire"', *Die Evolution filmischer Schwarzmalerei*, Marburg.

Taylor, J.R. (1979) 'The Bennett plays', in *Sight and Sound*, vol. 48, no. 2, pp. 116–18.

Wu, Duncan (1995) 'Alan Bennett: anarchists of the spirit', in D. Wu (1995) *Six Contemporary Dramatists*, London: MacMillan.

—— (2000) 'Alan Bennett, The Madness of George III', and 'Nicholas Hytner', in D. Wu (2000) *Making Plays: Interviews with Contemporary British Dramatists and Directors*, London: MacMillan.

Other articles on Alan Bennett (selection)

Adams, T. (2000) 'Behind the fringe ...', *Observer*, 29 October, p. 3.

Church Gibson, Pamela (2002) 'From dancing queen to plaster virgin – Elizabeth and the end of English heritage?', *Journal of Popular British Cinema*, p. 5.

de Jongh, Nicholas (1990) 'In search of the Garbo of Primrose Hill', *Guardian*, 13 December.

—— (1999) 'This Van is merely a vehicle for Dame Maggie', *Evening Standard*, 8 December, p. 20.

Hellen, N. (1998) 'Bennett pens TV child sex drama', *Sunday Times*, 10 May.

Kingsley, Madeleine (1988) 'Mr Bennett is a gentleman!', *Radio Times*, 6–12 August, p. 83.

Lahr, John (2000) 'The odd couple!', *The New Yorker*, 24 January, p. 88.

Lewis, P (1990) 'Rhyme time TV', *Sunday Telegraph*, 7 Days Magazine, 3 June, p. 54.

Lewis-Smith, Victor (1998) 'Bennett knows his bunions', *Evening Standard*, 7 October, p. 31.

—— (2000) 'Working class hero', *Evening Standard*, 6 November, p. 39.

McKechnie, Kara (2002) 'What's he really like? Alan Bennett and his

204   Bibliography

persona on stage', in Programme booklet *The Lady in the Van*, Leeds: West Yorkshire Playhouse.

Parker, Ian (1998) 'Her master's voice', *Observer Review*, 11 October, p. 11.

Preston, Peter (2001) 'Behind the fringe', *Observer Review*, 2 September, p. 15.

Reynolds, Gillian (1998) 'Alan Bennett's extraordinary people', *Daily Telegraph*, 6 October, p. 21.

—— (2000). 'A week of Alan Bennett at his brilliant and angry best', *Daily Telegraph*, 5 September, p. 21.

Sexton, David (2000) 'Bennett's battle-axes', *Sunday Telegraph*, 12 March.

—— (2001) 'National treasure', *Sunday Telegraph*, 23 December, p. 20.

Wells, John (1995) 'Bennett's golden treasury', *Daily Telegraph*, 25 March, p. 2.

Secondary sources

Aaron, D. (ed.) (1978) *Studies in Biography*, London: Harvard University Press.

Afton, Richard (1979) Telelvision review column, *Evening Standard*, 1 March.

Albee, E. (1962) *Who's Afraid of Virginia Woolf*, New York: Atheneum.

Amis, Martin (1993) 'A poetic injustice', *Guardian Weekend*, 21 August, p. 6.

Anderson, Linda (2001) *Autobiography*, London: Routledge.

Anon. (1959) *The Armchair Theatre*, London: Weidenfeld and Nicolson.

Anon. (1995) *Directors: Platform Papers*, London: National Theatre.

Ashley, K., L. Gilmore and G. Peters (eds) (1994) *Autobiography and Postmodernism*, Amherst, MA: University of Massachusetts Press.

Aston, Elaine and George Savona (1991) *Theatre as Sign-System: A Semiotics of Text and Performance*, London: Routledge.

Auden, W. H. (1976) 'Musee de Beaux Arts', *Collected Poems*, London: Faber & Faber.

Banks Smith, Nancy (1979a) 'Afternoon Off', *Guardian*, 5 February.

—— (1979b) 'All Day on the Sands', *Guardian*, 26 February.

Barnes, Julian (1979) 'Old Crowd', *The Spectator*, 3 March.

Barry, Peter (2002) *Beginning Theory*, 2nd edn, Manchester: Manchester University Press.

Barthes, Roland (1968) 'The death of the author', in R. Barthes (1977) *Image, Music, Text*, New York: Fontana.

Batchelor, John (ed.) (1995) *The Art of Literary Biography*, Oxford: Clarendon Press.

Baudrillard, Jean (1995) *The Gulf War Did Not Take Place*, Bloomington, IN: Indiana University Press.

Bechman, Helga (1997) *Das filmische Universum des Stephen Frears*, Alfeld/Leine: Coppi Verlag.

Beckett, Samuel (1984) *Collected Shorter Plays*, London: Faber & Faber.

Bennett, Alan (2001) 'Alan Bennett gives a personal view of 25 years of the National on the South Bank', *The National Theatre Website*, accessed 19 July 2002, www.nationaltheatre.org.uk/platforms/Alan_Bennett_NT25_article.html.

Bharucha, Rustom (2000) *The Politics of Cultural Practice: Thinking Through Theatre in an Age of Globalization*, London: Athlone Press.

Bignell, Jonathan, Stephen Lacey and Madelein Macmurraugh-Kavanagh (eds) (2000) *British Television Drama: Past, Present and Future*, Basingstoke: Palgrave.

—— (2002) *Media Semiotics: An Introduction*, 2nd edn, Manchester: Manchester University Press.

—— and Stephen Lacey (2005) *Popular British Television Drama*, Manchester: Manchester University Press.

Bloom, Harold (1975) *The Anxiety of Influence*, Oxford: Oxford University Press.

Brandt, George W. (ed.) (1981) *British Television Drama*, Cambridge: Cambridge University Press.

—— (ed.) (1993) *British Television Drama in the 1980s*, Cambridge: Cambridge University Press.

Brissett, David and C. Edgley (eds) (1990) *Life as Theatre: A Dramaturgical Sourcebook*, New York: Aldine de Gruyter.

Brooke, M. (2002) 'Alan Bennett', entry in screenonline Encyclopedia, London: British Film Institute, www.screenonline.org.uk/people/id/504794/index.html.

Bull, John (1994) *Stage Right: Crisis and Recovery in British Contemporary Mainstream Theatre*, London: St Martin's Press.

Burke, Sean (1992) *The Death and Return of the Author*, 2nd edn, Edinburgh: Edinburgh University Press.

—— (1995) *Authorship*, Edinburgh: Edinburgh University Press.

Buruma, Ian (1995) 'The great art of embarrassment', *New York Review of Books*, 16 February 1995, pp. 15–18, accessed 1 July 2002. www.nybooks.com/articles/article-preview?article_id=1986.

Cardwell, Sarah (2005) *Andrew Davies*, The Television Series, Manchester: Manchester University Press.

—— (2006) 'Television aesthetics', *Critical Studies in Television*, vol. 1, no. 1.

Carpenter, Humphrey (2001) *That Was Satire That Was*, London: Victor Gollancz.

Caughie, John (1980) 'Progressive television and documentary drama', in T. Bennett et al. (eds.) *Popular Television and Film: A Reader*, London: BFI/Open University Press.

—— (1995) *Theories of Authorship*, London: British Film Institute.

—— (2000) *Television Drama – Realism, Modernism, and British Culture*, Oxford: Oxford University Press.

Cave, Richard Allen (1987) *New British Drama in Performance on the London Stage*, Gerrards Cross: Colin Smythe.

Chandler, David (2000) 'An introduction to genre theory', accessed 3 October 2002, www.aber.ac.uk/media/Documents/intgenre1.html.

Clayton, Sylvia (1979) 'All Day on the Sands', *Daily Telegraph*, 26 February.

Clemen, Wolfgang (1972) *Shakespeare's Dramatic Art*, London: Methuen.

Clifford, S. and A. King (2002) 'Losing your place', Website Common Ground: *England in Particular*, accessed 7 May 2002, www.commonground.org.uk/Local_Distinctiveness.html.

Cockshut, A.O.J. (1984) *The Art of Autobiography*, London: Yale University Press.

Colliers Encyclopaedia (1984) New York and Toronto: P. F. Collier.

Columbia Encyclopedia, accessed 12 November 2002, www.bartleby.com/65/st/streamco.html

Cook, John R. (1998) *Dennis Potter: A Life on Screen*, 2nd edn, Manchester: Manchester University Press.

Cooke, Lez (2003) *The Television Drama Book*, London: British Film Institute.

Copjec, J. (1993) *Shades of Noir: A Reader*, New York: Verso.

Creeber, Glenn (2001) *The Television Genre Book*, London: British Film Institute.

Davison, Peter (1982) Contemporary Drama and the Popular British Tradition in England, London: Macmillan.

Day-Lewis, Sean (1998) *Talk of Drama*, Luton: University of Luton Press.

Docherty, Thomas (ed.) (1993) *Postmodernism: A Reader*, London: Harvester Wheatsheaf.

Donaldson, I., P. Read and J. Walter (eds) (1992) *Shaping Lives: Reflections on Biography*, Canberra: Humanities Research Centre.

Eliot, T.S. (1999/c.1932) *Selected Essays*, London: Faber & Faber.

Encarta Online Encyclopedia, accessed 25 April 2002, www.dictionary.msn.com/find/entry.asp?refid=1861736279.

Eyre, Richard (2000) *Changing Stages*, London: Bloomsbury.

—— (2003) *National Service: Diaries*, London: Bloomsbury.

Felix, J. (2000) *Genie und Leidenschaft – Künstlerleben im Film*, St Augustin: Gardez Verlag.

Financial Times (1991) 'A question of being English', 23 October.

Fletcher, Kim (1991) 'A familiar figure on the Courtauld stairs', *Sunday Telegraph*, 11 August.

Folkenflik, Robert (ed.) (1993) *The Culture of Autobiography*, Stanford: Stanford University Press.

Frears, Stephen (1998) 'Foreword', in R. Kelly (ed.) (1998) *Alan Clarke*, London: Faber & Faber.

Freeman, M. (1993) *Rewriting the Self: History, Memory, Narrative*, London: Routledge.

Gervais, D. (1993) *Literary England*, Cambridge: Cambridge University Press.

Giles, J. and T. Middleton (eds) (1995) *Writing Englishness*, London: Routledge.

Goffman, Erving (1959/1990) *The Presentation of Self in Everyday Life*, London: Penguin.

Grenfell, Joyce (1976) *Joyce Grenfell Requests the Pleasure*, London: Futura Books.

—— (1977) *'George – Don't Do That': Six Nursery School Sketches*, London: Futura.

Guiness, Alec (1997) *My Name Escapes Me*, London: Viking.

Hacker, J. and D. Price (1991) *Take Ten: Contemporary British Film Directors*, Oxford: Clarendon Press.

Hall, D. (2000) *Far Headlingley, Weetwood and West Park*, Leeds: Far Headingley Village Society.

Hassan, Ihab (no date) 'From postmodernism to postmodernity: the local/ global context', accessed 28 October 2002, www.ihabhassan.com/postmodernism_to_postmodernity.htm.

Hill, A. (2001) 'A bad case of writer's block deepens the dark mood of Alan Bennett', *Observer*, Sunday, 9 December 2001; *Guardian Unlimited*, accessed 19 July 2002, www.books.guardian.co.uk/news/articles/0,6109,616371,00.html.

Hodsdon, B. (1990) 'The mystique of mise-en-scene revisited', *Continuum: The Australian Journal of Media & Culture*, vol. 5, no. 2; accessed 4 November 2003, www.mcc.murdoch.edu.au/ReadingRoom/5.2/Hodson.html.

Hoggart, Richard (1957) *The Uses of Literacy*, London: Chatto and Windus.

Hunt, A. (1993) '*Talking Heads*: Bed Among the Lentils', in G. W. Brandt (ed.) *British Television Drama in the 1980s*, Cambridge: Cambridge University Press.

Innes, Christopher (1992) *Modern British Drama*, Cambridge: Cambridge University Press.

Jay, P. (1984) *Being in the Text*, Ithaca, MI: Cornell University Press.

Johnstone, Ian (1983) 'A question of being English', *Sunday Times*, 13 November.

Jolly, M. (ed) (2001) *Encyclopedia of Life Writing*, London: Fitzroy Dearborn.

Knight, Peter (1979) 'Daft, but all clever stuff!', *Daily Telegraph*, 5 February.

Kris, Ernest and Otto Kurz (1981) *Legend, Myth and Magic in the Image of the Artist*, New Haven, CT: Yale University Press.

Lacey, Stephen (1995) *British Realist Theatre: The New Wave in its Context 1956–1965*, London: Routledge.

Larkin, Philip (1988) *Collected Poems*, A. Thwaite (ed.), London: Faber & Faber.

Lay, Samantha (2002) *British Social Realism: From Documentary to Brit Grit*, London: Wallflower Press.

McAfee, A. (2002) *Lives and Works: Profiles of Leading Novelists and Playwrights*, London: Atlantic Books (on behalf of the *Guardian*).

McCourt, Frank (1997) *Angela's Ashes*, London: HarperCollins.

McGovern, Jimmy (2001) 'Whose story is it anyway?', *Observer*, 18 February.

Mann, W.J. (2005) *Edge of Midnight: The Life of John Schlesinger*, London: Arrow.

McQuillan, Martin (2000) *The Narrative Reader*, London: Routledge.

Mecklenburg, Norbert (1986) *Erzählte Provinz: Regionalismus und Moderne im Roman*. Königstein: Athenaeum.

Medhurst, Andy (2001) Keynote address given at the 'Other(ing) England' conference, University of Buckinghamshire and Chilterns, June.

Monk, Claire (2002) 'The British heritage-film debate revisisted', in C. Monk and A. Sargeant (eds) (2002) *British Historical Cinema*, British Popular Cinema Series, London: Routledge.

Moss, S. (2002) 'Harold Pinter', in *Lives and* Works: Profiles of Leading Novelists, Poets and Playwrights, London: Guardian Books.

Mrozek, B. (2003) 'Die Tyrranei der Intimität', *Der Tagesspiegel*, accessed 26 August 2003, http://archiv.tagesspiegel.de/archiv/26.08.2003/713566. asp.

Murray, James (1979) 'All Day on the Sands', *Daily Express*, 26 February.

National Theatre website, Alan Bennett's *The History Boys*, accessed 23 February 2004, www.nt-online.org/?lid=7785.

Nelson, Robin (1997) *TV Drama in Transition*, London: Macmillan.

Nevin, C. (1991) 'Our national treasure', *Independent*, 24 November.

O'Connor, G. (1994) *Alec Guinness: A Master of Disguise*, London: Hodder and Stoughton.

O. Henry Page, accessed 4 April 2002, http://ppl.nhmccd.edu/~dcox/ohenry/crit9.html.

Olney, James (1988) *Studies in Autobiography: International Symposium of Autobiography and Autobiography Studies*, Oxford: Oxford University Press.

O'Sullivan, Tim, J. Hartley, D.Saunders, M. Montgomery, and J. Fiske (1994) *Key Concepts in Communication and Cultural Studies*, London: Routledge.

Oxford English Dictionary Online, accessed 25 April 2002, www.search.oed.com/.

Paget, Derek (1990) *True Stories? Documentary Drama on Radio, Screen and Stage*, Manchester: Manchester University Press.

Pelzer, D. (2000) *A Child Called It*, London: Orion.

Pinter, Harold (1973) *Monologue*, London: Covent Garden Press.

—— (1991) *Plays Two*, London: Faber & Faber.

Prince, G. (1982) *Narratology: The Form and Functioning of Narrative*, Berlin: Mouton Publishers/Walter de Gruyter.

—— (1988) *A Dictionary of Narratology*, Aldershot: Scholar Press.

Reynold, Gillian (1998) 'Alan Bennett's extraordinary people', *Daily Telegraph*, 6 October.

Rhiel, M. and D. Suchoff (eds) (1996) *The Seductions of Biography*, London: Routledge.

Robbins, Bruce (2006) '"Martial Art" Review of Science and Reflectivity, Pierre Bourdieu', *London Review of Books*, vol. 8, no. 8, p. 18.

Rolinson, Dave (2006) *Alan Parker*, The Television Series, Manchester: Manchester University Press.

Rose, Margaret (1995) *Monologue Plays for the Female Voice: An Introductory*

Study, Torino: Tirrenia Stampatori.

Russell, Willy (1988) *Shirley Valentine*, London: Samuel French.

Scarr, R (1996) 'Alan Bennett – political playwright', *NTQ*, no. 48, p. 309.

Segal, M. (1993) *London at Home*, photographs, foreword: Alan Bennett, Manchester: Cornerhouse.

Selden, R. and P. Widdowson (1993) *Contemporary Literary Theory*, 3rd edn, London: Harvester Wheatsheaf.

Self, David (1984) *Television Drama: An Introduction*, Basingstoke: Macmillan.

Shaw, V. (1983) *The Short Story: A Critical Introduction*, New York: Longman.

Shubik, Irene (1975) *Play for Today*, London: Davis-Poynter.

Sierz, Alex (2001) *In-Yer-Face Theatre*, London: Faber & Faber.

Silver, Brenda (1999) *Virginia Woolf Icon*, Chicago, MA: University of Chicago Press.

Sinfield, Alan (1977) *Dramatic Monologue*, London: Methuen.

Spengeman, W.C. (1980) *The Forms of Autobiography*, London: Yale University Press.

Spilka, M. (1977) *Towards a Poetic of Fiction*, Bloomington: Indiana University Press.

Stam, R. and T. Miller (eds) (2000) *Film and Theory*, Oxford: Blackwell.

Sutton, M. (2006) *A Private Function*, www.dvdtimes.co.uk/content.php?contentid=5315, accessed 10 March.

Tulloch, John (1990) *Television Drama: Agency, Audience and Myth*, London: Routledge.

Turner, Graham (1990) *British Cultural Studies*, London: Unwin Hyman.

Walker, Alexander (1983) 'Running the tap over a traitor', *Standard*, 17 November.

Wesker, Arnold (2001) *Plays: 2. One Woman Plays*, London: Methuen.

West Yorkshire Federation of Women's Institutes (WYFWI) (1996) *West Yorkshire Within Living Memory*, Newbury: Countryside Books.

Willett, James (1977) *The Theatre of Bertolt Brecht*, London: Methuen.

Williams, Raymond (1977) 'Realism and non-naturalism 1', in the official *Programme of the Edinburgh International Television Festival 1977*, p. 30.

Wilmut, R. (1980) *From Fringe to Flying Circus*, London: Methuen.

Woolford, J. and Karlin, D. (eds) (1991) *The Poems of Browning*, London: Longman.

Wu, Duncan (1995) *Six Contemporary Dramatists*, London: Macmillan.

—— (2000) *Making Plays: Interviews with Contemporary British Dramatists and Directors*, London: Macmillan.

Index